THE HOUSE OF GOODBYES

By Jeff Pillars

Copyright © 2018 Jeff Pillars.

All rights reserved. No part of this book may be reproduced in any form without written permission from the author.

ISBN-13: 978-1986942980

ISBN-10: 1986942988

SPECIAL THANKS AND ACKNOWLEDGEMENTS...

To John Isley, Billy James, Ed Lowe and Randy Brazell for keeping me gainfully employed so that I may continue this reckless mission of mercy.

To Jackie Curry, Marci Moran, Terry Hanson, Andy Abdow, Marty Lambert, Cookie Eddings, Jay Wilson and Barbara Conrad for their love, understanding and support.

To Kathy Fenner for always being there for Gail in an emergency.

To Jason Saine, NC House of Representatives, for his ceaseless work in stopping the epidemic of puppy mills in North Carolina.

To Dr. Wesley Campbell, for her honesty, her wisdom and for caring for, and sharing the love of, a little orange tabby girl named Speck.

To Kathy Currlin and everyone at Atrium Animal Hospital. You've taken our path from sickness to health and from this life to the next. You've worked miracles and given your hearts to our four legged family.

To Rodney and Dash for making Clover's last mornings so wonderful and exciting.

To Dr. Knox and the staff of Faulkner Animal Hospital for treating us so right over the years.

To Dr. Skip Severt and Brown Creek Equine Hospital for having a great bedside manner with the ponies...even when the news wasn't always good. They have seen us through some very tough times.

To John Causby at Groundcrew Studios who has always looks out for my financial best interests in the voice over industry. Lean times or fat, John has always been my cheerleader.

To Dave Nickel whose carpentry skills and ingenuity have given first class homes and top drawer shelter to countless little souls. And also goats.

To Alan Peacock for keeping my old jalopy running so I can go to work and the vets and sometimes a movie. Sometimes.

To Jimmy Hill, our former farrier who spent years putting up with our pain in the ass ponies just to make sure their hooves were cared for.

To Joe Gatto, Brian Quinn, Sal Vulcano and James S. Murray aka The Tenderloins aka "Impractical Jokers". You've given me the gift of laughter when I thought I'd never be able to laugh again.

And to all of you who have been on similar journeys. You, who love the lost and forgotten. Who care unconditionally; sacrifice endlessly; and grieve eternally. If not for you, I'd be doing this all by myself.

In profoundly respectful memory of Robert D, Raiford. He loved old dogs, too.

Jeff Pillars

To my wife, Gail,

to my daughter, Haley,

...and to the creatures who shared, and share our lives.

The House of Goodbyes

INTRODUCTION

"When you allow an animal to touch your heart, you also give it permission to someday break it."

—Jeff Pillars

"Let's get a dog", my wife said. "Sure, why not." And that's how it started. That's how it always starts. A dog. One dog. That's all. Then one dog turned into another. After all, you don't want the first dog to get lonely. Then you find a poor stray…an abandoned puppy…a lost kitten…an orphan bird… and another…and another. We were up to seventeen dogs at one point. Over the years, our home, wherever that home was, became an ark for the forgotten. Rescues, strays and other peoples discards. Cleaning up after the negligent, the inconsiderate and the cruel who view pets as "disposable". We gave these furry afterthoughts a home. And love. And a story.

I never started out planning on this being my life. I never planned on being the lead dog of an ever changing pack. I had other life goals. I had dreams of being a full time actor. Early on I had success in TV and film. I traveled the world working with John Cherry III, creator of the "Ernest" franchise, writing and acting in several films. A role in a TV movie led to Hollywood meetings for my own sitcom. Then I became a very successful cast member of a long running, nationally syndicated radio show, writing and performing my own characters and song parodies. I still have a very successful career as a voice actor with clients on five of the seven continents. Remember the original Windex Crows? I was one of them. For fourteen years. But those things all ebbed and flowed. The one constant in my life was my wife, Gail; my daughter, Haley and the animals. No matter what happened; good times or bad; they were always there.

I've always believed, rightly or wrongly, that animals are like people. It's how they're raised. Bad dog, bad pet owner. Period. We raised ours with love. And discipline. Discipline without cruelty. Cruelty is for the ignorant. Even the ones we "inherited" when they were grown responded to the simple act of love. And that love and devotion has been returned tenfold. They look into your eyes with a knowing. A look that says "you are my world". A look that says "thank you." I see this show where people have to have some new age looking guy come in and help them deal with their cats. What the hell is that? We've got almost seventy and there's not a psycho in the bunch. Look, it doesn't matter what the animal is. Love and respect begets love and respect. Even my old iguana would hold my finger, rest his head on my hand and seemed to smile. Feral barn cats that won't let me touch them, still come running when they're called, their tails straight up and curled like a question mark, a sign of affection and acceptance. That's all they want from us, really. Our love.

The more time I spend around people, the more I love my animals. I've never trusted people who don't like animals. Once upon a time, one of my best friends was dating a woman who didn't like animals. She was a real elitist "theatre" type. He'd bring her over around the holidays and you could see the disdain on her face. Constantly brushing at any dog hair, real or imaginary, that dared land on her TJ Maxx mark down. Constantly pulling on my friends arm, indicating she wanted to go. The contempt in her eyes made my blood boil. I hated her. Still do. And so did my dogs. Especially the females. A bitch can smell a bitch. A dislike for animals displays a certain unseemly arrogance. A condescending superiority that bespeaks a loathsome personality trait often found in serial killers, terrorists and coffee snobs. And when it comes to those who would abuse animals; any animals; I have little patience for that species of human. I'll address it in length here, later. Suffice to say, my views are indeed controversial.

I've come to accept the idea that God has chosen me for this life. To do what most others can't, or won't. Give homes to the homeless that cross our paths. Understand, we don't go looking for these lost souls. They find us. Through one circumstance or another, our destinies intertwine and another charter member takes up residence. I don't know how they are sent to us. That concept is beyond my pay-grade. All I know is that you just know.

I christened our homestead "The House of Goodbyes". I call it that because when you accept a pet into your life, you are immediately accepting the inevitability of their exit. And if you do it right, that pet will be in your life long enough to make that goodbye powerfully emotional and extremely painful. You have to embrace the fact that this isn't about you. It's about them. If that pet isn't in your life, it will make little difference to your world. But without you; without your kindness and love, that pets' life is a roll of the dice. You can't save them all. But you can do something.

The cost of this adventure hasn't just been emotional. Take the cost of a normal family caring for one or two pets and multiply it by fifty. And that's a conservative estimate. This mission has cost us a small fortune. As of this writing, we're still pretty well in debt. Our pack seemed to get old all at the same time. Caring for the elderly, two legged or four, is costly. And when you're dealing in innovative health care, that cost goes up more than just a tick. In the past, we only had access to conventional veterinary medicine. We treated them the best we could with what we knew and what the vets we had access to. They still lived very long lives in most cases. But with the discovery of "New Age" pet care, our monetary output increased. Financial tensions can destroy a family and it certainly put a significant strain on our relationship. Thankfully, I've always been a pretty good earner. Not to pat myself on the back, but God made me a pretty capable voice actor. And a busy one. But, good as that income is, we still struggle. I've learned not to worry too much. No matter what the emergency, God always saw fit to make sure that "a little something extra" wound up in the pay pipeline to take the tension off. I'm grateful every single day that the Good Lord has my back. And despite my colossal imperfections and failings, he never lets me down.

As long as we've brought God into the conversation, I urge people to never hesitate to pray for your animals, as well as yourself. I've come to find great comfort in having faith to lean on. I'm not a perfect guy, in fact, far from it. I'm sure that God sometimes shakes his head and says "Man, Fat Boy, if you weren't taking such good care of my creatures, you'd be picking my sandal out of your crack." He's seen me through some very difficult times. He's given me miracles. Sometimes the miracle I needed, not the miracle I wanted. There's much to the supernatural world that people have a hard time accepting. Accept it with an open mind and an open heart.

I've started and stopped this book a dozen times. I'm not much of a writer. Not unless there's a fart joke in there somewhere. I've actually written quite a bit. Screenplays, comedy bits, commercials, song parodies etc… But not a book. At least not one like this. One so close to my heart. I'd always get just so far into it before I'd land on a difficult memory and emotion overwhelmed me. And then I think, "Who the hell cares about some washed up B-movie actor and his pets?" I mean everyone has stories, right? But something happened that makes me determined to push forward with it. When my old Lab mix, Shemp, passed away, I wrote a memorial to him which I read on the air along with the poem, "Two Old Dogs" about our daily routine of chores around "The Compound". I actually wrote the poem some weeks before he passed away. At the time I felt like I jinxed his timeline. Predestined his demise. I felt horrible. When the time came, I almost didn't read it on the air. I'd written several like it in the past, but at the last second, I choked. After all, I'm supposed to be the funny guy. The guy who does the crazy voices and the funny bits, not serious, emotional commentary. But this time I followed through. My voice cracked. Tears flowed. But I made it through. I made it all the way through. I walked, sniffling, back to my office. I was disappointed that I hadn't delivered the piece more professionally. But it happened how it happened and I couldn't get it back. The phone started ringing almost instantly. Our FB page blew up. Every time it was replayed, it retriggered a response. It was overwhelming. What I assumed would only be a dozen or so requests for the written piece, turned out to be thousands. Story after story from our listeners, chronicling stories of faithful friends fallen. One listener called saying they heard it on the way to say good-bye to their old dog. I wept through all of them. Clearly, I had struck a chord. There was a whole big world of "pet survivors" out there. Of course there was. I just hadn't even thought about it before. But "Two Old Dogs" had everyone in tears. Everyone. From housewives to truck drivers, our affiliates were experiencing a deluge. What I discovered is that through a personal story and a simple piece of amateur poetry, people found a common voice and a degree of healing. Memories, either years, or just days old, were given a voice. Someone called me "The Pet Lover's Poet Laureate". Perhaps that's jumping the gun, but compared to some of the other things I've been called, I'll take it.

So, off we go. I'll tell their stories individually, in the order they left. Some chapters will be longer than others. Some were here longer. Some had long, complicated stories. Others, while remarkable, had relatively unremarkable lives. But their stories will be told faithfully. Just as they were faithful to me.

Jeff Pillars

THE HOUSE OF GOOD-BYES

Let me tell you of a journey
That has taken many years.
It's taken many dollars
Many smiles and many tears.

We welcome the forgotten
With loving open arms.
We calm their fears with kindness
And shelter them from harm.

We do all this full knowing
That someday we'll eulogize
The beasts who shared their lives with us
Here at the House of Goodbyes.

It's not the life we planned for
In our free and wistful youth.
We gave up what some would call a life
To pursue a higher truth.

To rescue the abandoned
The sick and lost and old.
Shade them in the blinding heat
And warm them from the cold.

It's a life long dedication
To the love that never lies.
But it always ends with Rest in Peace
Here at the House of Good byes

We've never questioned how or why
Our flock will ebb and flow.
We tend to them the best we can
Till God says it's time to go.

We simply carry forward
And understand the price.
We give them all that we can give
Till they reach paradise.

A lifetime of joy; with a last sad refrain.
It's an all too familiar reprise.
All roads lead to the Rainbow Bridge
From here at the House of Good-byes.

. . .

PASSED

What follows are the stories of our faithful fallen. Their stories deserve to be told. A proper record of their days on Earth and by our side. By the time this book comes out, there's a good chance we'll have lost another. Or a few. Or even many. With the sheer volume of lives we care for at the compound, someone is always on the way out. Some of the stories illustrate the unique way they came into our lives. All of them relate the tragic, often poignant, way they left us. They say that animals don't know death the way we do. They don't dwell on it or worry about it because they don't understand it. Death takes them by surprise. Dear God, I hope that's true. I hope all of them, including yours, pass on to the next world in peace and without fear. I know that's not practical, but I hope.

CANINE

LADY

aka
[Lady Butt; Baseball Head; Lightbulb Head]

We frequented a little Mexican restaurant in Matthews, NC. Usually for Sunday lunch. Haley was little then, probably four or five, and she liked to visit the pet store a few doors down. On this particular Sunday there was a pair of Pomeranians in the window. One, in particular, was infatuated with Haley. It seemed that the feeling was mutual. When it came time to leave, Haley started to cry. She didn't want to leave the dog behind. Even though we couldn't afford it, we took her home. Little Haley Pillars had her first dog. She named her Lady.

To put it mildly, Lady was full of piss and vinegar. Like most Pomeranians, size was not a barrier to bravado. But her feistiness was reserved for people who were NOT Little Haley Pillars. She was connected to Haley at the hip. Whatever Haley wanted to do, Lady was up for it. Get stuffed in a doll's highchair for a tea party? OK. Take a nap in a fort dressed in doll clothes? Fine. Get wadded into a form fitting onesie and put on display at the local festival "Pet Parade"? Giddy up! I clearly remember on Haley's fifth birthday, which is in mid March, it snowed. And if that wasn't odd enough, it was thundering. We got about a foot of snow and Little Haley Pillars was still new to the whole snow thing. We bought a plastic sled at the hardware store and Lady sat patiently as Haley pulled her around the yard in the middle of a blizzard. That's love.

Despite her adorable, almost Disneyesque, fox-like appearance, she could turn fierce if you went after her with the dreaded "two fingers". Two fingers was something Haley and I came up with. You would hold up two fingers, index and middle, like claws. The minute Lady saw that coming, she'd start to curl back those little lips. Her little ears would lay back. Those big black eyes got even bigger. Then the high pitched growl would come. Low at first. And then, when you moved in to get her with those dreaded "two fingers", she'd attack. This wasn't "friendly dog playing" attack, this was "attack attack"! She'd really lay into you. And if you tried to run, you'd lose. She'd chase you. Chase you until she caught you. She was such a ferocious little monster. But once she thought you'd learned your lesson, she was back to being a sweet little "Poperamian" as Haley called her.

Lady was devoted to Haley heart and soul. She couldn't wait for her to come home from school. She'd sit with her while she did little art projects or school work. If Haley had a party, Lady was right in the middle of it all. I honestly don't think Lady knew she was a dog. I think she believed Haley was just her best friend. Her peer. It was so touching to see her follow Haley around. That's why it was so tragic that she only lived five years.

Lady got sick just all of a sudden. I remember I was getting ready for a trip back to LA for meetings on a movie. Lady was clearly not well and I was worried. I sat on the couch to put my shoes on and she walked over and looked at me. I spoke to her and she curled her tail up, but it only lasted a moment. I hoped Gail would take her to the vet. I left for the airport with an uneasy feeling.

The entire flight I was anxious. When I landed in LA, I called home to check messages. This was before everyone had cell phones, so I had to hit the pay phone. The very first message was from Gail. She was crying. I could barely understand her. Then I heard it. Lady was dead. My heart stopped. When I finally got Gail on the phone, she told me the story. She had put Lady in a pet carrier in the bathroom and went to work. She came home on her lunch hour and found that she had passed away. Then, when she went to take her little body to the vet, her car wouldn't start. It was awful. I felt so bad for Gail. To this day, she still doesn't like to talk about it.

We hustled our grips to the hotel and headed to our first meeting. Before I walked in the door, I called home to check on everyone. Haley had just gotten home and found out Lady was gone. She was inconsolable. I did my best to reassure her that everything would be OK, but the loss was too great. She cried and cried. This was her first experience with death and there I was on the other side of the country. My heart hurt. Especially for her. That night I cried myself to sleep in my hotel. When I got home from the trip I talked to her about how important it was to remember Lady. I even managed to get a smile out of her when I reminded her of some of the silly, crazy things she used to do. Those memories will last a lifetime. But in truth, Haley was robbed. Five years wasn't long enough.

. . .

PIPPIT

aka
[Chivvy; Chivvy Cheese; P.I.; Pippit Marie; Pee Feet; Pom-A-Pip; American Were-Poo:]

Pippit was our first dog as a married couple. One of the dogs we actually bought and paid for. She was a Pomeranian-Poodle mix. I named after the dog in "Jaws" that goes missing on the beach right before the Kintner boy met his doom. She was a crazy little white ball of trouble. We almost adopted one of her brothers. He was an apricot colored chip off the old block. We would have named him Ole, after professional wrestler, Ole Anderson. But finances prevented us.

We were living in a tiny townhouse in Charlotte, NC. Our second apartment and one that felt safe enough to have a dog. Before Pippit came along, we got a black and white Dutch bunny, named Bobby. Bobby was much bigger than Pippit and really didn't appear to be concerned with her one way or the other. Pippit, on the other hand, was fascinated. "What the hell kind of dog is THIS?" Pippit was always after Bobby, trying to get her to play. Bobby put up with it for a while and then she'd jump up on the sofa and stretch out. Pippit would crane up on her tip toes and look up at the reclining Bobby and yip, yip, yip. Bobby yawned. Gail said, "Be careful, Bobby. One day she's going to be able to get up there." Well, that day finally came.

Bobby was in her customary state of repose on the divan and all of a sudden, Pippit leaped up on the sofa! The novelty of that action surprised Bobby, and she sat up, startled. "What is going on here?" Pippit was just as surprised. Once the initial shock wore off, Bobby sprang off the couch and made a run for the steps. Pippit leapt off after her but the steps were a bit daunting for an itty bitty Pom-a-poo! But as Pippit got older, and was able to scale the staircase, this scenario changed. Pippit would chase Bobby up the steps. You'd hear clattering and bouncing around overhead and a few minutes later, they come back down the steps, this time Bobby chasing Pippit. It was pure slapstick. When they were exhausted, they'd relax and nap or Bobby would leap into the safety of her cage, which frustrated Pippit no end.

Pippit ruled the roost. She was whip smart. She was the first dog, so she got lots of attention. She quickly learned how to spell. She knew what "t-r-e-a-t" meant and what "r-i-d-e in the c-a-r" was all about. She knew the names of all her toys. Froggie. Shoe. Pork Chop. We'd line them up and tell her which one we wanted. She'd pounce on it and then pick it up and run away, staying just out of reach. If she knew you wanted something, she'd make sure you didn't get it.

Pippit needed a playmate. Gail and I were both busy and working and Pippit was lonely. We needed another dog. That's when we adopted Katie. Katie was a black and white Spaniel mix. Katie was just a baby but Pippit was full grown so little Kate was getting all the "cute baby" attention. Pippit didn't care much for the competition. To get even she'd drag Katie backwards by the tail, with Katie voicing her displeasure the whole time. Once Katie got a little older, Pippit couldn't get away with crap quite as easily. They were so funny together.

"P-A-R-K". Just spelling it sent them into a frenzy. Pippit loved to chase the ball. LOVED IT! She'd do it for hours. She also earned the nick name, "Circus Dog" because of her fearless character and willingness to do dumb little stunts. Gail would hold Pippit up on a concrete pylon and I'd place one end of a board on the pylon and hold the other end right under my chin. Gail would let her go and she'd nonchalantly walk the plank over to me.

Pippit was a natural performer even when she didn't want to be. At Christmas, I used to hold her up in the air, her front legs in one hand and her back legs in the other. Then I'd sing "Jingle

The House of Goodbyes

Bells" and I'd move her legs together and apart, together and apart, so it looked like she was one of Santa's reindeer prancing across the sky. She'd put up with it for a few minutes then she'd start to bite at my hands, all the time wagging that tail. I did a similar thing to the theme from "Superman: The Movie". As the theme song played the opening strains, I would hold Pippit up on her hind legs like she was standing. And when the musical chord struck where Superman would take flight, so would Pippit. I did it a hundred times and a hundred times it was funny. We also did a mock PSA for "The Pet of the Week". I'd hold her on my lap and say "And this is Pippit, our Pet of the Week. She's an adorable Pomeranian Poodle mix…" When I did that I'd sit her up on her butt and start to tickle her. "She's kind and patient and wonderful with children…" About that time she'd start to growl and mumble. "And ideal for a family…" about which time she'd viciously attack me. Good times.

We soon were on the move and rented a house north of the city. A huge, unfenced yard with a small fenced in yard just off the sun porch. We were up to three dogs now. Pippit, Katie and Peanut, a gangly Schnauzer-Poodle mix. Pippit loved having more room to cause trouble. The house was in an unusual weather corridor. If it snowed, we always got it. Pippit, never a wall-flower, would bound off the front stoop and into the snow, disappearing when it was a bit too deep. She'd suddenly reappear from beneath the drift, in her glory. One day, standing in the kitchen I watched Pippit playing in the back yard. What I saw made my heart stop. In a dead run, headed for the back yard, was one of the biggest Doberman's I'd ever seen. It leaped and cleared the fence. I ran for the door. When I got outside, there was Pippit on top of the Doberman, wrestling away. They played like puppies. The Doberman, whose name escapes me, made regular visits. It was always a treat for Pippit. And me.

In a few years, we finally gave up being renters and bought a little house in Mint Hill, just north east of Charlotte. Yards were smaller but both were fenced. Pippit loved her unsupervised freedom. When I came home from work, she would always come to meet me at the gate, doing her little sideways run. She'd lie out in the sun until her belly turned black as night. Over the years, Pippit developed a love for Christmas. She'd sniff out her favorite presents, stretch out under the tree next to them and fiercely guard them from other dogs. And us. If you tried to reach for one of her presents, she'd growl, baring her fangs and her little wafer thin tongue would quiver. I'd scold her. "Pip. Pit. Mah. Rie!" She'd just wag her tail, satisfied she'd gotten her way. She was a natural guard dog. My friend, Frank Williams, was a frequent guest and became known as Pippit's boyfriend. She'd set on his lap, gazing at him adoringly. If you made a move towards Frank, she'd become possessed. Her eyes bulged and she'd growl loudly. If you dared to touch him? She'd launch on you! Nobody was allowed to touch her boyfriend but her! We called her "American Were-Poo in Charlotte"!

As she grew older, her health waned. To me, it seemed overnight. But I think, in truth, I was still not "tuned in" to my pets. Or maybe I just didn't want to admit she was starting to miss a step. She lost one eye to an infection. Then, shortly after, lost the other. She still managed to get around. Her personality was still there, although her enthusiasm was fading. But every single night, without fail, she still found her "spot", sleeping right between my legs like a little white log. Until one night. I was sleeping soundly and suddenly felt a trembling against my leg. I pulled back the sheet to see Pippit in the throws of some sort of seizure. Her teeth bared and her tongue sticking between. I screamed for Gail. We wrapped her trembling body in a towel and she started releasing her bowels. We grabbed our daughter and sped to the ER, to no avail. It was some sort of aneurysm. The time had come to say good bye to our "first born". When it was over, I looked at her small, still body, wiping the tears away to see her clearly. She was gone. The drive home was awful. We walked into the house and Gail got Haley to bed. I went into the bedroom and when I saw where she and I had last laid together, I fell to the floor in tears. I don't remember sleeping. But I remember crying. A lot. She was our baby. My baby. It still stings to this day.

KATIE

aka
[Kay-Tee-NO!; Katie Bird; Conehead Kate; Katie Topknot; KATE!]

Pippit needed a friend. So Gail picked out a little black and white Sheltie Spaniel mix. Gail named her Katie. She was a talker from the beginning. As the "little sister", Pippit put her through her paces. She'd come up behind her and grab her by the tail and drag her backwards. Baby Kate would puppy growl and yap her displeasure. "You'll be sorry when she gets older, Pippit!", Gail would say. She was sort of right.

As she got older, Katie was a bit of a clown. She always sought her Mom's favor. She'd hover and stare, begging for attention like she'd never been pet in her life! She was also a real park hound like Pippit. We'd set on the ground in the ball field and throw the ball. Pippit would RACE to get the ball. Katie? Eh, not so much. She'd run out about half way and lay down, waiting for Pippit to return. Then she'd jump up and try to intercept her, chasing her all the way back.

During this time, I was going back and forth to Greensboro to work at the Barn Dinner Theatre. It was about 90 miles north of Charlotte. It wasn't ideal being that far away, but I needed to work and we needed the money. Also at that time, Gail was cast as "Golda" in "Fiddler on the Roof" at a local dinner theatre. One night, Katie escaped from the small back patio area of the townhouse. Gail was beside herself. But what could she do. She had to go to the theatre. When I called home after the show, she told me what had happened. I lost it. I didn't have a car, so the tech guy drove me back home. I went out the back door and out into the alley way behind the apartment. I was desperately calling for Katie. Then I heard something. A familiar whine. I raced (back when I was physically capable of "racing") down the alley and found Katie in one of our neighbor's patios. She was terrified. I brought her back to Gail. It appeared that she may have been hit by a car, but we didn't know for certain. She was so happy to see Gail. In reality, we were amazingly fortunate to have found her. She was never the same after that. She did her best to never let Gail out of her sight.

Katie was a clown. We'd lie on the bed and ask "Where's Katie?" Katie would crawl under the bed and then she'd pull herself out from under the bed, looking up at us with a big smile on her face. She'd lay on her back looking up at us and then she'd duck back under the bed. "Where's Katie?" She'd poke her head back out, smiling, and so happy that we were entertained. She was always doing silly things. Long before the Klingon's developed a "cloaking device", Katie was the innovator. One day, while Gail and I were in the tiny kitchen, Gail turned around and burst out laughing. Katie had somehow gotten herself under a rag rug and was setting there in the corner, wagging her tail. "Where's Katie?" Her tail went into overdrive. Gail even took a picture which has since gotten lost in the shuffle of life. I'd love to find it.

As I said before, Katie was a talker. If she made eye contact with you, all you had to do is say "KATE" and she'd bark and bark at you. She was verbal with the other dogs too. Not a growl, per se, but more of a grumble. An agitated mumbling. This got worse after she got lost. Gail said she thought she might have a mushroom growing in her head. I knew better. She was just afraid of anyone getting between her and her mom.

Katie seemed forever youthful. She was always so happy and carefree. She didn't fuss with the other dogs that joined the family. She'd run with them and carry on, entertaining them as well as us. As long as she could be with her Mom, all was right with her world. That's why it was so heartbreaking when Katie got kidney disease. This was back when we were relatively new to pet ownership. We didn't know the signs to look for. We didn't know the treatments available. Homeopathic options were unknown to us. We took Katie to see Dr. Brenda Yerchek. She confirmed Katie's kidneys were beyond treatment. Total renal failure. Poor little Katie wandered around panting, clearly in pain. There was nothing else we could do. We had to let her go. I couldn't bear it. We were all out in the clinic lawn. I said goodbye to her and walked away. Dr. Yerchek administered the shot while Gail held her. Katie was in her happy and safe place as she left this world. And her beloved Mom was the last thing she saw.

...

PEANUT

aka

[Peanutty; Pawmutt; The Goat; Goater; Tennessee Walking Goat; The Big Chinese]

I was walking trash to the dumpster down the alley between the townhouses. I saw two cats attacking something I assumed was a rat. It was a puppy. I little hurt puppy. So tiny. Curly dark hair that was coming out in clumps. It was a little girl. No bigger than a peanut. So that's what we called her. Her first days with us were touch and go. We had a big blue milk crate with a closable lid. So that's what we kept her in. Gail would wake many times during the night to check on her, certain that the next time she looked at her would be the last. She was a pitiful little thing. One thing that stood out about little puppy Peanut was that tongue! Man, oh, man! Gail always said she hoped Peanut would grow around her tongue. When she'd yawn, it was like a furry chameleon. That wide, bubble gum pink tongue would unroll. It was adorably ridiculous.

Peanut slowly grew strong. Her mangy skin healed and her fur grew in thick, full and curly. She was grayish silver with long, gangly legs and a tail that curled skyward. She fell right in with Pippit and Katie. They were the Three Stooges. Peanut never realized that she was growing up. The little stool in the kitchen she used to hide under as a puppy, now only concealed her head. That didn't stop her from trying. When it stormed or something scared her, she buried her head under that plastic stool. It was funny and touching at the same time.

Life in the townhouse was not without excitement. "Garbage Adventure!" The uttering of those two seemingly incongruous words brought a stampede of twelve little paws to the front door. Pippit, Katie and Peanut would scramble down the sidewalk ahead of me as I walked the trash to the dumpster. Then we'd come back. That was it. We didn't stop for ice cream, there was no wildlife interaction, no cat butts to sniff, just garbage to the dumpster. But they LOVED it! They'd get a chance to say hello to Travis, the Bichon Frise that lived on one side of us. Or Precious, the crabby little Pekinese that lived on the other side. No matter her interaction with any other animal, poor Peanut was always the submissive. She'd tuck her tail and lower her head. It was just her accepting her role in the pack.

A pivotal moment in Peanut's life was when she learned to fly. That's right. Fly. I remember that it was summer. We were outside the front of the complex in the common yard, like a Quad at a college. The dogs were wandering around and goofy Peanut suddenly decided to leap up into Gail's arms! And I mean LEAP! She was airborn, baby! And she was thrilled. Suddenly, she discovered her super power; the thing that made her special. It was like a kid that figures out they're good at something. She wouldn't stop. She'd leap into your arms at a moment's notice. And even though she was slender and slightly built, if she got a running start, you better have had your feet braced because she'd take you down like a ten pin. It was hilarious. This simple little act made her so happy! She did other tricks. She "sort of" shook hands. And by "sort of", I mean that she'd offer her paw, but when you tried to shake it, she'd pull it up and away, like she was a doggie germaphobe. But she made up for that quirk with the "Goat Walk". To get a treat, she'd stand on her hind legs and hop/walk to you to get it, looking like some sort of circus goat. She liked all treats. Some of her tastes ran to the extreme, shall we say. When Haley was a baby, we constantly had to hide her dirty diapers from Peanut. If you let your guard down, in no time flat, the diaper would be licked clean. Peanut would look up with a very satisfied look on her face. Not to mention a very crisp moustache.

Peanut loved any kind of play, but she was most fond of "Blanket Game". I think all dogs have a jones for attacking your hand under the blankets. Peanut was a Jedi Master. If she saw you try to sneak your hand under the blankets, she'd go on point, eyes wide with anticipation. The second you bumped the blanket with your finger or scratched the sheet, she'd launch her attack. She'd bite your hand and jump on it. She was unstoppable. Her other favorite game was tug of war. With anything. We learned early on that toys were fine, but for a dog, there was nothing like a pair of old gym socks knotted together. She'd lock those iron jaws on and shake her head furiously. The sound she made can only be described as "otherworldly". The closest way I can explain it is that it sounded like "Gloop and Gleep" from the old cartoon, "The Herculoids". Google it. Totally worth it.

She also liked to help me get dressed in the morning. "Peanutty, help daddy put his pants on!" She'd run into the bedroom and when I'd put my foot into a pants leg, she'd grab on and jump at it. I honestly don't know how it started but she did it up till the end. She always wanted to play. Nothing ever illustrated that better than one night, when we were all playing on the bed. I had a big rubber bug prop. It was horrible looking and it had a big pair of pinchers on the front. I'd put my fingers in the pinchers and used it to go after Peanut. She acted horrified, jumped off the bed and ran away. She came back a second later and dropped her ball in front of the rubber monster. "Will you play with me?" she seemed to say. I said she'd made a ball offering to the Bug God. Gail and I laughed for days about it and I remember it clearly to this day.

Peanut seemed to love everyone and everything, but she had a real soft spot for Bobby the Rabbit. They would be out in the yard together and Peanut would do her best to garner her attention. Sometimes it worked. Sometimes not. But she always tried. Bobby got pneumonia and passed away suddenly. I buried her out in the back corner of the yard. The next day I let Peanut out and when it came time to come in, she was nowhere to be found. But I did finally find her. She was lying on Bobby's grave. I've never seen anything so sad in my life. I sat there with her for a while and talked to her. It was just another example of her loving heart.

Peanut, who was always a good eater, got super fussy with her food. She would only eat from your hand. I also noticed that she had started walking with a wider legged gait. She was not her usual self. Not perky and happy. She was sick. We took her to see our vet. She was extremely dehydrated. He put her on fluids and suggested that we take her to the hospital for overnight treatment, which we did. The next morning, the hospital called. She started having seizures overnight. I was completely blindsided. I went to pick her up to take her back to her regular vet. On the ride back, she insisted on sitting on my lap. And during the trip, she had seizure after seizure. I just cried and held her tight. Her doctor said her x-rays showed some questionable things. He asked if he could operate to see if he could remove anything. I called Gail to come immediately. She cried as she tried to comfort Peanut, who had another seizure. We left the doctor to do his work. A while later he called. She was riddled with cancer and he suspected that it had moved to her brain, causing her episodes. We made the decision, as long as she was under, to go ahead and let her go. I hated not being able to say good-bye, but it was for the best. An undeserved, inglorious end for such a happy go lucky girl. She left behind a void that will never, ever, be filled.

BROWNIE

aka
[Brownie the Clownie; Brown Hound; Brown Dog]

We moved out the apartment and into our first house on Denbur Drive, just outside the Charlotte city limits. It was a single level house with a huge carport and an even huger yard. The yard was unfenced save for a small parcel outside the back door. Our neighbors were quiet for the most part. Except for the asshole across the road.   Pure white trash. And what made this knob even "white trashier" was the way he treated his dog. She was a little German Shepherd mix. Tan in color with really beautiful and unique facial markings. He kept her in a crappy pen and tied to a rope. It pissed me off on a daily basis. But I was always taught to never rub another man's rhubarb. So, I minded my own business. Until one day. The day he beat her. That was it. The minute he left his house, I went across the road, cut the rope and took her. I hoped and prayed that he'd come to get her because, baby, I was ready. In those days, I could eat sawdust and crap two by fours. I was a force to be reckoned with. But he never came. Lucky for him because I would have straight up murdered his ass.

We learned that she'd been named "GI Joe". Really? You stupid hick. Gail renamed her Brownie and she was hurt. She had a broken leg, but it didn't warrant a cast or surgery, just rest. She remained timid and uncertain, but she was happy. The look in her eyes was one of gratitude. In short order, she grew to understand that this was her home now. Her previous owner was not coming back. She was overjoyed. And she showed it in every movement and every look. She even smiled when she was sleeping.

Brownie was a smart, smart girl. She learned what words meant. When you spoke to her and she cocked her head, you knew she was doing her best to understand what you saying. She'd even listen to Little Haley Pillars! Haley, only a toddler, would jabber away at Brownie and she'd listen trying to figure out what message the baby was sending. She was terrific with Haley. Haley would crawl on top of Brownie and pull her ears and twist her nose and Brownie took it all in stride.

Brownie loved to play and was a fiercely focused fetcher. She would chase that ball to the point of exhaustion. Many times Gail and I had to ask her to stand down and let someone else play. It drove her CRAZY, but she obeyed, frantically looking at the other dogs chasing the bouncing ball and then back at us, eyes imploring she be released to chase along. She also had a little trick to prolong the game. She'd only bring the ball back just so far and then drop it. You had to ask her to bring it to you. And she would. A little. Again, you'd ask and again, she'd bring it a little bit closer. Finally, one of the other dogs would jump in and grab it and bring it back. That gave Brownie the chance to fade back and be ready for the next throw. Clever girl.

Brownie befriended another hard luck story. Buster, a robust little rat terrier mix, immediately attached herself to Brownie. The feeling was mutual. They were definitely an odd couple. They looked like the Laurel and Hardy of the dog world. They'd nap in the sunlight together. Spend time in the yard together. It made me smile that these two lost souls found each other.

Brownie was a top notch watch dog. Though she wasn't big, no one doubted her ability to rend ass. She was the first to catch and kill possums and coons. She could also sniff out a snake. At the house on Vagabond Road, in Mint Hill, she was bitten by a copperhead more than once. She and Dolly both would find a snake and then raise hell until you came to see what the commotion was. She always seemed so pleased that she'd done her job.

Gail was the first to notice that something was amiss with Brownie. She saw that she was getting confused easily. She'd stare off into space as if deep in thought. A vet visit confirmed our worst fears. Brownie was in the early stages of canine cognitive disorder, a dog's version of Alzheimer's. It was so heartbreaking to see this smart, alert, vital dog slowly lose her faculties. Those eyes that, at one time, looked into your soul, now merely stared past, or through, you. She didn't recognize our voices sometimes or that we were even in the room. Every day, you could see her slip farther and farther away. When she started walking into the corner and not be able to figure out how to get out, we knew what we had to do.

Haley said good-bye to her and gave her one last hug. I think somewhere there is a picture of that moment. We put Brownie in the car and headed to the vet. In retrospect, the silver lining was that Brownie was unaware of the entire thing. She just lay in the backseat. In days gone by, she'd be the one to sit and stare out the window, taking everything in. Not now. I don't remember if she walked into the clinic or I carried her. But when we put her on that table, she laid perfectly still, as if welcoming what was coming. She slipped away quietly. We both kissed her one last time. I was relieved that she was finally at peace, but I will always be haunted by what took her.

...

BUSTER

aka

[Buster Bear; Pigglin; Pig Wigglin; Booster]

To support my theatre habit, I worked in the warehouse at Morris Costumes. Masks, magic tricks, novelty pranks. It was heaven. But it didn't pay a whole lot. In spite of that, once in a while I'd splurge and go to McDonald's for lunch. One of those days, I got more than just lunch. As I pulled into the lot to go to the drive through, a junker sedan pulled in, opened the door and a little brown dog got tossed out. I was torn between wanting to follow the asshole and beat his brains in or rescue the terrified dog. I chose the dog.

It was a little rat terrier mix. Mostly brown and white, with a black mask like "Bandit" from "Jonny Quest". "Come on, buster. Let's go." She didn't fight, probably still in a daze from the ordeal. She was scared and pitiful. The one thing that stood out was her tail. Part of it was missing. What was left was obviously infected. You could see exposed bone and it smelled awful. According to the vet, it looked like her previous owner had unsuccessfully tried docking her tail using a series of rubber bands. What?! What kind of low rent scumbag does something like that? And when they realized that the "operation" was a failure, they just decided to throw her away. As I sit here years later, I hope and pray that Karma paid him a visit.

Buster healed up just fine. Why did I name her Buster? If you could have seen her, you would know. She was a sweet little pudding. What was left of her tail was barely a nubbin. But when she was happy, that little digit wagged like lightning. In fact, her whole body wiggled. She wasn't fat, just thick. Short, stumpy legs and a tongue as big as a tennis racquet. Buster was one of a couple dogs we've owned that was just content to be a dog. I can't figure out any other way to say it. She didn't think she was a little person. She didn't act like she was trying to impress anyone. Just a stumpy, cheerful little pudge.

Buster's life was pretty unspectacular and that was just fine with her. She ate like a little piggy. She loved her long naps. Especially in the sun. Buster would lay out in the yard, belly to the sky and those stumpy little legs sticking straight out. Sometimes that sight caused me to stop short. For all the world, the little sausage shaped dog, laying in the yard looked way too much like road kill. I don't mean to be insensitive, but sometimes she looked like a bloated armadillo that lost a fight with a pick-up truck. I'd have to knock on the window or open the door and say "Pigglin! Are you OK?" She'd raise up her head and give me the stink eye for having disturbed her slumber. Then she'd drop her little round head back to the ground. I bet I did that once or twice a week. I never got used to it.

Some dogs don't like storms. Buster HATED them. I've never had a dog, before or since, that reacted so badly to thunder and lightning. It was frightening to behold. At the least, distant rumble of thunder, Buster would start to pant and shake. Full body tremors. Her eyes would grow wide and she'd look for someplace safe. It got so bad sometimes that she'd throw up! Thick, yellow foamy bile. Gobs of it. And there was no consoling her. Even after the storm had passed, she'd still be nervous and unsettled. I often wished that I could create a sound proof room to shelter her from it all.

Buster was never a "trick dog". Not that she didn't get it, she chose not to participate. She'd sit there while the other dogs sat, shook hands and the usual cadre of "good dog" stuff. Not Buster. She'd look at you like you had beans growing out of your ears. Until one day... We were handing out treats, asking all the other dogs to shake hands and before we could give Buster hers, she raised her paw!!! To make sure it wasn't just a coincidence, I did it again. And again. And once more. She was actually doing a trick! We made a big fuss over her and she was delighted. Pippit and Katie and Brownie would speak on command. Especially Katie. Well, what do you know? All of sudden, little Pig Wigglin' started speaking! You didn't even have to ask. Just look at her and hold up a treat. Yap! Yap! Yap! I think she was just as impressed as we were.

Buster was relatively low maintenance, medically. She had to have operations on both hind legs to repair cruciate ligament tears probably about six months apart. But she seemed to bounce back with spirit. It was only when we lost Brownie that things shifted. She knew Brownie wasn't coming back and it showed. She still hung in there, but it was like her smile was gone. I tried to give her extra attention and she enjoyed it, but it was never, ever the same.

We began to notice she was limping on one of her hind legs. It's been so long ago, but I want to say it was her right leg. The limp turned into her just holding the leg up when she walked. And it literally just hung there. There was no support whatsoever. We took her to the vet and they couldn't see any cause for it. But she was able to get around just fine so we were hoping she'd get her mobility back. So much for hoping. Soon the other leg did the same thing. She was scooting around using her front legs and her back legs were useless. She became unable to control her bodily functions, pooping and peeing without any control whatsoever. So, we tried to get her one of those doggie wheelchairs. The ones where you put their back legs in a harness and it allows them to get around after a fashion. She didn't take to it. Buster was struggling. She was clearly in pain and no one had any answers. If it had been today, I know I could have gotten answers from the vets I know. Back then, there was no acupuncture, no tui na, no physical therapy. It hurt too much to watch her struggling. She was panting all the time and clearly not at 100% physically or mentally. This was before cell phones and I had no way to contact Gail. So, I bit the bullet and took her to the vet to let her go. She didn't deserve to have to wait. She was quiet on the ride over. Her head was back and her eyes closed, panting heavily. Once inside the clinic, she was agitated and anxious but once she was sedated she fell asleep very quickly. The final injection was administered and she slipped away. I looked at her for a long while, remembering the discarded little dog all those years ago. I said a quiet thank you for the life and happiness I was able to give her. And the mercy I could give her at the end. I got home and sat on the front porch waiting for Gail and Haley. Breaking the news to them broke my heart all over again.

...

ROXIE
aka
[Rox; Bug; Waxie; Bug-A-Loaf; Rocka-Buga-Loaf; Peek-a-Sneeze]

The family of one of Haley's little friends had moved from a duplex to a house in a neighborhood. The entire development was in a wooded area. On this particular day, we discovered that they had found a little Pekinese. She was a bit older and very scared. She was the sweetest little thing. We learned that the little dog had been hanging around for a couple of days. During that time, they provided her water and little else, hoping she would get hungry and leave. People are such damn idiots. She wasn't skin and bones yet but she was thin. Who in the world would let this little old dog get so lost? Some people shouldn't own pets. We agreed she'd be a good addition to the pack. We took her to her new home.

Upon closer inspection, we found that she was slightly deformed. She had weird, crooked front legs. One of her big eyes was obviously not functional. After a vet visit we also learned that her jaw was not fully formed! It didn't connect on one side. Gail named her Roxie. I don't know why, but it did seem to fit. What a ridiculous little spark plug she was. She had a personality at least a hundred times her size. Happy and crazy for such a disadvantaged little dog. Even when she lost her left eye, it made little to no difference to her. She was back in action in no time.

Roxie was the originator of the "Nummy Dance". Whenever it was time to eat, she'd scamper to the rug in front of the refrigerator and merrily bounce from one front foot to the other. Sometimes we'd pretend we couldn't find her food and she'd lose her little Peke mind. Her short legs made it easy to for her to get down and dirty in the food dish. She made short work of anything. She was always eager to try new things. When we sat at the table for dinner, Roxie was always in the mix, going from me to Gail to Little Haley Pillars looking for handouts. Some things she liked...some she didn't. The way she rejected new offerings was hilarious. She'd eagerly take it into her mouth and if it was good, it was gone. If, however, it did not meet please her persnickety palate, she'd smack her lips around it and then unceremoniously drop it on the floor. My modest literary skills somehow prevent me from painting an adequate picture of the process, but it was hilarious. Even funnier is when she'd spit out the offending morsel, she'd raise her head right back up again and wait for what was next. Another of her most favorite treats was pizza crusts. She wasn't really interested in the actual pizza but there was something magical about those delicious warm bits of golden brown dough. When it was gone, she wasn't convinced. You had to show her. Then she'd go pull her scam on someone else. Pudgy little crust hustler.

When it came to playing, she didn't let her physical problems get in the way. One of my favorite things to do was to sit on the living room floor and wait for her to wander into view. I'd say "ROX!" She spin her head in my direction and like a stumpy, little, chubby, flat faced bullet, she would shoot across the floor and throw herself at me. Literally. She'd dive into my crossed legs, gleefully. I'd grab her and hold her down and wrestle her around. When we were done, she'd give me little kisses and cuddle up with her dad. She was a natural comedian. Even at bedtime.

When day was done and we were all creeping to bed, I'd hoist Roxie up on the bed with the family. I'd kneel on the floor and get face to face with her. I'd stare at her and furrow my brow and open my mouth. She'd do the exact same thing. Then I'd start to make kind of guttural growling sound. She'd do the same. We called this "The Wind Up". Then, at the same time, we'd lunge at each other, snapping our respective jaws. Anyone who's ever owned or spent time with a Peke knows what I'm talking about. We'd do it over and over and over again. She never grew tired of it. One of her other unforgettable schticks was to lie on her back next to Gail. Upside down, Roxie looked like a Sea Monster. Gail would tease her and Roxie would gurgle and snap at Gail. It kind of freaked her out but Roxie was having such a good time, she couldn't say no to her.

Every once in a while, Roxie would experience what the vet called "False Heat". So, even though she was spayed, she still experienced the symptoms of being in season. When this happened, she became infatuated with Haley's little Pomeranian, Lady. Roxie would make a fool of herself, flirting with Lady. I created a character for Lady called "Count Von Biscuit" who was an evil super villain. Roxie was his wealthy dowager wife who was always hammered. "Gadzooks! Drunk again! You disgust me!" And all the while Roxie would rub her face all over Lady and act trashy. It could have been a sitcom.

Roxie took ill rather suddenly. She was leaking from her butt and there was dilute blood there. We took her to the vet immediately and they said it was probably nothing. We took her home but something just wasn't right. She wouldn't eat anything. Gail decided to keep her in a pet carrier next to the bed to keep an eye on her. In the middle of the night, Gail woke me up in a panic. Roxie was in her carrier, struggling to hang on. She jerked and lurched suddenly. I didn't know it at the time, but that was probably the moment she passed away. We all crammed into the car and raced for the ER but it was too late. Roxie was gone. I stroked her little round noggin and kissed her good-bye. Then I went home and called the vets office and left a profanity laced tirade that I don't remember. Basically, I accused them of sending Roxie home to die. I know vets are human and make mistakes but when a dog is leaking dilute blood from their anus, it might be worth looking into. I made the mistake of trusting my vet when my instinct told me to take her to the ER. I let Roxie down that night. There might not have been anything they could do, but she at least she wouldn't have passed so horribly. One of the many regrets that haunt me to this day. She deserved better. Much, much better.

...

SANDY

aka
[Sandy Cotton Candy, Flower, Dog Belly]

On her way home one night, Gail saw a dog by the side of the road. Some sort of Chow mix. She was scared and the encroaching thunderstorm wasn't helping. Gail tried to lure her with some food. The starving dog came to eat and Gail made her move, lunged and caught the stray. Gail spent a moment comforting her and then got her in the car and got her home. She was a mess. We sat in the living room and, taking turns with the tweezers, picked ticks off her. We stopped counting somewhere around seventy five. She was a flop-eared sad sack. She looked horror struck. We got her cleaned up; to the vet and in no time, she was the newest addition to the pack. Her name was Sandy.

Sandy wasn't a typical Chow hybrid. She didn't have an unpredictable nature, as some Chow blends can be. She was gentle and loving, even with the other dogs. She was especially fond of Haley's new Pom, TC. Sandy would lie on the floor and let TC chew on her lips and stand on her chest. Sandy would lay there and wag her tail. She never had a dust up with any of the other dogs that I can remember. Sandy lived in a state of being

The House of Goodbyes

grateful. Grateful to have been saved, grateful to finally be safe and grateful, most of all, for a loving family. More than anything else, she was grateful to Gail and she showed it with every breath. She loved Gail.

Sandy wasn't much of a fetcher or player. She was a lover. All she wanted was attention and she knew how to get it. She did a thing called "Dog Belly". She'd slowly roll over on to her back, tuck one arm down and stick the other one straight out in front of her. When she did this, she expected her belly and chest to be scratched. No excuses. When you looked into those soft eyes and that precious face, it was impossible to refuse.

If you had ever wondered if The Great Houdini had ever been reincarnated, the answer is yes. He came back as Sandy. Short of shackles and padlocks, she could not be contained. We added Sandy to the family when we were living at Vagabond Road. Our neighbors put up a fence to keep their dogs in. But Sandy didn't know it was also meant to keep her out. If you looked away for a second, over she'd go. Oh, she knew if you were watching, trust me. She wasn't causing any trouble or attacking their dogs. She was just stopping in for a visit. The neighbors were sort of assholes about it, although their dogs were a pain in the ass and had gotten out and raised hell in the neighborhood many times. Sandy wasn't mischievous, she just didn't like to be penned. When we moved to Mineral Springs we had pens with seven foot fencing. Sandy climbed it like a circus monkey. She didn't even break a sweat. We even tried creating a canopy of fencing along the top. Didn't stop her. So, we gave up and she won. We never put her in the pen again.

As with most of our dogs, things went south with Sandy very quickly. It was mid November. Sandy wasn't herself. It hurt her to go up and down the steps. She was uncharacteristically lethargic and withdrawn. She ate sporadically. Gail took her to the vet and they sent her to that veterinary specialist clinic that I'm not fond of. But they do have good doctors. We spoke with Dr. McFadden, the veterinary oncologist. Sandy had lymphoma. But she thought, since Sandy was so stout that she'd respond to treatment. So, the Wednesday before Thanksgiving, we admitted her for treatment. Gail went to see her every day. She was beside herself. The Monday after Thanksgiving we got the call we'd been dreading. Sandy was fading. We needed to come right away. We piled into the car and got there as fast as we could. Haley couldn't bring herself to be in the room with us. They brought Sandy in and she was very still. She tried to raise her head for Gail but she was too weak. Her skin was almost white and her pulse was thin. Gail spooned with her on the floor and sobbed uncontrollably. With tears in her eyes, as well, Dr. McFadden gave Sandy her final injection. She passed very quickly. At last, she was out of pain. She was only around ten years old, but those were ten years she never, ever would have had, if Gail had not worked so hard to rescue her. In the end, we were grateful to her for giving us all the love she ever had to give.

. . .

SADIE

aka
[Pug; Pugsley; Sadie Bug]

While Gail was at the stables, they found a dog. A pug. It was pretty plain to anyone with a clue that she was an escaped puppy mill dog. Or a discarded one. She was thin and her skin was bad. She was salt and pepper, grayish in color, with the trademark curly Pug tail and big eyes. One eye was not in good shape. She was going to be a real project. Nobody wanted her. Nobody except Gail, that is. She didn't even call me, she just brought her home. She was scared, but you could see that underneath it all, she had a big personality. That's an understatement. Gail named her Sadie. I don't think I ever called her that. It was Pug.

Step one was to get her healthy. In her first weeks with us, Sadie needed to be crated. She had mange and her skin could be contagious. So, it was shampoo and lotions and pills, which she put up with like a good patient. We'd take her out to potty and she would look around and then look back, like she was being cast out. Seeing that made me cringe. How horrible must her life have been? Eventually, she realized this was home. She'd trot around the yard like a dopey, happy idiot. When it was time to come back in she'd lope up the steps, head bobbling and pig tail wagging. But her euphoria stopped when she realized it was back to her crate. She would dutifully walk in and sadly sit there. She looked so pitiful. You could tell she'd been caged before. I made sure once she was better, she'd never set foot in a cage again.

In case you don't know, Pugs are notoriously bullheaded. Sadie was stubborn enough for twenty Pugs. Compound that with her chronic "selective hearing" and you have the recipe for a supremely irritating dog. If she hadn't been so adorable, it would have been maddening. To illustrate, Sadie loved cat poop. Worse than love, it was an addiction. She was a crap junkie. And with all the cats we had running around, there was a fix on every street corner. All the dogs ate cat poop, but they weren't fixated like The Pug. You'd let her outside and watch her put her nose to the ground and go treasure hunting. She'd find a kitty pickle in the grass and dig in. "Pugsly! PUGS-LY!!!!! You stop that right now! No!" She didn't even cock an ear. So, I'd start towards her, cussing a blue streak. She waited until I got right up on her, making sure she didn't miss a morsel, and then she'd scamper away, smacking her poop covered lips, her ears flapping backwards and looking over her shoulder. I was mad as hell, but I just could never stop laughing.

Sadie's bad eye was becoming a problem. At some point in the past, the eye had popped out and the previous owner just put it back in without going to a vet. I hate people. Now it was starting to protrude, becoming more pronounced. She would have to lose the eye. No big deal, because she had no sight in it. We had a great surgeon who did a great job. She came through with flying colors and her new look gave her even more personality. And when you're not the prettiest thing in the world, personality counts for a lot. Believe me, I know.

My mom came down to visit. She'd been used to our dogs over the years but she'd never seen Sadie before. It was a match made in heaven. Well, for Sadie anyway. For some reason, she took a shine to mom. She'd follow her everywhere. When my mom was in the kitchen having coffee, Sadie would stare at her with her one eye, big smile on her face and doing that hard breathing that Pugs do. Mom wanted to ignore her, but she couldn't. When mom sat on the couch to watch TV, Sadie was right there beside her. Mom said "You are the ugliest dog I've ever seen!" but Sadie heard "You are so beautiful!" She was actually depressed when mom went back to Michigan.

We had a bad run of copperhead encounters on Vagabond Drive. In the spring and summer it was like they were everywhere. One night, there was a small copperhead on the sidewalk so I hustled the dogs in the house, got the shovel and took care of business. When I came back in we checked everyone for bites. Here came Sadie, looking sadder than I'd ever seen her. She sat down and lifted up her left front paw. It was swollen and still swelling. She'd been bitten. The look on her face was like a kid who got hurt doing something they shouldn't have been doing and then having to tell their parents. It was a combination of guilt and embarrassment. How could you not love that face? We took her to the ER and got her patched up. For the next two weeks she didn't want to go outside without Gail or me.

Pugs snore. Sadie abused the privilege. I used to take her back to the bedroom to nap or sleep at night. She always made herself comfortable right away. Unlike any of our other dogs, Sadie wasn't a bed hog. She always gave me my space. She liked to be near me, instead of on me. About the time that one big eye closed, the logs began to be sawed. She'd roll over and expose that hog belly and I'd reach out and just put my hand on her. It's funny, but her snoring never bothered me. It never kept me awake. It was like white noise. I'd drift off to sleep with that little blob of snorting love beside me.

It was midnight, or thereabouts. The bedroom door opened. It was Gail. "I think we need to take Sadie to emergency." She'd been in the back yard and all of a sudden, she just lay down and wouldn't get up. Gail got her in the house but she did not want to move around. I came into the hall and Sadie was lying at the top of the steps. She looked up at me and I knew that something was very wrong. We took her to the ER in Matthews. She was really struggling. They immediately took her to the back. The vet on call told us that she was having trouble breathing and her tongue was a little blue. It could be congestive heart failure. He wanted to keep her overnight in an oxygen room. We agreed. I went back to kiss her goodnight. It broke my heart to see her like that. The image I'll always have burned in my memory is her looking over her shoulder at me as I left. I thought about staying there and just sending Gail home but I didn't. I should have.

The phone rang very early in the morning. Sadie was in bad shape. Very bad shape. While Gail was on the phone with the vet, Sadie went into cardiac arrest. The vet asked if he should resuscitate. I just shook my head "no". I knew there really is no coming back from something like that. So we let her go. Sadie was gone. My Pug. I went out on the front porch and just screamed my head off, tears pouring out of my eyes. It was only later that I found out what a horrible reputation that ER clinic had. I will forever be haunted by the possibility that things would have been different if we'd gone somewhere else. Probably not. But we never went back to that ER ever again.

...

BUDDY

aka
[Bud Bud; Buddy the Beagle; Beagle Boy]

Gail told me there was a dog in the pasture. How in the hell did he get into the pasture? All I could think was that someone knew we took in abandoned dogs and just dropped him over our fence. At least they didn't put him out on the side of the road. Assholes. I went out to see an old, shop worn, Beagle. He was in pretty bad shape. His skin was a mess. And it appeared that he was crippled because he was having such a difficult time getting around. He was a true hard luck case and we had to do what we could for him. It was one of the best decisions we ever made.

Gail and I decided on the name Buddy. Buddy the Beagle. A trip to the vet revealed he wasn't crippled. The pads of his feet were all torn up. He was eaten up with fleas and worst of all, he had heartworm. We had to make a decision. If he had the heartworm treatment, he'd need to be confined with limited movement for six weeks. The cold weather had set in and he'd need to stay in the big holding cage in the garage. We decided that, after everything he'd been through, he deserved a shot. Totally worth it.

Good Lord, what a character! Buddy wasn't fazed by anything. We made him a heated fort inside of the big cage. In the morning, you'd go out and say "Bud Bud, you want breakfast?" You'd hear a snort and he'd stick just his nose out of his fort. Just his nose. Nothing else. Then you'd hear, "thump thump thump", his tail banging against the wall. Then he'd stick his head out. He had the happiest sad hound dog eyes I'd ever seen. He'd gobble up his chow, go out on his leash to potty and when you said, "Come on, dude. Gotta go back to your room", he'd walk right back with you and retreat to his fort. He was a wonderful patient and the six weeks flew by.

Once Buddy was in general population he showed his true colors. Goofy. Buddy loved the outdoors. He would go sit in the yard and just soak up his rural domestic bliss. We got the impression that this was probably Buddy's first real "family". I don't mean owner, I mean family. He loved attention but wasn't demanding. He appreciated a treat now and then and a good long scratch behind the ears. Buddy was quite old and I was thankful that at least the end of his life would be filled with love and acceptance.

Buddy did lots of crazy stuff. Most of it had to do with barking. Beagles have a unique bark. It's really more of a bellow. Buddy got plenty of use out of his. He didn't bark at normal dog stuff; squirrels, cats, cars, people; Buddy barked at…the litter box. I'm not making this up because who would believe it? In the laundry room, the wash tub has a litter box underneath, behind a cabinet door with a cat door in it. One night, we were sitting in the kitchen and all of a sudden we hear the Buddy Bellow. Over and over. We got up and ran to the laundry room to find Buddy with his head stuck in the door. He was barking and wagging his tail. What an idiot. But that wasn't even the weirdest thing. In the spring, we always get those big, white grubs. Sometimes we find them in the driveway or on the sidewalk, but some of the dogs would sniff them out in the yard and dig them up and eat them. They must have tasted like pumpkin pie because they ate the hell out of them. But they did it in peace and quiet. Not Buddy the Beagle. You could stand in the garage and watch him. He'd amble out into the yard, nose to the ground and tail going a mile a minute. Then he'd stop. Bingo! He'd dig and dig and dig. His little fat feet furiously moving the dirt away so he could get at his treasure. And when the grub was finally revealed, rather than just gobble it down, Buddy would bark at it. Not just bark, but bark AT IT! You could watch him look down and bark at the grub. When the grub was finally appropriately humiliated, then Buddy ate it. He was so pleased with himself.

Buddy started having trouble breathing. The vet told us it was his heart. The heartworms had done enough damage to it that it was very weak. We kept him stable for a while but things steadily went downhill. It was Gail's birthday. We were cooking dinner. I went to the panty for something and found him sitting there struggling to catch his breath, I rushed him to the ER. They wanted to keep him overnight. Put him in the oxygen room and get him some air and then go from the there. I agreed and loved him up a little before I left, but I could tell he was in rough shape. The second I got home, the ER called. We needed to come back. Buddy was struggling and wouldn't last much longer. It knocked the wind out of me. The ER was so far away, it would have taken us forty five minutes to get there. I made the decision to let him go right away. Buddy was gone. We didn't have him many years, but while he was here, he was so happy. He felt safe and loved and like a real member of a real family. That was all that mattered.

...

LUCKY

aka
[Mister Big; Big Head; Beak Boy; Biggie; Collie-huahua]

The phone rang and Gail answered. I was watching TV but I remember her being very quiet. She came into the living room and said that Haley's babysitter had called. A friend of hers had a dog that had been wandering the neighborhood for a couple of weeks. They took it in and had it on a chain in the garage. They'd already made an appointment for animal control to pick it up. She said she knew how we felt about animals and she hated to see that happen to such a sweet dog and could we possibly take it. The house on Vagabond Road was small. We already had a lot of dogs and space was at a minimum. I said "Whatever you think" even though I already knew exactly what she was thinking.

In a short while she returned. She'd gone to a stranger's house in the middle of the night. In that stranger's garage was a full blooded Collie. White with black and brown patches. Little tiny eyes. Apparently he was barking too much so his previous owner put a rubber band around his nose to silence him and the skin had started to grow around it. That made my blood boil. Those scars lasted most of his life. What his owner didn't know, or didn't care about, is that he was deaf. He was thin and very scared. So scared that he wouldn't walk to the car. Gail had to carry him. How could I say no? This would be his forever home. Gail named him Lucky and he certainly was.

Lucky fell into the routine very quickly. His deafness didn't matter too much. He learned to sit with just a hand gesture. His eyes were always alert, his little eyebrows raised in constant interest. But when he was sleeping, forget about it. I've never seen a dog that was such a hard sleeper. I imagine that being deaf helped, but man, he sawed more logs than Paul Bunyan. As far as the other dogs, he was happy to have friends. Whatever they wanted to do, all he asked was to tag along. If he saw the dogs get up and run after something, he'd raise himself up and trot along with them, barking the whole time.

Lucky was quite the lover dog. He was so thrilled to have a family. He'd come over to you and put that giant dolphin beak head in your lap. And he'd look up, right into your eyes, like he was asking permission. All you could see was love. I'd hold his head and kiss him on his long, Collie nose. Then he would angle sideways so you could hug him if you wanted to. We always wanted to. And if you sat on the floor or the ground, you had a giant dog in your lap.

The summer is hot in this neck of the woods. Lucky had a long, thick coat. His first summer with us, we could see he was uncomfortable. Gail said, "Why don't we just shave him?" Well, that was a job I didn't want to tackle. So we took him to a groomer. He left a beautiful long haired Collie Boy. He came home a giant mutant Chihuahua. There's nothing quite like the sight of a big, shaved Collie prancing happily around the yard. Throwing himself on the ground and rolling merrily in the fresh cut grass. Then getting up, black, brown, white...and green. It was hilarious.

Being a big dog, Lucky started to have a little arthritis as he got older. We made sure there were rugs around so he could get up more easily. Turns out that would be the least of his problems. Lucky started having a cough. A sort of dry, hollow cough, but it persisted. It didn't seem like much, but after a while, we decided to take him to the doc. He wasn't acting sick. He was still dopey old Lucky. But after a few x-rays, we were informed that he had a tumor on one of his lungs. Cancer. Ugh. Why Lucky?

Regardless of his illness, his spirits never flagged. He lost weight, but he was still a loving, happy boy. His appetite would come and go, but would always take a treat. I tried to spend extra time with him, which he always loved. I'd sit on the grass and he come over and plop down in front of me. His favorite was getting his ears rubbed and scratched. He'd crane his neck and kind of groan a little. If you stopped, he'd give you a look like "Why?" Sometimes, I'd spoon with him. You could tell he really enjoyed it.

I remember it was a Thursday. I got home in the early afternoon. There was Lucky, sunning himself in the driveway, looking regal. I got out of the car and went over to love him up. He was struggling to breathe a bit. And when he took a breath, you could hear a rattle. A wet, thick rattle. We called the vet and they said to bring him in around five. We sat with him, knowing what the outcome of the visit would likely be. I cried. Gail cried. Haley cried. He was so happy. He didn't know what was going on. But we did.

We put him in the back of Gail's Jeep and I rode in the back with him. He was happy. He loved to ride. When we got to the vet in Waxhaw, he was merrily walking around the yard. The rattle was pronounced. After consulting with the vet, we decided it was time. The end was inevitable. I would rather have him go out on a high note. I didn't want to wait until he was at death's door and struggling. And the advancement and severity of his condition was unpredictable. Gail and I sat with him on the floor. Haley left. She couldn't bare it. Lucky laid there, a smile on his face, not knowing what was coming and certainly, in his mind, not ready to go. But, I knew we were doing the right thing. If he had gone home, there was a chance his condition would advance and he'd drown in his sleep.

There is nothing worse than having to put down a pet that is still alert and feeling OK. We positioned ourselves so he could see us. We kissed him and told him how much we loved him. He couldn't hear us but he could see us crying and he knew something was up. When they gave him the final injection, he simply lowered his head, slowly, until his chin was resting on the floor and that was it. He was gone. My beautiful old boy, who deserved a better end to his story, was gone. Although the trip home was only seven miles, it seemed like a thousand.

To this day, there is still a patch of grass by the carriage light that is yellowed and thin. Though it has been years, that's where Lucky always peed. When I see it, I have to smile. I think sometimes he comes back to pee. Just to make sure we know he's still around.

...

DOLLY

aka
[Dolly Marie; Polly Puddin'; Dolly Doodle; White Devil; Scooby]

I remember it was March of 1995. I'm usually terrible with dates, so the fact that I actually remember that is amazing. The neighbors two crazy dogs; Mo the Pom and Shaina the Spitz; had a litter of puppies. Spitzeranians. Four little, fat, white paper weights. I was laying on the day bed, talking on the phone, and Little Haley Pillars plopped this wobbly, furry, hot water bottle on my chest. I was nose to nose with Dolly.

As soon as Dolly was able to leave her mother, she came to live with us. What a smart and funny dog she was. So alert and curious. This was supposed to be Haley's puppy. But Dolly was a face biter. If you got too close to her, she'd nip at your face. Haley was quite young and it scared her. So, instead of Dolly being her dog, she became a member of our growing pack.

Dolly was a character. She loved to play. With anything. When we had our ferrets, Ace and Bandit, Dolly couldn't wait until we opened their cage door so they could come out and play. The ferrets weren't intimidated by her and they'd hop around and scurry like ferrets are want to do. When Dolly got too excited, she resorted to a tactic that she became famous for. She'd sit on them. Not try to bite them or hurt them at all. Sit on them. Butt to ferret. In wrestling, we'd call that her "finishing move". And the ferrets seemed to love it. She'd stand up and they'd leap to their feet and pounce at her and the match would start again and always finish the exact same way. In the end, the ferrets collapsed in their cage and Dolly would go sleep in the living room.

Ferrets aside, not much else that crossed Dolly's path survived. She had a hunter's heart. The Vagabond Road house had a laundry room off the kitchen and we put a dog door in so the dogs could go out into the back yard. Many times we found dead baby possums in our laundry room. Some not so dead. We also had a terrible problem with Copperheads. Every spring and summer it seemed someone would get bitten. Dolly was the first. We heard the dogs making a commotion in the back yard. Dolly came to the house with her lip and muzzle swollen. A trip to the ER and a hard lesson learned later and Dolly knew to keep her distance. One day she came to me barking. She ran out to the back hedge and went on point. She never took her eyes off that spot. I went out there to find the biggest, fattest Copperhead I'd ever seen. I'll stop here and tell you that I've always loved snakes. I would never intentionally hurt one. But there was no way I was going to let this monster harm my pack. Wearing only gym shorts and armed with a rock, I crawled into the hedge on hands and knees with Dolly at my side. Yes, it was stupid, but it had to be done. Dolly kept the snakes attention while I got it with the rock. We were a good team. Once we moved to Mineral Springs, her range of prey widened. Raccoons and skunks. She was ruthless. A stark contrast to her normally bright and happy personality. Dr. Jekyll and Miss Dolly.

The Mineral Springs property was a blessing and a curse. Dolly and some of the other dogs became outdoor dogs. Sort of. The previous owners had big touring bus that was parked under a big port. That became part of their covered area and a nice big heated and air condition dog house. Things were so busy then that I didn't get a chance to spend much time with the dogs. The years flew, but Dolly, being pure snowy white, never showed her age and never really had many health issues over the years. When she was fourteen or so, I noticed that she'd gotten a little weak in her hind legs. I considered it just a part of her age. Then one day, I noticed she wasn't moving around much. Not at all, in fact. She was laying in the yard under a tree…in the rain.

I took her to the local vet in Waxhaw. They did some x-rays and blood work. Dolly had spondylosis. It's a degenerative spinal condition. The vet coldly said her condition would continue to deteriorate until her quality of life would be so bad that she would need to be euthanized. She gave her six months. I am not a person given to accepting things at face value and I damn sure don't like ultimatums. I'm even less likely to accept that there is nothing that can be done. So, I started doing a little research. It was time to give conventional treatment the back seat. That's when I found my miracle. Atrium Animal Hospital.

Atrium dealt in alternative therapies. Acupuncture, herbal remedies and Chinese medicine. We started with Dr. Kim Hombs who did her acupuncture and prescribed some herbals. Then Kathy Currlin stepped in to do a Chinese massage technique called "tui na". Poor Dolly's back legs, once thick and muscular, had withered with atrophy. It was flesh on bone. But I was game to try anything. After about six months of therapy and treatment, Dolly was not only walking again, but running. Not her usual frantic gate but it was great to see her romping around again. And her back legs and thighs? Like Schwarzenegger. Huge. Solid. In just six months. The exact amount of time that the other vet said she had left. Believe me, I took great pleasure in walking into that clinic and telling the doctor, in front of a waiting room full of patients, that she was not only wrong, but full of shit. That vet retired only months later. Another bad apple kicked out of the bushel.

Now it was Dolly's turn to be spoiled. She slept in the bedroom with me. At first I kept her in a holding cage because she was having trouble controlling her bladder and would leak in her sleep. But a trip to Atrium and some special Tea Pills, and her problem was gone in less than ten days. So Dolly got to sleep wherever she wanted. She had a special pillow at the foot of the dresser. Just about every night, I'd hear her snorting and rolling around. She'd growl at herself. I knew what was coming. "RR-RRRRREP"! That was her bark. It meant one of two things. She wanted to play or she wanted to go outside. If it was early in the evening, it meant "Come wrestle with me!" And I always did. I'd get on the floor with her and she'd be so vicious. Then when she had enough, she'd give me kisses and roll over to go to sleep. I'd rub her back for a minute or two and then turn in. I never turned her down. Ever. But you could set your clock on the fact that you'd hear that "RRRRRREP!" again around 3:30am. "Time to go for a pee walk, Pop!" No matter how tired I was, I'd scoop her up and take her outside. In the moonlight, I'd see that little white shape moving down the fence row, sniffing along and looking for a perfect place to squat. Then she'd casually wander back and wait to go back to bed.

Her condition required her to take a lot of pills and supplements. It was fine at first. She gobbled up her pill pockets. But then she got wise to the whole scheme. At that point, it was her versus me. Outsmarting her wasn't easy. I hated using the Pill Popper to shove the pills down her throat. Seemed kind of mean. I did everything. I'd wrap it in chicken or ground beef. She'd take it in her mouth and roll it around. You could see in her eyes that she knew something was up. A second later, the meat was gone and the pill was defiantly spit out in front of you. "You little shit!" She was extremely pleased with herself. We had quite a streak of success when we found out she liked cat food. Unfortunately, it was very high end cat food. Not cheap. But as long as it got down her, all was well. We always managed to get them down her but it was never a breeze.

Dolly loved going to the doctor. She was so spoiled by everyone at the clinic. One of her treatments was Underwater Treadmill. This is literally a treadmill underwater. The idea being that it takes about a third of the dogs weight away and gives them full range of motion, helping to strengthen their legs and back. When her hair was long, it would gracefully wave in the water like sea weed. When they were done, the girls would dry her with a towel and love her up. She was in heaven. If it was a tui na day, she was so dramatic. She would throw herself down and expose her belly for Kathy. She loved getting her "spa day". All the massage and stretching was so good for her. Acupuncture, on the other hand, was different. Poor Dr. Hombs. She is the one who introduced Dolly to acupuncture and Dolly didn't like it. They had to muzzle her. There was a mark on her chart that said "WB". It meant "Will Bite", but I always said it was for "White Bitch". Then came Dr. Yen. She had a totally different approach to acupuncture. Dolly never so much as snarled at her. The pins would go in and Dolly would be laying there smiling at me and eating little Charlie Bear treats. One time, Dr. Hombs came in for something. Dolly was pretty deaf at this point but when she saw Dr. Hombs, she gave her little growl. Dr. Hombs is bothered by that to this day!

Dolly turned 17 on March 15, 2012! They threw a birthday party for her at Atrium. She wore a tiara and had big can of her favorite special food with a candle. She was so damn spoiled. She was doing very well but I could see her slowing down. Getting fussy about her food. Not wanting to wrestle as often. One day, when she was eating I noticed her back end started sinking to the floor. On her walks, if she stopped, her back end would slowly sink. Consulting with Kathy Currlin at Atrium, we decided it was just "age and stage". The years were catching up with her. The spondylosis in her spine was reaching a critical point. But she was hanging on. She'd look at me and I could see the love in her eyes. But I could also see the weariness. She was tired.

It was Saturday, October 27, 2012, I was going to run to Atrium to get a refill on one of her supplements. She looked sad that day, so I thought I'd let her ride along. She loved to ride. I'd keep one hand on the wheel and another on my Scooby. She was different today. Quiet and still. I fussed with her but I knew she wasn't feeling good. We pulled into Atrium. She sat up. I got out and went around to her door and when I opened the door, she was laying on her side panting. I picked her up and cuddled her for a second. I put her on the ground and she fell over. I tried to right her but she toppled over again. She couldn't stand. I scooped her up and ran into the clinic. "Something is wrong with Dolly!" They hustled me into the back and Dr. Barbara Butchko was looking at her. Her rear legs were not responding to any sort of stimulus. She was hurting. As I'd had to do so many times before, I had to make "the decision". It was time to say good-bye. We were taken to a room and I got on the floor with her. I was crying my eyes out. One after the other, everyone came to say good-bye to the dog who became a fixture there. It made me cry even more. I held her little white face in my hands and kissed her over and over. Kathy stayed with us as Dolly said good-bye. I cried on the way home. I cried the rest of the day. I cried myself to sleep. The next morning, when I got up, I saw her empty pillow at the foot of the dresser and I cried some more.

When I got her ashes back, I took a small amount and went to Atrium. I sprinkled the ashes in the landscaping where she always insisted on taking a sniff and a pee. It was the right thing to do.

A few weeks later, I was startled from my sleep by a familiar sound. "RRRRRRREP!" As clear as a bell. Not my imagination. And the time on the clock? Yes. 3:30am. Dolly had come back to let me know everything was OK. I got up, walked to the front door and opened it for her one last time. In the distance, I could have sworn I saw a small white blur walking the fence line.

. . .

TC

aka

[Pete; Pistol Pete; Popperjack; Pinecone Pete; Popcorn Pete; Popsicle Pete; T-Bone; T-Dog; Mr.T; Sir]

Once again, I was on the road. I was off to Capetown, South Africa, to do the movie "Pirates of the Plains" with Tim Curry, Dee Wallace and Charles Napier. It hadn't been that long since Haley lost her beloved little Lady. I hated leaving home. But Gail's favorite aunt, Vera, was there and Haley loved her. I still wasn't crazy about being that far away from my family. There had been talk about getting Haley another dog, but nothing was definite. Little did I realize… On one of my calls home, I got the news. Haley had a new dog. Another Pomeranian. She named him TC, for "Tough Cookie".

After seven weeks on the other side of the world, I returned home. My head was shaved, save for a long ponytail and my beard was thick and full. Little Haley Pillars was at the gate waiting for her daddy. On the ride home, she didn't ask about Africa. All she did was talk about her new dog. When I got home, I was shocked. I knew it was supposed to be a dog, but it looked more like a rat. A loud, virtually hairless, spastic rat. Light auburn in color with a rat tail that curled over his back. This manic little thing ran up to me and I picked it up. "So, you're TC?" He immediately started squirming and wiggling and I almost dropped him! I put him down and he launched, running all over the front yard like he'd escaped from a lunatic asylum. What had we gotten ourselves into?

Gail told me that although they had paid for TC, she felt like it was a rescue. The conditions were terrible. The people who sold TC were eventually busted as a puppy mill. I don't think TC cared too much about the past. He was too busy enjoying today. We've never had a puppy that was such a maniac. It seems like he ran everywhere he went and as fast as his little legs would carry him. He loved to play, but only what he wanted to do. TC didn't care about your stupid dog games. If you threw a stick for him, he'd run over, pick it up and run AWAY from you. If you tried to take the stick back? He'd lie down on the ground and bite the stick to pieces, one bite at a time. He knew exactly what he was doing and there was not an ounce of remorse on his face. Then he'd run past you, with that ridiculous taunting smile. He loved being a turd.

When he was a puppy, he was the wrestling dog. He was fearless. He'd go and attack Sandy, our Chow mix, who was easily ten times his size. Sandy, ever the good sport, would throw herself to the ground and TC would stand on top of her and bite and pull her lips. If you wanted a piece of TC, he'd take you down. He didn't realize he was the size of a popcorn fart. I promise you, if you mixed it up with TC, you'd quit before he did. He always found ways to amuse himself. Haley had VERY long hair that she kept in a braid. If she bent over, TC would latch on to it and Haley could lift him off the ground. He'd hang on for dear life and growl and squirm the whole time. On a moment's notice and without any provocation, TC would "low butt" run around the house. Low Butt running is where a dog runs frantically with their tail tucked and butts low to the ground. Occasionally TC would get tired and sleep. I guess. I personally never saw it.

TC was happy to accommodate all of Haley's ridiculous whims. He went to more tea parties than the Queen of England. He'd sit in the doll's high chair and eat Cheerios and little dog treats, while Haley would pour water into his cup. Halloween was her excuse to dress him up in outfits that other dogs would be embarrassed by. Not TC. He'd ham it up, shamelessly. Haley had one of those portable pop-up kid's tents and many days that was their fort. They'd nap and watch movies. The proof of TC's love for Haley was during Mint Hill Madness one year. It was a small town festival where we lived and we went annually. This year, Haley entered TC in the Pet Parade. Haley dressed him in a onesie that used to be on one of her dolls. It didn't have a butt flap so you couldn't see his tail. It was just creepy. Creepier still was when he walked in it. Oh my God, it was like some deformed little monkey. Then she pushed him around in a baby stroller. But if it made Haley happy, TC was all for it. They were inseparable. When Haley was in school, I'd take TC to go pick her up. He'd sit on my lap while we waited and it was so funny to watch him frantically scan all those kid's faces looking for his girl. His little ears would quiver in anticipation. When he'd finally see her, he'd whine and gurgle until she got in the car. Then he'd dive on her and smother her with Pom lovin'.

I don't know why, but I always called him "Pete". He just looked like a Pete to me. He knew that's what I called him and he was cool with it. As he got older, I could use that name to make him bark. He'd walk into the kitchen trying to hoark a treat. I pretended I didn't see him. His ears were up; his eyes were wide; his frustration growing. Finally, I'd look at him and the second we made eye contact, his ears would go back a bit and he'd get that low growl going. "PETE!" And that would set him off. He'd bark and bark until he got what he wanted. That never got old. He and I did that same routine, with minor variations, up till the last week of his life.

TC's haircuts were legendary. If you didn't cut his hair, he looked like a dirty cotton ball; a tumbleweed with teeth. When he had a puppy cut, there was no one cuter. He looked like a little fox and sometimes a bear cub. Sometimes we went a while between haircuts. He looked like a cartoon dust bunny. We never had a groomer that didn't love him and say he was easiest dog they ever groomed.

One day while we were downstairs, Haley let TC outside and all of a sudden he couldn't stand. Came to find out that TC had hurt his back. At the same time, he got vestibular disease, which is dog's version of vertigo. Their eyes move side to side, they can't focus and they walk in stumbling circles. Too many times, people assume their dog has had a stroke and have them put down. Vestibular just requires some time but it passes. We took TC to the vet in Waxhaw. X-rays showed that TC had spondylosis of the spine, which is a weakening and deterioration of the vertebrae. It also showed that he had an enlarged heart. We always knew he had a bit of a heart murmur but never this. The vet gave him six months to a year. Haley was sobbing. That was our last trip to that vet. And we started taking him to Atrium Animal Hospital.

Atrium is an integrated vet clinic. They did traditional medicine and holistic. Acupuncture and physical therapy. In his later years, TC needed all of that. Upon examination, we discovered that the other vet was, essentially, full of shit. His heart was NOT enlarged and his spine, while not perfect, was certainly not a death sentence. Atrium would become a second home for an aging and ailing little monster. They loved him and spoiled him rotten.

TC required therapeutic massage called Tui Na. He loved it and the therapist, Kathy Currlin. She'd massage and stretch TC and he'd sit up and lean back against her, giving her love. When he had to have K-Laser therapy, he'd wear goggles that made him look like a bug. He even used the Underwater Treadmill. The tank was big enough to hold a Great Dane and there was tiny TC in about three inches of water, plodding along like he was on a Sunday stroll in the park. He dominated that water tank. He always did great and it kept him strong. But TC would soon face his toughest challenge.

Haley was working and going to school and TC didn't see her as often. That made him become even more protective of Haley when she was home. When she would lie on the couch, TC would recline on the back of the couch above her head, monitoring her every move. He wanted to be with her every second she was home. If she was standing up, he'd bark his head off until she picked him up. When she did, he'd stop with that self satisfied look on his face. Around this time, TC started acting different. He wasn't eating as well, which was a big red flag. There's never been a dog so focused on food as TC. We attributed it to him being lonely for his girl. To be safe, we had a full blood panel done and found that TC was in the early stages of renal failure. It was hard news to take.

TC stayed in the hospital for a few days. He was not happy. I stood in the lobby and you could clearly hear his unmistakable "Gab! Gab! Gab!" It got so bad that all the vet techs took turns holding him so he'd just shut up for a few minutes. Again, spoiled rotten. After a few days on fluids and antibiotics, he was ready to come home. It became necessary for him to get fluids at home every day and that became my responsibility. Gail or Haley would hold him while I put the needle in under his skin. He was a patient boy getting his "squirts" but he was never happy about it. Getting a pill in him, however, required the patience of Job. You could try to hide a pill in food, but TC found it. You could wrap it in steak. TC would take it in his mouth, roll it around, swallow the steak and spit the pill out. The minute we found something that worked, it didn't work long. We went through hundreds of cans of high end dog food and even cat food looking for the "key". And it changed like the calendar. He went through a chicken phase, a beef phase, a tuna and sardine phase and even a pie crust phase. It was frustrating. But because it was TC, it was also hilarious.

TC had another stay at the hospital. His kidney values were getting worse. He was virtually deaf by this point and his eyesight was fading. But the King of Comebacks came back again. With a vengeance. He was a ball of fire and was extremely full of himself. But he didn't let that get in the way of being spoiled. One of his many quirks was he didn't like going up and down the steps anymore. So when he wanted to go out, he'd scamper over to you and turn sideways. That was the signal you should pick him up. He'd let you navigate the steps for him. You'd put him down and he'd scamper out to his favorite "poopin' tree". Then he'd "let you" carry him back up the steps and he'd retire to his pillow in the den. If he needed you, he'd let you know.

His last trip to Atrium was a pip. He had Tui Na that day. He was feeling good and wanted to let the world know it. I was standing in the lobby with Kathy. Since it was practically empty, I put TC down. Without warning he ran all over the lobby, stopping to bark at me like a maniac. He was on fire! Mind you, TC was over sixteen years old at the time. TC was sprinting like a Greyhound. I got him home and he ate like a pig and slept for hours, which is what usually happened after his rub down. The next day, his girl came home and got to spend the entire day with him. He was in heaven.

The very next night was a Saturday. February 21st. I remember because that was my dad's birthday. TC ate his dinner. I was the only one home that night, sitting in the kitchen and he walked over to me with that look in his eye. "Come over here, Pete. Come see your dad." He walked over and stood sideways. I picked him up and held him for a while. I don't know why. He let me know when he'd had enough and he snorted and went back to his pillow for an after dinner nap. I went back down to my office to write. I came upstairs about ten o'clock. I opened the door to the den. I saw TC lying on the floor just inside the kitchen door. My heart stopped. I ran to him, but I knew. TC; Haley's best friend for over 16 years; was dead. I sat on the kitchen floor holding his little body, crying and screaming "No, sir! No, sir! No, sir!" I called Gail. "Oh, Gail. TC's dead." I explained what happened. I told her she would have to tell Haley. I carried TC into the laundry room and lay him on a towel. It was the first time I'd ever seen his tail straight. I don't know why I remember that, but I can still see it. I drove him to the ER. I didn't want his little body at home when Gail or Haley came back. On the drive, I held him against my chest, wrapped in a towel, the same way I always did when we were going to and from the vet. I was releasing his remains to be cremated and I just didn't want to let him go. I finally kissed him for the last time and said good-bye.

On the way home, Haley called me. It broke my heart. TC had been Haley's rock. He was always there for her during the worst times of her life. When she was suffering from a crippling illness, TC was there. When she broke up with a boyfriend, TC let her know that no matter what, he loved her. The outpouring of sympathies was overwhelming. When Haley moved into her new apartment, she took TC's ashes with her. They will never be apart again. There is a reason this is the longest chapter in the book. While I've loved all my dogs, we have never had a dog, before or since, that had such an impact or made such an impression. There isn't a day that goes by that I don't think of him and smile. He was the dog of a lifetime, in a lifetime of dogs.

...

HEIDI

aka

[Blueberry; Bloofus; Bluetoof; Werewolf Puppy; Blueberry Blue]

When we first moved to Mineral Springs, we found a great groomer in Waxhaw. One morning she called and said that someone had dropped off a puppy. If we didn't take it they were going to take it to the pound. I didn't want to let that happen and so I hopped in the car and drove down there. I was presented with what looked like a baby werewolf. A fuzzy little auburn colored bear. Obviously some sort of Chow mix. Cute as a bug. She looked up at me with questioning eyes. I can still see it so clearly in my mind. How in the hell could I say no? So, I picked her up. "You looking for a place to crash?" She gave me many kisses and politely sat on the passenger seat as we drove to her forever home.

Gail named her Heidi, but I always have my own names for them. Heidi had those purple spots on her tongue from her Chow blood. I said it was like she'd been eating blueberries. So from then on I called her Blueberry, or variations thereof. She always knew I was referring to her. In her first few months, we kept her in the laundry room off the kitchen. We put up a baby gate so she could be included in the goings on and get to know the other dogs. God, she was cute. I'd look at her over the gate. "What do Blueberries do for their father?" She knew that meant to sit and she did. No matter how old she got, all I had to do was ask that question and she'd sit right down. She also loved to hug. When Gail would lean over the gate to love her up, Heidi would wrap her front legs around her neck and hold on for dear life. It's like she was saying, "Please let me come in! I don't want to be alone!"

Heidi had small ears. For a dog her size, they seemed unusually small. Not tiny, just small. They looked fine when she was a little puppy but when she got big, her ears didn't. It just seemed odd. Gail always said Heidi grew up but her ears never did. But her feet did grow. As a puppy, her feet were curious looking. That's why I called her the Werewolf Puppy. And when she grew, so did her feet and I don't think they ever stopped. When she walked in soft earth or mud, it looked like a shape shifter had been stalking the property.

Heidi grew into a big bear of a dog but she always acted like a puppy. Gail's puppy. She always followed right on Gail's heels. Especially after she was spayed. Her procedure didn't go well and she didn't react to the anesthesia normally. Once she was back to square, she attached herself to Gail's hip. Inseparable. If Gail was in her chair, Heidi was at her feet. If Gail was sleeping, Heidi was on the floor right next to her. And when Gail went to work in the garden, you couldn't keep Heidi away. She KNEW that at some point, the hose would come out. Her beloved hose. Yes, Heidi was a water dog. She'd get extremely animated when Gail turned on the hose. I couldn't even begin to calculate the gallons of water she wasted letting Heidi bite at the water stream. By the end, she was usually soaked nose to tail and gloriously content.

When the horses weren't in the pasture, I'd call for Heidi. "Blueberry. Pond!" She come flying to the gate, her little ears up and her tail wagging a mile a minute. I'd open the gate and she'd zoom out into the pasture. We'd walk down to the small pond and along the way, I'd find a stick and show it to her. She would crouch in anticipation. I'd throw that stick into the pond and she'd take a short sprint and then LEAP into the air and hit the water like someone dropped a cinder block out of a helicopter! She'd swim over and grab the stick and bring it back. Over and over. When we were done, she'd grab that stick in her mouth and trot back to the house to proudly show her mom.

Heidi never really had any health problems. She had a growth on one of her giant feet that had to be removed, but as I recall, that was about it. For some reason, I think it was a Wednesday afternoon. Gail texted me that she had to take Heidi to the vet. NOW. I ran upstairs and Heidi was clearly not well. It happened just all of a sudden. Gail opened the back of the van and when I bent down to help Heidi into the back, I could feel that her tummy was quite taught. Gail rushed her to Atrium. Later on, she sent me a text that Heidi was full of fluid. And there were complications. It was time to let Heidi go. I was dumbstruck. How? She was fine the day before and now she needs to be euthanized? I quickly finished chores and raced to the clinic. When I went in the door, I found Gail laying on the floor next to Heidi, sobbing her eyes out. I sat on the floor and stroked her head. "Hey, Blueberry Blue…" She was not doing well. The vet gave her a shot to sedate her. It didn't take. At all. Heidi was not ready to go. But she had to. Gail tried to comfort her but old Blueberry was not having it. After two more shots, she was finally sedated. She was struggling and it was time to say good-bye. I felt so bad for Gail. I'd been through this too many times and I hated seeing her crying over an animal she was close to. Even after the final shot, Heidi's heart beat for a while. She didn't want to let go. Finally it was over. I helped Gail up and out the door. I turned back and reached down and rubbed those ridiculously small ears one last time.

...

MILLIE

aka

[Baby Banill; Millie Vanillie; Baby Bue; Bubbanill; Bubs; Mono Me]

It sounds completely cliché, but it was a dark and stormy morning. Friday morning, to be exact. I was up early to go to "The John Boy & Billy Big Show", to do The Playhouse, a featured bit that was sort of a comedic "redneck theatre of the mind". I braved the downpour to run to my car, a beautiful maroon Reliant K station wagon. I started the car and before I could put it in reverse, I saw a dark object dart from underneath. A scared black hound dog puppy sat shivering in the car port. I got out and she came right to me. She had a wormy belly and a white star on her chest. I brought her to the house and woke up Gail. I handed her our new addition. I called her Midnight. Gail called her Millie. Gail won.

Millie was a gangly, silly puppy. When she ran, she was all legs and ass. Happy and goofy. And if a dog can have a single distinguishing mark, Millie had hers. One, single white hair on the very tip of her tail. Just one. But it always made me smile when I saw it. It was so ridiculously random. Like all of our rescues, it was always clear that Millie was just so happy to have a home. And stuff. Most of all, she loved her dolly. It was a small fleece figure of a man. She could not sleep without it. When bed time rolled around, Millie brought her dolly. She leaped up on the bed and kept it close. I remember one time, she couldn't find dolly. Gail accused me of hiding it but I would never do that to her. We got out of bed and looked all over the house. Thank God, it was a small house. Millie was by our side during the entire scavenger hunt. I think we finally found it stuck between the couch cushions. If she could have giggled and clapped, I believe she would have. She snatched the dolly from my hand and ran off. We found her on her spot on the bed, dolly safely tucked under her. Dolly continued to get smaller and smaller until one day it just wasn't there anymore. Millie was a big girl now.

Little Haley Pillars had a passion for fashion and Millie was her runway model. She gladly sat there while Haley dressed her in endless combinations of sunglasses and t-shirts and beads. Haley would bring Millie in to show her mom. Millie didn't have to be lead, she trotted right along with Haley. And when it was time for a wardrobe change, she gladly accommodated, eager to please. Although she was quite animated and silly, she really didn't do any tricks, per se. The closest she ever was what I called "Long Dog". Millie probably had some Doberman in her. She had a full chest and a narrow waist just like them. And when she was happy or very comfortable, she did the Long Dog. Front legs straight out in front and back legs extended all the way to the back. Hence, Long Dog. I'd rub her chest and her belly and she'd snort and snuffle and roll her head around. It got to a point where all I'd have to do was say Long Dog, and she'd assume the position. She loved the attention.

In the pack hierarchy, Millie was a submissive. She didn't seek to be dominant. It wasn't in her nature. She was happy just going with the flow. All the dogs loved to chase the ball. If there were too many dogs competing for the ball, Millie would just sit by and watch. But when you told the other dogs to stand down so Millie could have a turn, she sprang into action. She was so happy to have a turn or two and then was content to hang out and watch until her next chance to play. That was just Millie. Another trademark of her submissiveness was her trot. When she was out eating cat poop and you yelled at her, she'd come trotting back with this wide legged gate, her head down and smiling to show her teeth. And her tail? Weirdest tail ever. Like a backwards question mark.

Gail started to notice that Millie was beginning to act a little distant. A little bit absent in her gaze. I tried to dismiss it, but it was clear. Millie was in the early stages of Canine Cognitive Disorder. In other words, Dog Alzheimer's. To compound the problem, she was also having mobility issues. In the early stages of the disease, we took her to Atrium for Underwater Treadmill. She did very well and it helped to strengthen her back legs and lower back. It seemed to engage her, mentally, as well. But it was abundantly clear that Millie was beginning to lose her way and was easily confused. That's why it made me so happy when I'd take her to the pasture to do her exercises up and down the hill. She'd suddenly get a bee in her bonnet and off she'd go. Galloping around the pasture. Chasing Skittles and Chloe and bounding through the tall grass. Carefree and happy. Those were great days, but it didn't last long. Soon, she was having trouble just going up and down the three steps to the house from the garage. Once in a while, out of nowhere, she'd gracefully leap from the garage floor up to the laundry room floor. Just like in the old days. "Oh, Banill! You're so agile!" But those inspirational moments faded.

As her disease progressed, it was more trips to the vet. She usually pooped or even peed during the trip. Sometimes in the water tank she'd poop, too. At home, she'd wander around the kitchen like she didn't know where her food dish was. She'd eventually find it. Sometimes she'd eat. Sometimes she didn't. She also started "getting stuck". With her weakened back legs, she'd get stuck on the floor. Usually at night. In the morning, you'd find her sitting in her own poop, sometimes pee. She'd look up at you with those lost eyes. It was heartbreaking. I started keeping her in the back bedroom with me. She had many accidents. But there was still a little Millie there. The old Millie would appear during treat time. She loved her treats. She remembered what treats were. And rice pudding. Gail makes the most amazing homemade rice pudding and Millie loved it. Her big old floppy ears would raise up and her empty eyes would brighten, if only for a moment. It was sad and frustrating.

One night, Millie didn't eat. Not only didn't she eat, she went to her food and it was like she didn't know what it was anymore.

I offered her treats and got no reaction. This would be Millie's last night. The next morning, I called Atrium and said "It's time." Millie stood in the back seat most of the way to the vet. In her younger days, she'd be watching everything. Today, it was a blank stare. When I got her in the room at Atrium, she lay right down beside me. She never moved. I sat beside her, silent. I knew that she wouldn't know what I was saying. So, I just stroked her old head and cried. When the doctor came in to let Millie go, it was very quick. Like she just couldn't wait. I bowed my head and I prayed that she showed up on the other side, whole and well and able to run and play. I kissed her head and took one last look. There it was. That one single white hair on the tip of her tail. And through the tears, I smiled.

. . .

SHEMP

aka
[Shempers; Champ; Shempy; Big Foot]

I had stopped by PetSmart in Matthews, NC, to buy ferret chow on my way to a job. As I'm standing in check out, a young guy walks in with a young, Black Lab mix on a leash. "Where do I go to put this dog up for adoption?" "Sorry, sir. We don't do that here." The man paused for a moment, dropped the leash and left. Just left. Walked out. Leaving behind a very confused dog. He kept looking out the door, waiting for his master to come back. What he did was beyond cruel. The manager was about to call Animal Control and I said, "If someone can take him up the road to my veterinarian, I'll take him." I walked over to him and bent down, taking his head in my hands. "You wanna go home with me, bud?" He wagged his tail but he was still uncertain. They let me use the office phone to call the vets office. I said "Check him out and I'll be over to get him shortly." "OK, what's his name?" "Shemp".

I don't know why I called him that. I just always liked the name. And like his namesake, he was a forgotten stooge, too. The vet said he was in great shape. We made arrangements to have him neutered. He was young but not a puppy. He had sleek black hair, little tiny pig eyes and the biggest feet I've ever seen on a dog. Like a bear! I took him out to the car and he jumped right in. On the ride home, he was calm. Looking casually out the window, like he'd done it before. This ride wouldn't end like his last one. This time he had a home. It's like he knew this was the real deal. We were in the little house in Mint Hill at the time and adding another dog was putting us close to the tipping point. But Shemp was low-to-no maintenance. He went with the flow. You've never seen a happier dog.

The move to Mineral Springs was good and bad for Shemp. He was spending the majority of his time outside. We had turned one of those pre-fab sheds into a dog house. Heated and cooled. One door lead to the big covered area, complete with an old sleeper sofa for lounging and a kiddie pool for cooling off in the summer. The other door lead out into a long quarter acre run with big trees, lots of shade and soft grass. Shemp wasn't alone. Dolly, Sandy, Daisy and Rocky were out there too. We hated that they weren't in the house with the family but they seemed to do pretty well. Even though Rocky and Shemp were big males, there wasn't any conflict to speak of. Yet.

Gail was home alone and she heard a fight break out in the pen. Rocky had attacked Shemp from the front and Daisy was attacking his rear. This wasn't a pissing contest over a treat or a toy. This was a fight. And if Gail hadn't gotten to them, it would have been to the death. Gail got in the pen and threw herself on top of Shemp, punching and pushing Rocky and Daisy away, but the damage was done. They really tore him up. Gail got him to the vet. Many stitches later and a lot of pain meds, my boy was home. From that day forward, Rocky and

Shemp had to be kept separate. Even in their advanced age, the animus was still there and very, very real.

The fact that Shemp and Rocky didn't get along meant we had to bring someone in the house. It was Rocky. Shemp, due to his easy going nature, was safer to keep with other dogs. But it also generated a lot of guilt. Whenever everyone was outside, Shemp would stand in his pen and bark. He wanted to be a part of the family so badly. I spent time with him as much as I could. He always loved being able to come out of his enclosure. He'd bound around like a fool. Big smile on his dopey face. Every time I had to put him back, you could see his spirits sink. It really bothered me.

Shemp started to turn his nose up at food so I knew something was up. A trip to the vet and some blood work showed that he had kidney disease and was in the early stages of kidney failure. Now, I'll tell you, five years ago, I would have been inconsolable. That would have been all she wrote. But I knew that I could give him fluids at home daily and Atrium would know the proper supplements and herbals to get him back on track. None of this is a cure for the inevitable, but it keeps their quality of life intact. So, Shemp and I changed our routine.

Every morning, before I did chores, he'd come into the foyer for his fluids. If it was nice outside, we'd do it on the front steps. I'd bring his rig out and he knew exactly what to do. He'd come over and lay down. I'd put the needle in and turn on the flow. We'd sit there, me drinking coffee and Shemp just chilling. I'd mix his kidney supplements in some blueberry kefir and give it to him in a big syringe. He never once turned away or made a face. I think he liked the blueberry flavor.

Even though he was getting on in years, Shemp was still quite active. I started getting him out in the morning to do chores with me. It was a perfect fit. I'd open his door in the morning and he'd come flying out! He romped around like a simpleton until he shook a poop loose. Then it was time to go to work. He loved going to the barn in the morning. The cats freaked

The House of Goodbyes

out at first, but when they realized he was harmless, they became fascinated with him. Especially, Momma Girl. She had a storied history of loving on dogs. None of them liked it, but it didn't stop her. Shemp was no exception. "Shemp, here's your girlfriend!" You could almost hear him sigh in exasperation.

While I was in the barn, Shemp hung out in the side yard. He loved to sniff around and if it was warm, he'd lounge in the shade and do his roll and snort. But every so often, the temptation was too much and he'd sneak into the paddock to scavenge for cat poop. We've had a lot of dogs and all of them, at one time or another, had a thing for "kitty pickles". If only someone could capture that flavor in a dog treat, they'd make a fortune. Although the real thing is much less expensive. I'd go out and scold him and he'd scamper back to the side yard, like he'd really gotten away with something.

I started to notice Shemp was acting "off". I can't really describe it. It was just a feeling. He wasn't being himself. Seemed a little low. He still liked his walks. He loved his morning snort and roll. But I could see it in his eyes. And his eyes said "I'm tired". I was getting ready to leave the house, but something told me to check on him. I opened his door and he looked up at me. But he wouldn't get up. I called him again. Nothing. Finally he struggled to his feet. He came out, sort of wobbly like. He got to the concrete driveway and he started to poop. Soft, wet, viscous. He laid down and wouldn't get up. I put him in the backseat and raced to CARE in Charlotte.

I got to CARE and got Shemp out of the car. He wouldn't stand up. He was hurting. I carried him into the clinic and they took him into the back. I had that feeling again. The doctor came in and said "He's really in a lot of pain." I explained about his kidney issues. She agreed that this was probably the end. I knew in my heart it was time. A few minutes later they rolled Shemp in on a cart. He looked at me with those little brown eyes. He looked so sad. I held his old grey face in my hands and told him how much I loved him and what a great friend he'd been to me. He gave me a little kiss and that's when I started crying. The doctor gave the sedative and Shemp was asleep in no time. When the doctor started to give the final injection, she'd barely pushed the plunger and he was gone. It was shocking. He was gone in an instant. He was ready. I don't often sit with my dogs when they're gone, but I did this time. He looked just like he looked when I was doing his fluids. So peaceful and still. Finally I stood up, leaned over and kissed him one more time and left behind the best work mate I'd ever known.

...

ROSIE

aka

[Rosie Toes; Miss Rose; Toes; Thunder Toes; Boxer Hound]

Gail was on her way to work. She took an unusually circuitous route which was always under construction. This particular morning, the traffic was especially bad. As she creeped towards the intersection, she saw a Boxer running around in the road. People were slowing down and going around her. Gail found the chance to pull over, walked into the road and called her. The Boxer bounded over to her. "Do you want to go for a ride?" She helped her into the Jeep. The Boxer rode all the way to the house with her head on Gail's shoulder. For the next two weeks, Gail drove through all the neighborhoods looking for "Lost Dog" signs. Nothing. So we had another dog. A Boxer. Gail called her Rosie.

Rosie was brown with the docked Boxer tail, but her ears were uncut. She was so precious. How the hell could someone lose a dog like this? Regardless, she was home now. She was so happy and was always doing "The Boxer Wiggle". Anyone who has ever owned or known a Boxer knows exactly what that is. Any sort of excitement, be it minor or major, produced a full body wiggle. Rosie's little stump tail would whirl! She was happiest when she was with Gail. She was another of Gail's babies. Gail was her savior.

Rosie was a world champion sleeper. She'd take naps with me from time to time, but when bedtime came around, she went looking for mom. Every night, she'd wedge herself next to Gail, contently snoring like a broken duck call. I don't know what Rosie's life was like before she came to be with us, but it sure must have been bad. Rosie had the most amazing dreams/nightmares of any dog we've ever had. Everyone's dog has doggie dreams. Rosie's were a full blown production. Her face would twitch, her legs would move, she make crying sounds and she'd shake all over. All you could do was either wait for it to pass or gently love on her until she woke up. I felt sorry for her, but sometimes it was a laugh riot.

When it came to grasping the concept of size, Rosie was a "D" student. She was certain that no matter how small your lap was, she fit on it. There was no telling her otherwise. If you sat down in our house, Rosie was going to find a way to get on top of you. She loved everyone and assumed the feeling was mutual. She wasn't aggressive about it. She was very subtle in her approach. She'd climb up on the chair or couch one leg at a time, hoping you wouldn't notice. Before you knew it, you and Rosie were one. Once on top of you, she looked you in the eye and if you made eye contact, chances were pretty good you'd get a Boxer kiss or twelve. It was the same thing at bedtime. She'd wedge herself next to/on top of Gail. Rosie always had to be touching you.

Everyone has a super power. Rosie's was being a Cat Magnet. Cat's loved Rosie. I don't think she was particularly fond of cats but just got to point where there was no use fighting it. If Rosie was taking a snooze, you could pretty much count on a cat sleeping on her. One cat in particular looked on Rosie as her mom. Dulcie. When Dulcie was quite young, she'd climb up on Rosie, take her ear in her mouth and nurse on it while kneading the side of Rosie's head. Even if Rosie was sitting in the kitchen, any cat nearby was mysteriously drawn to her, rubbing all around her. All Rosie could do was sigh and accept it.

Even in her later years, Rosie was fast. Like Millie, she was built for speed. Before we had our fences up, we had to be careful not to let Rosie out untethered. One time, Rosie and Millie bolted on us. In an instant they disappeared into the woods. Gail jumped in her Jeep and after a while found them two streets over, standing in the road, wondering how they got themselves there. The fences went up shortly afterwards. That kept them from escaping but not from running. One of Rosie's "triggers" to erupt into a run was a successful poop. She'd trot out of the house and start down the driveway. She had a favorite spot just to the left of the driveway. She'd do her business and then she'd scratch at the ground doing her peel out and then leap into the air and run back to the house. I called it the Poop Run. And like all other Boxer's she did the full body wiggle when she ran. Her footfall was so heavy and loud, it earned her the nickname "Thunder Toes".

Rosie had many quirks. She was a talker. She talked to Gail all the time. If she felt like she wasn't getting enough attention, she'd put her head on Gail's leg and start to whine. The whine turned into a grumble; the grumble, to a bark. Until Gail either pet her or let her outside. If there were any other dogs around and Rosie thought they were getting the attention that she should be getting, she would walk up and wedge herself between you and the offending canine. She was not shy about it, either. She was also a "fart startler". Meaning that she'd be surprised at her own poots. She'd cut the cheese and turn around looking for where the sound came from. And when it came time to eat, you better put her food in a bowl. A lot of times we fed the dogs off a spoon. Maybe it was because of the shape of her steam shovel jaw or maybe just because she was a klutz but Rosie could NOT eat off a spoon. She would sort of tip her head sideways and try to snatch the food as it fell off of it and it never ended well. The other dogs got used to hanging around to snatch up everything she dropped. I'm surprised she didn't starve.

Rosie's brown face had been white for a few years but she hadn't really shown many other signs of age. She was slower now, but was still funny old Rosie. That changed all of a sudden. Rosie was suddenly unsteady on her feet. She had a hard time staying up. She looked sad. Rosie was sick. Very sick. Gail had to take her to the vet. I had to work and then I had a very important recording to do. I helped Rosie into the back of the van and she immediately lay down. I held her face and kissed her. "Come back to me, Toes. Come back to dad." I'll never forget, I had stopped at Arby's to get a sandwich and before I could pull in the parking space, my phone rang. It was Gail. I could tell by her voice, the news is what I feared. We were going to lose Rosie Toes to cancer. Son of a bitch. There are times as a pet owner when only one parent was there and this was one of those times. I hated not being there with Gail because she was so attached to Rosie and needed the moral support. Haley went with her. Gail said Rosie passed quietly. Which is probably one of the few times she was ever quiet.

...

OLIVER

aka
[Wallaceford; Wally Balls; Mr. O; Walleed Sheik Balls; OllieVar]

The folks at one of the riding stables Gail frequented were caring for a stray. A Schnauzer. At least that's what they thought. His fur was so overgrown and matted with sticks and debris that no one could tell. The boys at the stable gave him a "haircut" and sure enough, it was a Schnauzer. Gail named him Oliver. He was grown, but young and of all the dogs we've ever owned, he was the square peg in our packs round hole. I don't know any other way to describe it but he was like that kid on the playground than nobody ever wanted to play with because he was such an oddball. He wasn't a loner, he liked other dogs. But he was just so damn socially awkward. Like the guy at the party that goes around asking people to pull his finger.

Oliver started his stint with us as an outdoor dog. He was bunked with Lucky the Collie and Buddy the Beagle. But when he wound up having eye surgery for cataracts, he was moved to the house. Oliver had a habit of sticking his nose in everyone else's business…and butts. It seemed like he irritated everyone. He was a tender little guy but a hopelessly irritating nerd. If two other dogs were in a dust up, Oliver had to butt in and make things worse. If you were walking with an armful of groceries or something heavy, Oliver would step directly in front of you at the worst possible moment. It was like having a dog version of Jerry Lewis underfoot. Always the wrong thing at the wrong moment.

Oliver fancied himself a hunter. As long as whatever he was hunting was defenseless. Yeah, he was dick. Before we had two thousand cats running around, we had lots of baby birds to be rescued in the spring. If Oliver saw you trying to catch a baby bird, he did everything he could do to push past you and get the bird. You could hit him, push him, yell at him, but you couldn't stop him. It made Gail absolutely furious.

    Oliver started to gain weight. Check that. He got fat. FAT fat. The little twenty five pound dog blew up to fifty one pounds! He looked like a beer keg with a moustache. Conventional weight loss didn't work for him. Once again, Atrium came through with the right prescription and some herbal supplements. It took a while but he eventually got back down to his fighting weight. It was not the first of health issues. Oliver suffered from horrible skin problems. Many times he'd cry out loud because the itching drove him crazy. It was hard to keep under control. What worked today might not work tomorrow. Special shampoos, lotions and pills. It seemed like a full time job. Grooming became a regular necessity. If the hair near his tail got too long, he was prone to what we called "mud butt". I don't think an explanation is necessary. And while he looked elegant with the typical Schnauzer moustache, for Oliver is was highly impractical. Like so many dogs before him, Oliver had a jones for cat crap. He loved it. He was addicted to it like it was crack, no pun intended. So we kept the moustache trimmed. Dingleberries on the backside is normal. In the front? Well, that's just gross.

    I started to notice that he was starting to be uncertain in his movements. Like he was searching for his next step. A trip to the vet confirmed that Oliver was losing his eyesight. He had something called SARDS, which is a rapid onset retinal deterioration. In a short time, little Wally Balls was completely blind.

    His blindness didn't slow him down at first. He'd hop down the steps to go outside. He'd find his way out to potty and back. He found that food dish come hell or high water. His blindness tended to compound his being irritating. After all the times he'd been a pain in the ass when he could see, the other dogs were conditioned to be pissed off when he'd run into them. It was by accident, of course, but the other dogs didn't know he was blind. They just thought he was being a jerk. They'd snap at him or growl. I felt so bad. I could tell it got to him. Not everyone disliked Oliver. Our old black cat, Bianca, loved him. Gail has a wonderful picture of them sitting together. Bianca would notice Oliver sitting alone and go over and snuggle up to him. It was so touching. I know it was a comfort to him. It must have been to her, as well. When Bianca passed away, Oliver was finally alone.

When Oliver went for a walk, he started to not come back. We'd find him far from the house, walking in circles. I'd put a leash on him and walk him back. If he was being lead, he was fine. When I wasn't there, Gail had to take the four wheeler and find him. He didn't have any mobility issues. Sometimes he'd wind up all the way down at the front gate. Almost a hundred yards. Still, he could go up and down the steps to the house. He still chowed down like he was on a starvation diet. The vet said it was some sort of neurological disorder. Possibly a tumor. His quality of life wasn't what it once was, but he was hanging in there. So, we did too.

Late one afternoon, I noticed Oliver was more off balance than usual. Then he just sort of jerked and fell into the bushes. I went over to him and said "Wally, what's wrong!" His eyes were open, but he wasn't moving. It was time. I put him on the front seat of my old Hyundai. He just laid there. He wasn't breathing hard. I put my hand on him and talked to him. At the ER, the doctor agreed that he'd run his course. I held him as he passed away. He went so quickly. On the way home, all I could think about was all our other dogs who had passed on seeing him cross that Rainbow Bridge, looking at each other and going, "Oh, great."

...

DAISY

aka

[Daisy Jane; Fudgie O'Wonders; Fudge; Fudge Puddle; Fudge Pocket; Pudge; Spitbull; Daisy Dew Drop; The Beady Eyes of Love]

I was sitting in my office writing when Gail stepped into the doorway. In her arms was a little white and brown puppy. The homeliest puppy I'd ever seen. Apparently, the story was that a woman up the street found a Boxer/Pitbull mix wandering the streets with a litter of puppies. One of them ended up in her father's yard. He wasn't going to feed or water it so it would go away. She came to our house. She said she knew we had a lot of dogs and wondered if it was ours. Gail told her we were over stocked at the moment. The woman said she was going to keep it for another week and if she couldn't find the owner, she was taking it to the pound. Gail told her to call if they came up empty handed. One week later, the woman's truck came up the driveway. A few moments later, little Daisy came to her forever home.

That homely little puppy blossomed. What a sweet girl. Little tiny pig eyes, a whip-like tail and a big, broad smile. She was so happy and loved her brothers and sisters. Her favorites were Rosie and Big Dumb Clover. They'd wrestle each other and fall asleep together. Sisters of different mothers. You had to monitor her play because she truly didn't know her own strength. She was one, big muscle. You had to tell her to be sweet. Unchecked, the situation could have escalated. That monitored play included interaction with people. She never bit anyone but when she played with me, I marveled in the potential damage that could be inflicted with those massive, powerful jaws. Her toenails were nothing to sneeze at, either. When she'd throw herself to ground to wrestle, she'd kick those lethal talons. If you weren't careful, she'd shred the flesh on your arms and legs. I still have scars.

While she was sweet as pie with people, she had a dark side. In trying to find space for all the dogs, we had to keep some separate and pair up the ones that got along best. We made the unfortunate mistake of putting Daisy and Clover in an area we call "The Side Yard". It's a little over a quarter acre between the house and the barn. It was in this space that Daisy's aggressive side showed itself. First, she killed our old barn cat, Bruce. That was devastating. Bruce was a sweet boy. And if that wasn't bad enough, Gail found that both Daisy and Clover killed and mutilated several kittens that wandered into their area. It was odd because in the house, Daisy was horrified of cats and kittens. Her expression was one of sheer terror. I could never deduce how she differentiated between house cats and feral. We immediately took steps to remedy the situation.

Eventually Daisy wound up in the far pen with Clover. It was difficult for me because they both wanted to be part of the family so badly. I did the best I could to spend time with them and give them some extra attention. Despite my terrible guilt, they seemed to enjoy the outdoor life. They had a custom built doghouse that was heated and air conditioned. But we hadn't anticipated some of the cats making their way to their pen. We lost Dusty and Tom Kitty to Daisy and Clover's savagery. There was no real alternative to the situation. We just had to hope and pray that the cats would steer clear of them. The irony is in their later years they seemed to lose interest in the pursuit of anything but uncatchable squirrels and the occasional skunk or possum, which they did catch.

Daisy loved having her belly rubbed, especially when she was rolling and snorting in the grass. I noticed that she had a lesion on her tummy. When it didn't respond to ointment, the vet deduced that it was cancer. The vet removed them but warned us that this particular type of cancer could spread. Tendrils would leech outwards from the original lesion and find other places to grow. There was no way of ever knowing where it would go or ever getting all of it. I knew then that this would be the thing that would someday take her from me.

In her recovery, Daisy had to wear an Elizabethan Collar, or the cone of shame. She wore it with ease. She never had a problem with it. But to be safe, she had to spend a lot of time in the house again, for monitoring purposes. She loved it. I always made sure she got to go out to visit Clover for breakfast and dinner. They'd merrily trot down the driveway for their walk. Later on, when we adopted the goats, they enjoyed going down and barking at them. They were quite easily pleased. And the goats seemed to like it, too. This was usually the time that Daisy would do her number two's. I've never seen a dog look so guilty for pooping. She'd try to go behind one of the crepe myrtles to obscure the view, but she knew I was watching. She'd be in the middle of her business and turn and look at me. "Why are you watching, dad! I'm dropping two's!" When she was done, she'd leap into the air and run, she seemed so delighted with herself. It's sounds pathetic, but it was one of the best parts of my day. It always made me laugh. But, for me, bedtime with Cuddle Fudge was my favorite.

Daisy was the best cuddle hound I ever had. She always lay right beside me, with her back against my right side, her head toward my feet and her butt under my arm. She was such a sound sleeper, but sometimes had little dreams that made her whine and twitch and sometimes even kick her legs. All it took was to gently pet her. "It's ok, Fudge. Poppy's right here." She'd raise her head, flutter her beady eyes and reach up and give me a pig nose kiss. Then she'd drift off to sleep. If I ever woke up at night, I'd always roll over to look at her. She usually had a big smile on her face. That smile usually faded with the dawn. She hated to get up in the morning. "Come on, Fudgie. Let's go potties." She'd roll away from me and pretend not to hear. "You can come back and sleep while Pa works". Nothing. "Fudgie! Let's go!" She'd get up and stretch and yawn. She'd do her business as fast as she could so she could get back under the covers.

I started to notice that Daisy wasn't doing her spins as much. She was also starting to have issues with peeing in the house. She was on and off her food and I knew something was up. Gail took her to the vet in Lancaster, SC, for blood work and x-rays. The vet said the x-rays looked no different than they did a few months earlier. I wasn't satisfied. I took her to CARE in Charlotte to see the specialist. An ultra sound revealed she had a large mass in her chest. It was also wrapped around the arteries leading to her heart. They wouldn't even try to operate because it was very likely she would bleed out during the procedure. That goddamn cancer came back under the radar. I just sat in the room and cried. My poor, poor, Fudge.

In the coming days, I did my best to spoil her. Treats, which she didn't always take because she was sick. Rides in the car, which were great at first, but as she got sicker she lost interest. So I just loved her up as best I could. It got to a point where her breathing was short and rapid. If I waited much longer, she could have a heart attack or worse. I decided I would take her in the next day and say good-bye. That night, I didn't sleep. I just held her and watched her sleep, hoping she'd make it till morning. All night long, she still smiled.

The next morning, Gail and Haley said good-bye to her. I have tried, when possible, to spare my family from being present at the end. They've seen and been through so much with losing our flock. I insisted that it be me alone that stayed with her at the end. Daisy was sad that morning. I could tell she didn't feel good. She rode in the car, taking one last look out the window. When we got to Atrium, Daisy went right inside. She lay right down in the room and Dr. Colleran came in to give her a sedative. My heart hurt so bad, I could barely breathe. Having to let a beloved pet go when they still have a smile on their face is soul crushing. But when you think of the alternative, the idea of leaving with a smile doesn't sound so bad. Daisy slowly slipped into unconsciousness. I lay beside her on the floor and told her how much I loved her. Many of the other vets and vet techs came in to say good-bye. That was touching but somehow made it even more painful.

When the time came, Dr. Colleran knelt beside her, tears in her eyes, and gave her the injection. Even with her heart in a compromised condition, Daisy held on for longer than any other dog we've had. "It's OK, Fudge. You can go. Poppy will see you soon. Go on, now, Daisy Jane. It's OK." And then...she just let go. My little Spitbull had gone on to see all her other brothers and sisters and sit in that long line to wait for Poppy and Mommy. I stayed with her for a long time. Just petting her and kissing her face. I got up to leave and didn't look back. I think sometimes you just have to do that. I still keep her collar in the car. So she can always go for a ride with Pa.

...

ROCKY

aka
[Rock; Rocket; Rocky Bug; Mr. Meat Loaf; Rock-a-Doodle; Rocky Bug-a-Loaf]

Gail went to pick up Haley at her boyfriend's house. Her boyfriend's grandparents ran a small country church next door to their house and Gail pulled into the parking lot area. There was a large dog running around. She asked about him. The story was quite sad. There was a guy riding a bike and the dog was running along behind him. The police pulled the guy over in the church lot, arrested the guy and threw the bike aside. Then they drove off, leaving the dog behind. He'd been hanging around for days, apparently waiting for his man to come back. On top of that, no one had bothered to feed him. That was all Gail needed to hear. The terrified dog wouldn't get in the car. He was terrified. Gail had to pick him up and put him in the back seat. He cowered in the corner. Ironic, because in very short order, riding in the Jeep would be one of his favorite things in the world. Gail got him home. This was going to be a process. We agreed his start in life was indeed rocky. So that's what we named him. That was the day Rocky got a new name and a new home.

Though we were never certain, we think Rocky was more than half Mastiff. He was light tan in color with a big, thick solid build. Very muscular, with a giant mailbox head. But his two most striking features were his eyes and his tail. Rocky had the most soulful eyes. He didn't look AT you, he looked INTO you. His eyes said everything. You could see exactly what he was thinking. Happy. Sad. Frightened. Sleepy. Hungry. It wasn't even a guess. You knew precisely what he was thinking and feeling. He also had another emotional barometer. His tail. Rocky's lethal weapon. It was like a fur covered nunchuck. If he was overly happy or nervous and you came within the proximity of his tail, you were going home with a bruise. If he was lying on the floor and you said his name, you'd hear "thump thump thump", which would change in tempo depending on his mood, excitement or enthusiasm. So fervent was his wag that he even hurt is tail a couple of times. He was such a blockhead.

Rocky must have had a horrible early life. He was terrified of everything for almost two years. If you raised your voice, he'd cower and tremble. We tried to give him a bath and he screamed and screamed like he was being tortured. If you touched his ears to hard, he yelped. It was so distressing. I can't imagine what he must have gone through to come to this. But once he knew he would always be loved; he'd always be safe; he'd always have food and water and shelter; he settled into his life. We have never had, before or since, a more grateful, thankful dog in our lives. Rocky took nothing for granted.

The one thing you would immediately notice about Rocky was he was very emotionally needy. I think it was from how uncertain his life used to be. He was eager to love everybody because he so badly wanted to be loved and accepted in return. If you sat down, Rocky would instantly put his head on your leg and look into your eyes, tail wagging a mile a minute. All he wanted, more than anything in the world, was to be loved. Just a pat on the head and a kind word. Sometimes it became too much and you'd have to tell him to cool it. As he skulked away, the look in those big sad eyes made you feel like a criminal.

Once he accepted that he wasn't going anywhere, Rocky blossomed. He loved to run and play. He didn't fetch. He didn't do "dog games". Rocky ran with pure, unadulterated joy. He did a thing that a few of our dogs have done. The spin. The butt goes low and they spin in circles. Rocky did it a little different. He actually combined it with running. It's hard to describe, but he would spin and keep moving in the direction he was going, his tongue flapping in the breeze, his ears back and a big, stupid look on his face. When Rock did that, you knew he was on top of the world.

One of my biggest disappointments was the fact Rocky and Shemp had such a rivalry. When they were outside together in the pen, everything was fine for a while. But when they had their big dust up that sent Shemp to the hospital, nothing was ever the same after that. It kept us from bringing Shemp into the general population. I hated to see Shemp in the pen, barking and barking to come out. We had to put Rocky in to let Shemp out. It just never felt like a complete family because of this rift between them. I tried once and Shemp leapt on Rocky's back and took the back of his neck in his mouth and shook his head. I dove on them and pulled them apart. Shemp was bent on revenge and I had to drag him back to his doghouse. That relationship just never, ever mended.

Old Rocket aged relatively gracefully, slowing down in the usual ways dogs do. Unfortunately, he was diagnosed with kidney disease. Not really unusual for his age. He handled it very well. With the help of Atrium Animal Hospital, we created a potent potion of supplements and herbals mixed in blueberry kefir. He took it twice a day from a big syringe. He liked his Blueberry Squirts. Rocky also required fluid therapy morning and night.

I've said it before, but I'll say it again. If your dog has kidney disease, learn to give subcutaneous fluids at home. It gives them a much better quality of life for a longer period. Rocky learned the drill and knew it well. I'd bring his fluid rig in and put it by his bed. "Rock! Come get squirts!" You'd hear his trademark nails on the kitchen floor. He'd walk right in and sit on his bed. I made sure he got lots of lovin' when he came in. He'd lie down like a good boy. Rocky was a sensitive soul and the needle sometimes made him squeal. But once I found the right gauge needle, all was well. Sometimes the fluid flowed like water from a faucet. Sometimes it seemed to take forever. Regardless, I made the most of the time with him. I'd talk to him and sing to him and that dang tail would go thumpity thump.

I knew my time with him was short, so I'd take him to the pond in the mornings and evenings. He loved it! I'd go to the gate and call him. His eyesight was fading, but he saw well enough to know where he was going. I'd open the gate and he'd do his jaunty little trot down to the water. For a dog who, once upon a time, was so terrified of the getting wet, he sure seemed to be over it now! Rocky went right into the water, wading up to his chest. He lapped at the pond water and splashed around. It made me happy that he enjoyed it so much. When he was done playing in the water, he'd find a spot in the weeds beside the pond, literally throw himself to the ground and merrily roll around, kicking his legs into the air. He'd stop for a second and then go back at it with fervor. "You big dummy!" Thump thump thump.

Another one of his guilty pleasures was "The Rubber Brush". It was a rubber pad with big rubber teeth used to groom out shedding hair. He'd find a spot in the pasture, usually in the shade, and he'd throw himself to the ground and roll around. I'd go up with the rubber brush and just go back and forth. He'd close his eyes and when I stopped, he'd roll over so I could do the other side. When that side was done, he'd roll over on his back so I could do his chest. That was his favorite. And right when he was about achieve the ultimate in nirvana, Momma Girl showed up.

The House of Goodbyes

Momma Girl always gravitated to the ailing dogs. She did with Dolly and Shemp. Now it was Rocky's turn. But she took it a bit further with him. When Rocky was lying down, Momma Girl would fall to the ground beside him. She'd roll around when he did. Then she'd scootch closer. And closer. And closer. Finally, she'd reach towards his face with her paws, lick and kiss him and then start giving him love bites on the head, cheek and muzzle. Sometimes she'd lay across his head. Rocky just sighed. Secretly, I think he loved it.

Rocky had been slowly getting worse. A trip to the vet revealed his kidney values were the worst yet. The doc gave him two to three weeks. It was not what I wanted to hear. But I guess Rocky didn't hear her. He just kept going. But the Thursday before Thanksgiving he took a very sudden downturn. He was getting up off his bed and he yelped. I don't know what happened and never will. But Rocky was very suddenly gravely ill. His eyes drooped and he looked positively morose. The next day we took him to Atrium. They came to the van with a stretcher and Rocky never, ever tried to get up. Sick as he was, he still wagged that dangerous tail. Gail and I lay on the floor with him, giving him the last love we would ever be able to give him. Then it was thump…thump….and then he was gone. It wasn't two weeks or even three weeks after his prognosis. It was four months. Rocky held the Reaper at bay for four months after being given two weeks. He was happy right up to the end. You can't ask for more than that. Except for more time. He deserved more time.

...

Jeff Pillars

CLOVER

aka
[Big Dumb Clover, Clover Bear, Clovis; Clovi-Opis; Clovie]

Gail was going to visit her mom and on the opposite side of the road she saw an old station wagon pulling away from the shoulder. Left in its wake was a little black and white puppy sitting on the road side watching the car disappearing in the distance. Gail almost stopped but had to get on with her errands. Two and half hours later, as she returned home, there was that little dog sitting on the side of a hill and desperately scouring the passing traffic for its owner to return. Gail stopped and called out, "Do you want to go for a ride?" The little black and white puppy bounded to her and she helped her into the car. She could still see the wear marks on her neck where she'd been on a collar. A terrible thing for a dog of any age, let alone a puppy. But Clover's misfortune turned out to be quite fortunate. That's the day Clover came home.

Clover was such a gangly, dopey puppy. Perennially happy, even when scolded. Joyful in having brothers and sisters to love and play with. Especially Daisy and Rosie. She would gallop and galumph around the yard like an idiot. I'm sure she could have been very fast, if she cared to get anywhere in a hurry. She was too busy loving life. If championships could be given for cuddling, Clover would have been champion of the universe. People, dogs, furniture, toys, whatever. As long as it let her snuggle, she was good to go. Clover was a real love dog.

Clover got fat. There's really no other way to put it. The once lithe and athletic dog became…well, me. She retained her "jolly" but got a lot more "jowly". I look back at pictures of her and I can't believe it's really her. But to me, the chubby, merry Clover is my favorite. It all started quite suddenly. She developed a number of fatty cysts on her chest, belly and inside of her back legs. Her vet determined that they weren't a potential threat and we had them removed. It was after that that she beefed up on us, cause unknown.

Clover's weight became a problem. She ballooned up to over ninety pounds! Good old Clover was still happy but very lethargic. A special blood test showed she had developed Cushing's Disease. After some trial and error we hit on the right meds, which were extremely expensive, but totally worth it. With the meds and a change of diet, Clover trimmed down to a solid seventy pounds. Still adorably chubby, but not a walrus.

If Clover had one quirk that stuck out, it was her ability to lose a collar. I can't begin to tell you how many she lost over the years. We would scour the pen and yard to find it and rarely…rarely…ever found it. It was like pixies removed her collar in her sleep and had a cache of them in a hollow stump on the property somewhere. We'd replace it and sure enough, three or four months later we were off to the store to find another one. We started to buy several at a time to save a trip. I had a sneaking suspicion that Clover was taking them off and burying them in the yard. I couldn't prove it, but I think she was sniping me.

Clover's happy heart can be illustrated in no better way than her love of toys. If the Animal Planet had ever done a show about animal hoarders, Clover could have been the pilot episode. I noticed this first when Clover was out and about the yard with the other dogs. She found some old stuffed toy, picked it up in her mouth and wouldn't put it down. She carried it around for nearly thirty minutes! When we finally went back to her house, she walked in the front door, out the dog door, down the ramp and into her enormous pile of cedar shavings. She buried the toy and then came back. So a day or so later, I "accidentally" left another stuffed toy in the yard. Sure enough, she found it and wouldn't put it down. She took it back and this time put it on her bed. In short order, she had about twenty stuffed toys of various shape and size. Some were exclusively for the dog house, others were relegated for the cedar shavings. If you moved them, which I did, she'd put them back where they belonged. I've never seen a dog take such joy in the accumulation of toys.

Once she had spent so much time outside, with a heated and air conditioned doghouse, she didn't really care too much to be in the house. We brought her in from time to time, but she just seemed uncomfortable. I felt horribly guilty that she was left out there alone, especially after Daisy passed away. Clover was the last dog left outside. So I made it a point to spend as much time with her as possible. She loved to go on "sniffs". So, after Daisy passed away and Clover was basically left alone, we started our "two a days".

In the mornings, I would load my pockets with treats and we'd take our hour long sojourn to the Church lot next door. The Church Lot was an adjacent piece of property owned by the local Methodist church. It was heavily wooded with a wide driving path and a small pond covered with duck weed. It was so serene and peaceful. Clover was in her glory! She would wander off into the woods. I would sit on an old stump and watch her. She'd find a particularly attractive smell and roll and roll in it, kicking all four legs in the air. She'd stop for a moment and then start right back in again. I tried to let her be as free as possible and let her explore unfettered. From time to time, she'd do her best to chase a squirrel or a rabbit. She wasn't quite as agile in as she once was but she had fun and that was all that mattered.

The morning jaunt was punctuated with Clover coming back again and again for treats. I'm so surprised that Clover maintained her girlish figure with the number of treats she consumed. Let's see, she had joint supplement tablets that she gobbled down; she always begged for some Apple Jacks or Fruit Loops that I gave as treats to the goats; many dog crackers on the walk; and then a blueberry dog cookie and a piece of chicken jerky treat when she got back to the house. To be honest, I really think she wore those treats off on her walks.

Most mornings, we'd have a visit from her boyfriend, Dash. Dash was an insane Black Lab mix owned by my neighbor, Rodney. Dash would spot me and Clover and literally drag Rodney all the way to us. Dash would flirt with Clover and act the fool. I always kept extra treats in my pocket in case Dash came along. Clover was more interested in Rodney. Clover had a trick to get attention and she used it all the time. I called it "The Topple". Clover would go to her object of affection and throw herself to the ground. This indicated that she was expecting chest and belly lovin'. She did it everywhere she went. When we went to Atrium for her Underwater Treadmill therapy to keep her legs strong, she would throw herself down before and after treatment. Allyson, her therapist, was so smitten by Big Dumb Clover that she always waited for it to happen so she could love her up. Rodney never let Clover down. He always generously indulged her and she often lay there for a minute after he and Dash had left. She was so dramatic.

In the evenings, we took a different route. We'd go for a walk into the pasture. A sad, but true, fact about Clover is that she loved poop. Cat poop, horse poop, any poop. It was her snack of choice. And the pasture was full of it. I tried my best to monitor her antics but she was so sneaky that she'd always get away with at least a couple tender stinky morsels. She also loved grasses. Not all grasses, just particular grasses. When she found wild mint, she'd go crazy. All her life she was a grazer. Not surprising as she was built like a cow. I had an old stone bench put on the side of the hill overlooking the pond. Just inside the shade line, so we could beat the afternoon heat and spend time together. She'd get tired of exploring and looking at the neighbors chickens and come back to me. She knew I had treats and after she'd had a few, she'd throw herself to the ground for belly rubs. She luxuriated in the attention and l enjoyed making her happy.

Years ago, Clover had a terrible bout with a kidney infection. So bad, we almost lost her. She was in the hospital for days. The dead giveaway for most dogs is loss of appetite. Clover would fool you because she would eat, even when she didn't feel good. She was a true chow hound. But that Saturday morning in June, Clover didn't want breakfast. She didn't even want treats. I knew something was up. I had visions of the last bout with kidney issues. I hurriedly finished chores and took her straight to Atrium. Dr. Credit said she was slightly dehydrated and her kidney values were only slightly off. No signs of infection. Something else was going on. I agreed that she should stay. I said good-bye to her and she dutifully went to her "room" with a smile on her face. That would be the last time I ever saw that smile.

I didn't hear anything all weekend. No news is good news. Monday morning the phone rang. It was Dr. Credit. Clover had taken a very bad turn. Her vitals are dropping. I asked her to be honest with me. She said "I think it's time." I hung up the phone and broke down in tears. Gail and I raced to Atrium and they hustled us into a room. They brought Clover in on a stretcher. Through tears I said "Oh, Clovis". She didn't even have the strength to raise her head, but she feebly wagged her tail. Gail lay on one side of her and I spooned her from behind. She never raised her head. She just moved her eyes. I kissed her over and over and over. I stroked her face and under her chin. As I moved my hand down to her chest, she tried to raise her front leg like she used to do in "The Topple" but she didn't have the strength. I had been in this situation twenty times before. But this was more poignant somehow. Clover had been doing so well. The day before she went to the hospital she walked in the woods for almost an hour! She was exploring and rolling and having a wonderful time. I guess, in the end, that's all you can ask for. To be happy till the end.

We let Dr. Credit know it was time. Gail and I sobbed as Clover's big, happy heart beat its last. I rubbed her big belly one more time before I left. On the way home, I tried to be thankful that we gave her a life and love and a home that she never would have known if Gail hadn't stopped her car. I tried to be thankful. But Clover deserved more time. Time I couldn't give her. I can't look at a dog toy without missing Big Dumb Clover.

FELINE

EMMA

aka
[Em; Auntie Em; Emmers]

We were living in Mineral Springs, but Haley was still taking dance classes in our old stomping grounds of Mint Hill. There was an elderly cat hanging around the dance studio. A brownish diluted calico. The owners were feeding it by the front steps at night. The old cat was kind and friendly and appreciated any attention. When word came down that the local exterminators were going to be rounding up all the feral cats, the owners of the studio started looking for someone to take her in. This was clearly not a feral. She was a sweet old girl who was down on her luck. We don't know how she came to find herself in this situation but we weren't about to let her life end in some ruthless, cruel round up. She had clearly been someone's pet. Maybe an elderly person who could no longer care for her. Or maybe she had outlived her usefulness to a family and was cast out. Maybe she escaped a bad situation. Whatever the case, she was coming home with us. She wouldn't end her days like this. Gail brought her home and named her Emma.

Emma was a loving, precious old gal. Very easy going and got along well with the other cats. She was warm when it was cold. Had shade when it was hot. She had food whenever she wanted it and she was in no danger. She seemed so grateful; so appreciative. She was happy. Emma wasn't with us for very long. As I said, she was old and her age caught up with her. She got sick and her bodily functions were misfiring. Rather than letting her suffer, we chose to let her go. She passed quietly in the vets' office. I wish she'd had more time to spend with us. We have the solace in knowing that she ended her days in comfort and safety. Without fear. Without uncertainty. And with love.

...

DUSTY

aka
[Big Dust]

Dusty was not with us very long. He was part of the rescued barn litter which included Blackie and Tina and a handsome lad he was. A sturdy, very light colored diluted calico with a curious nature. When they became teenagers and were spayed and neutered, Gail decided to let them come and go as they pleased. Dusty was adventuresome. He liked to roam. One day he roamed right into the far dog pen. We found his body a day later. Seems a shame he was taken so soon. Dusty, we hardly knew ye.

...

TOM KITTY

aka
[TK; Tom Tom]

Josh, Haley's boyfriend at the time, had found a tiny little kitten and given it to his sister. Gail and Haley went by one day and saw the kitten. It was a handsome Siamese mix but he was suffering from a severe upper respiratory infection and its eyes were filled with white, sticky goop. These were old school country folk and they didn't spend money on vets. There would always be other cats around to replace it. Gail asked to take it because it clearly was not going to survive otherwise. They didn't want to let the kitten go because it was the little girls "pet", but they finally relented and just in time. Gail was able to nurse him back to relative health. But his tenure would be short lived.

Gail named him Tom Kitty because that was a nickname given to Haley's boyfriend by his grandmother. He was a beautiful cat. You could clearly see the Siamese and his eyes were bright blue. What a sweet, laid back, cool cat. His favorite thing was climbing up the tree by the bird feeders and lying across the branches with his legs dangling on either side. He was pretty devoted to Gail and followed her most places. That would prove to be his undoing.

One summer night, a powerful thunderstorm rolled through. At that time, Daisy and Clover were still in the far pen. Gail went out to the dog house to sit with them, hoping her presence would comfort them from the sound and fury of the storm. Apparently, Tom Kitty followed her. Gail said at one point, Clover excused herself and went outside. This was curious because she was so unnerved by the storm. But she returned moments later. The next day, we found the body of Tom Kitty behind the doghouse. What we think happened is that Tom Kitty climbed the fence into the dog's pen looking for Gail. Clover heard the meows, went out, attacked and killed him and then came back. Son of a bitch. That was just horrible. Gail still blames herself but what's the point in that? Shit happens. And it's going to happen, no matter what.

...

BELLE

aka

[Baby Belle; Bella Diablo; Belly]

Gail was on her way to work, driving her old Jeep Cherokee. We were living in Mint Hill then and she was only five or six miles from home. Up ahead she saw something on the center line of the road. It was a very small black and white kitten. She stopped immediately and jumped out. She made a run for the kitten as cars sped around her, not really caring for the safety of the tiny, helpless animal in the road. She scooped it up, jumped in the Jeep and sped away. It was only when she stopped at the stop light did she get a good look at it. "Dear God, what have I done?" The kitten was a mess. Missing its left eye and the other one was white. She drove straight to the vet's office, thinking he would most likely put the poor thing out of its misery. They were busy, so she just dropped it off. Later on, she was surprised when the vet called and said he could likely save the eye. On the way home, Gail stopped and picked up Belle, our first cat.

What a little scrapper this kitten was. Sweet, but tough. A real fighter. That's why Gail called her Bella Diablo because she was the Devil Kitty. Once Belle had regained her strength, we built a ten foot by twelve foot cage outside behind the tool shed. We thought she'd flourish in the fresh air, but that was not the case. She got sick and dehydrated and the consensus was that it was for the best that she be brought in the house. She did just fine amongst the canine population. I don't think she thought she was a dog or anything like that. I think she just adapted to her surroundings and made the best of it. Once she made an example of a couple of the dogs, they knew not to mess with Devil Kitty.

Belle did pretty well once we moved to Mineral Springs. She sort of ruled the roost in the newly found Kingdom of the Garage Cats. She was a chubby, cycloptic enforcer that was not afraid to let you know when you, or anyone else, crossed the line. The only one who got cut any slack was Gail. That was mom. Always. She never forgot her kindness. Oh, sure, she let me pet her as long as I didn't go too far. She was funny like that.

Before we had the fences put up, we had a problem with stray dogs invading our property. They got used to terrorizing our cats. It was typical of some of the local trash to not keep tabs on their pets and let them run free. Not cool. We think that one day, Belle went beyond the perimeter and out past the heavy brush and the tree line. I was outside and heard a cat screaming. By the time I got in the direction of the sound, it had stopped. In my heart, I knew it was Belle. A couple days went by and she hadn't returned. We had to accept the hard truth that she never would. This was hard pill to swallow considering the incredible odds she beat early in her life. But that, as they say, is the way of the world. I'm sure, in the end, Belle got her licks in. She didn't win, but I know she went down swinging and whatever did take her knew they'd been in a scrap.

. . .

BOO

aka
[Boo Boo; Boo Berry; Boo Berry Biscuit]

It was the year of the "Great Plague". Gail couldn't go to the barn without having to bury one or two young cats, dead from some sort of illness that swept through the population. It was truly gut wrenching to see these sweet young kittens one day and the next they were gone. Taken by what we now believe was coronavirus. On one occasion, Gail found the body of a tiny black kitten. By this time, she'd become almost hardened by all the loss. She decided to finish chores and then bury it. Once done, and having already dug the hole, she took the hay fork and slid it under the small body. Then she saw it twitch. The kitten was still alive. And where there is life, there is a chance. She carried the frail black kitten to the house and made it as comfortable as could be in a crate in the laundry room. She gave it fluids, orally and subcutaneously. Many times a day she'd look in on the sick kitten, fully expecting to find it dead. One morning, she looked and the little black kitten was sitting up looking at her. A miracle. The poor kitten looked like some sort of wide eyed, unkempt dust bunny. That's how she got her name. Gail would pick her up and show her to Haley and say "Boo!"

Boo was quite the character. She was short legged, chubby and resembled a skunk that God forgot to stripe. She'd scramble around on those comically stubby legs and it was absolutely adorable. She had the perfect meow. A sort of metallically squeak with a trilling 'r' and a curious, inquisitive lilt. Like she was asking questions with each one. She was also a bit of a talker. All you had to do was say her name and she'd trit-trot in your direction, talking and beeping the whole way. She was just so precious. Another hysterical compliment to her personality was the way it could turn on a dime. Many times, Gail and I would try to corral her or get her to go outside and she'd meow and meow and then suddenly hiss. It got laughs every single time. She was just the quirkiest little butterball ever.

I noticed that Boo started isolating herself. She'd hide under chairs or behind the sofa. Then she started sneaking into my office without my knowing and hiding under my chair. Then I'd unintentionally lock her in overnight and she'd tear the carpet to shreds trying to get out. Something was clearly wrong. We discovered that Boo had an abdominal tumor and it was growing quickly. There wasn't much that could be done. We brought her home to try to make her final days happy and comfortable. It was so sad to see this funny, oddball cat; one who dramatically beat the odds early in life; slowly losing her battle to a far bigger opponent.

When it came to the point that she couldn't walk a few steps without having to lie down, it was time. Gail took her on her final ride and she went very peacefully. We weren't allowed to keep Boo for very long, but while she was here, she gave us so much joy. She was so silly and loving and weird. A bitter finale for a great, great performer.

...

TIMMY

aka
[Tiny Tim; Tim Tim; Timmy the Tiger; Tim Burton; Timber Toes]

Gail was at the barn where we had our horses stabled. That's where she met Timmy, or Tiny Tim as she called him. It was partly due to his puny stature but also because it was Christmas time. Timmy was old enough to crawl up barn ties and scamper around ably without getting underfoot. Gail took a liking to him and started making sure he had food and a warm bed on top of her grooming box. Timmy took a liking to Gail, too. The other riders in the barn took great joy in telling her that when Timmy would hear her Jeep coming down the long drive, he'd leap from wherever he was and race down the wide barn aisle to greet her. And when Gail saddled up Ranger and headed to the arena, Timmy scampered along in lock step. He'd goof around and watch from the perimeter until they were done. Then he'd trot along with them back to the barn where Timmy rubbed around her legs while she groomed Ranger. Gail recounts the time that a poor Cardinal found its way into the barn. Timmy promptly pounced on it and gobbled it up in ten seconds. Timmy never let his sweet side get in the way of his survival. Timmy was the man.

Gail got the bad news that the barn was closing. She made arrangements for the horses but she wasn't about to leave Timmy and his barn mate, Bianca, behind. She brought them from the barn to our house in Mint Hill. Timmy was used to ruling the roost in a big, expansive area. Now, he and Bianca were confined to a small ten by twelve cage in the back yard. Though he didn't really show it, I'm sure it must have been frustrating for Timmy. But then again, maybe it was nice to feel safe and secure, away from all the dangers that living in the barn involved. Nah, Timmy would rather have the danger. That's why the move to Mineral Springs was so great for him.

    Timmy was the king. It was fun to watch him sort of take stock of his surroundings and get the lay of the land. He quickly staked his claim and it wasn't unusual to see him patrolling the property. That was never more clear to me than when I took a stake out on the back patio to wait for those damn stray dogs that were sneaking in through the back wooded area and chasing the cats. I got up early and sat on the cement bench to wait for the trouble makers. I had a cup of coffee and I sipped and listened for any crackle or noise in the woods. After a minute, Timmy jumped up and sat next to me. He was watching and waiting, too. Sure enough, here they came. A big Boxer and smaller mutt with a little Chow in the bloodline. I waited for them to get closer and before I could stand up, Timmy launched! He leapt off the bench and made a bee line straight for the unsuspecting Boxer, who backed up, bug-eyed and was all elbows and assholes trying to make its escape. The terrified mutt was right behind. Timmy chased them INTO THE WOODS!!! I heard sticks cracking and a final YELP and then it was silent. A few minutes later, Timmy strolled back through the bushes, with a real "Jack Reacher" look of satisfaction on his face. "Good boy, Tim." He brushed against my legs and purred. An iron paw in a velvet glove. After that day, Timmy made a part of his rounds to work the perimeter, even after the fence was up. Gail worried about him going over the fence. Me? I worried about who he went over the fence after.

    Timmy was a very loving boy but at the same time, fiercely independent. He did his own thing. Some days you saw him, some days you didn't. Maybe for a couple days. That didn't mean he wasn't there, he was just laying low. But if some other cats caused a ruckus or the dogs raised hell, Timmy appeared to set everyone straight. Even when he got older, he was still tough. But he was pickier about his battles. Slowing down is a part of aging, but not Timmy. He was going strong even though we noticed he'd lost some weight. Something wasn't right with Timmy and Gail took him to the vet. The bad news was Timmy had cancer. Cats of a certain age are prone to cancer and Timmy was not exempt. The vet said to just keep an eye on him. We'd know when it was time. Timmy the Tiger hung on for a good while. He wasn't as fast or as spry as he once was, but he was still Timmy. He wanted a bit more attention than in days past. He slept a good bit more. But that personality was still there. Still and always Timmy.

It was on Easter Day, I forget the year, when it happened. I was feeding the dogs in the near pen and saw Timmy staggering towards the dog house. He crawled underneath and started to yowl. I knew this was it. I went to get Gail and we got on our hands and knees and had to dig Timmy out from under the dog house. He was in rough shape. Easter dinner was put on hold. I drove like hell and Gail held Timmy. He groaned and yowled a few times. It was hard to take to see our old boy in such dire straits. We got him into the ER and the vet got him hooked up with an IV port. They brought him in and we immediately told the doc to give the shot. This had to end. We kissed him, told him we loved him and said our good-byes. Timmy, with his final breath, spat a hiss at the world and then…he was gone. It was so sad to lose him, but so typical of Timmy to have the last word. He lived a great, long life and today, when I think of him, I smile. Timmy was one of a kind.

...

SASSY

aka
[Sassers; Growly Moon Face Cat; Sastobell]

Sassy was Gail's mom's cat. She got her as a kitten from a litter born at a nearby barn. By the time she got there all the other kittens were taken and little Sassy was the only one left. When they got her home they found she was being nearly eaten alive by fleas! They gave her bath after bath until the fleas were gone. Fleas can be dangerous to a kitten and can leave them dangerously anemic. She called the other people that had taken kittens to warn them but it was too late. All of Sassy's other litter mates were dead. Sassy was the sole survivor.

Sassy was a beautiful Siamese mix with bright blue eyes. She came by her name honestly. She was a ball buster from a very early age. She was the Queen and if you didn't know it, she'd make damn sure you learned. A very little Haley Pillars didn't seem to have any problem with her. She'd carry Sassy around in the pouch of her sundress. Sassy went along for the ride like a Queen in her carriage.

Gail's mom moved south from Michigan to be with her daughter and granddaughter and Sassy came along. She made the trip in a cage in the back of her big conversion van. When they got here to Mineral Springs, Gail went to unload Sassy and bring her into the house. Unfortunately, Gail's mom failed to tell her that she hadn't attached the bottom of the cage. Gail slid the cage out, the bottom dropped and Sassy, terrified and in unknown surroundings, bolted. In a flash, she disappeared. One day turned to into two. Then a week. Then two weeks. No Sassy. It was a horrible time of year, as well. December in North Carolina isn't always snowy but it is cold and Sassy wasn't used to it.

Christmas was approaching and everyone was depressed at Sassy's absence. Gail and Haley made up flyers and posted them around. They offered a reward and added "Bring Sassy home for Christmas." Well, Christmas day came and there was no Sassy. But, life goes on. Gail and Haley were taking some hot mash down to the horses as a Christmas treat. On the way back to the house, Haley thought she heard a cat meowing. Out of the woods came a tired, hungry and scared Sassy. Haley picked her up and brought her into the house. Sassy was home at last. They'd gotten their Christmas miracle. After that, Sassy was never too interested in going outside. When she did, she stayed close to the house. She wasn't going to go through that again.

Sassy and I didn't really hit it off at first. I tried to be nice to her and she'd growl at me. "Sassy! Be nice!" Growl. She also incurred my wrath by taking the opportunity to piss in as many places as she possibly could. It's not like there weren't litter boxes available, but nooooooo! Sassy ruined parts of the new laminate flooring. She peed on walls and if you left laundry on the floor, that got peed on too. It was infuriating. And if she wasn't pissing on it, she was shredding it with her Wolverine sharp claws. Chairs, sofas, carpeting, it didn't make any difference. And brother, if you caught her and chastised her, she'd give you, what I called, "The Death Stare". It was almost as if she was saying "You're move, Fat Boy. I dare you. Bring it, don't sing it!" It was that stare that always had me second guessing her.

As time went by, Sassy and I actually became friends. She had favorite spots on the backs of certain chairs and the back of the sofa which was up against the half wall in the living room. I'd always stop and rub her head and the bridge of her nose. "Hey old girl! How's trick's, Growly Moon Face?" She purred and purred. When she was on the back of the couch, she'd throw herself down and show me her belly. I'd lean over the wall and pet her and pet her. She was so beautiful. But I learned the hard way, that no matter how tempting it was to rub her belly, it was, in reality, a trap. She'd hiss and swipe at your hand

and try to bite. When you would recoil in horror, she'd lay the trap out again, showing her belly and acting all kittenish. Burn me once, Sassy...

Sassy had gotten old and started to slow down. When she was diagnosed with cancer, she really slowed down. She got fluids to keep her hydrated and her appetite was on and off. It hurt my heart to see her so sick. She started coming in my office to spend time with me while I was working. She slept on the chair and when she had the strength, she'd come up on the desk and sleep while I worked. I'd reach over and pet her and say her name and she would purr and opened her eyes and looked at me. When Sassy looked at you with those big blue eyes, it was like she was looking into your soul. Many times I just looked into her eyes and stroked her head. Sometimes it was so profound it made me cry. Isn't that odd?

Gail came down to the office to see Sassy who was really starting to slip. I looked at Gail and just said "Tomorrow." Gail nodded. So, in the morning we put Sassy in the carrier and went off to Atrium. Sassy was very frail and weak, but not so much that she didn't give us some love before we let her go. It was always a satisfying feeling that Sassy and I became close, not just when she was sick, but before. She taught me a lot about how to reach out to an unfriendly cat and bridge that animosity with gentle understanding. I'll never forget Sassy.

. . .

BEAU

aka
[Bobo; Beau Bro]

Gail rescued a beautiful little black cat from the barn. She assumed it was a girl and called her Beatrice, which, in my mind, is a perfectly awful name for a cat. One day she noticed a small pair of boy nuggets had descended. At that moment, the tragedy of the naming of Beatrice was rectified and the little black cat was rechristened Beau. Much, much better.

Beau was cooler that his spastic, manic brother, Pogo. Very casual and friendly. But during their formative years, an emergency occurred. Little Haley Pillars became very, very ill. Gail's attention was directed to her and the boys sort of grew up on their own. They didn't have as much human interaction except for me. I fed and watered and cleaned litter. They'd mill around sometimes and ask for pets, which I obliged, but I didn't really have a schedule that allowed for "quality time".

Beau had long, luxurious black hair. He was always slender but I didn't realize just how thin he'd gotten. Although he showed no real behavioral signs, it was clear something was wrong. Gail took him to the vet and he was suffering from some sort of blood disease. They sent him home with meds but he couldn't tolerate them. They made his mouth bleed. She took him back the very next day. I was on the road when she called me. Beau was in very bad shape. His blood work numbers were all over the map. They had no idea what was wrong. The choices were to bring him home and isolate him from the other cats and hope they land on some sort of cure or we could simply let him go. My advice was to let him go. He was so sick and I can't imagine that being removed from the only place he'd known as home and left alone was going to really do anything for him. If the meds didn't work, he'd simply flounder and sink deeper and die in pain. We agreed to let him go. Beau passed peacefully with Gail at his side.

This is another instance of the tremendous guilt I feel when something like this happens. How did we miss this? If we'd caught it sooner, could we have done anything? None of that matters now. I just wish Beau had gotten a shot at a longer run. I would like to have gotten to know him better.

. . .

CLARK

aka
[Clarkie Soft Face]

Gail was down in the paddock one day after cleaning stalls. She stopped to watch the kittens playing because, seriously, how can you resist? A few of the kittens were interacting with their mother when a little white kitten came bumbling up. The mother cat wheeled around and hissed and drove him off. The little white kitten fell back on his butt. Gail said the look on his face was a combination of utter shock and profound, unspeakable sadness. It broke her heart, so she went over and scooped him up and cuddled him with absolutely no resistance from the kitten. She couldn't return him to that harsh realm with a clear conscience, so up to the house he came. He was dubbed "Clark".★

Clark was slow. Not mentally, he just did everything at a snail's pace. Every step measured and always employed an "economy of movement". In other words, he was lazy. Or so we thought. After a visit to the vet, we learned that Clark had a serious heart murmur. A four or five on a scale of six. He could suddenly die in two days, a week, next month, a year or live a long life. They just had no way of knowing. We had to accept the inevitable but as long as he was with us, he'd be safe, loved and as happy as we could make him. But the other cats had a different plan.

Clark seemed to be everyone's whipping boy. They bullied him a good bit. But Clark was pretty good about it. If any of the cats snapped at him, he just sat down and waited it out. After a few minutes, whatever the problem was had dissipated and Clark was at ease once more. It really got me that he was pushed around his whole life. But animals adapt and Clark was no exception. I made sure I always gave him attention before the other cats. I called him "Clarkie Soft Face" because he had a chubby mug and his features were rounded and soft, almost like a stuffed toy. I think sometimes it embarrassed him when I'd fuss over him and chuff his chubby cheeks. He sure looked it, anyway.

Clark was a long haired cat and prone to matting. We had to "catscape" him on many occasions. We were concerned that because of his sensitive nature, it might prove to be difficult or even traumatic. But Clark loved it! He sat so patiently and never, ever fussed. Even on his undercarriage. A sweet, patient boy under the worst circumstances.

I remember that it was chilly out. I went out into the porch enclosure to check on the cats and make sure the food and water had been filled. There, laying half in and half out of his bed, was Clark. He had passed away. It was as if he'd just woken up, stepped out of bed and died. His eyes were closed and he showed no signs of struggle. Clearly, his heart had finally given out. And now ours was breaking. The little, quirky, down on his luck cat that found a new family after his own pushed him away…was gone. I wrapped his body in a blanket for transport to the vet for cremation. But before I let him go, I chuffed his chubby little cheeks one last time.

Author's Note: As to the naming of the three white cats, there is differing of opinions. Gail thinks that she and Haley named Clark and Lewis. Not true. Because Lewis was such a nerdy cat, I named him "Lewis" after "Lewis Skolnick" from "Revenge of the Nerds". Clark was named after "Clark Griswold" from the "Vacation" movies. Let the record show…you know, for posterity sake.

BLACKIE

aka

[Big Black; Big Baby Black]

Gail found three tiny kittens in the hay barn. Tiny. Tiny tiny. So small she thought they were some sort of miniature cats. We'd been having trouble with hawks, so Gail didn't want to take any chances. She named the black kitten Blackie. Not very original, but it worked. From that tiny little kitten grew a giant beast! It was stunning! Blackie was a big, lumbering, intimidating cat with medium length black hair and a big, fat tail. His long, white fangs extended down below his lips. They gleamed against the black of his fur and made him look like some sort of prehistoric sabre tooth monster. It was all for show. Despite his appearance, he was an absolute doll baby. Blackie was a living contradiction on four paws.

Blackie was one of the lucky ones. He was an indoor/outdoor cat. You always knew when he wanted to go outside. Dear God, in heaven, you'd hear this low, guttural yowl, over and over. You'd follow that sound to find Blackie at one of the doors. He'd let out another yowl and then when he turned to see you, he let out this demure, sweet little "meow". And that's exactly what it sounded like! For all the world, it sounded like he actually said "meow!" The two sounds were in such contrast to each other, I looked forward to it. I'd go over to let him out and he'd look up at me and I'd reach down and rub his head. "Big Black! You are a precious boy!" With a very satisfied look on his face, out he'd trot, so pleased and full of himself. Such a character.

Blackie became fast friends with Bear. Bear was blonde long haired cat who also started out life as an astonishingly small kitten. And now, here were these two behemoths hanging out together. They were always together. Gail says "I don't think

I have a picture of them when they aren't in the same picture!" Fast friends.

Gail was sitting in her chair just outside the garage one night while the dogs were doing their business. She noticed Blackie come up as far as the car, lie down and stare at her. Then he started calling to her. Gail knew something wasn't right. She went and picked him up. He was limp but he was purring. Gail loaded him into the car and rushed him to the ER. They wanted to keep him for observation. This is when we found out that cats don't just purr when they're happy or content. Sometimes the purr when they are in tremendous pain or stress. Gail no sooner got home when the vet called and asked us to come back. They didn't know if Blackie would make it that long. As far as they could tell, he had a sudden onset of kidney failure or something similar.

They escorted us to the back of the hospital and there was Blackie in a holding cage, sedated, his pupils dilated and his breathing labored. We took turns leaning into the cage, loving him and saying good-bye. With the quick push of a syringe, Blackie was finally out of pain. It all happened so fast that it took a while for the entire thing to sink in. It wasn't until a few days later when I let one of the cats out. It made me think of Blackie and the way he behaved when he wanted out. I stopped and took a breath and cried. I remember it so well.

. . .

BIANCA

aka
[Baby Binaca; Bianc]

Timmy had a friend at the barn. A slender black female Gail named Bianca. She would hang around when Gail was there. She arrived one day to find that Bianca had been seriously injured when she was mauled by a dog at the barn. Unbelievably, no one had even bothered to check and see if she was alright! What the hell is wrong with people?! Gail took the time to clean her wounds and nurse her back to health. During that time, Bianca became attached to Gail and vice versa. When the barn was shut down, Gail knew that Bianca would be coming home to live with us. She found her forever home and came to our little house in Mint Hill. She did quite well in the backyard cage. She seemed quite content. Bianca was a sweet, sweet girl. But things would get much better when we pulled up stakes and moved to the house in Mineral Springs.

In her new surroundings, Bianca flourished. Even though she had plenty of room, Bianca was a homebody. She never strayed far from the garage. She had an enclosed heated bed for the cooler months where she got "breakfast in bed". I'd put wet food in a dish and put it next to her bed on the feed table. Her head would dart out from behind the curtain and take a bite of food and then retreat back into her fort to eat it. She would repeat that process until her chow was gone. I called it doing her moray eel impression. In the summer, she'd lounge in the cool shade of the shrubbery near the front of the garage, sometimes venturing as far as the big swing under the tree to sit with Gail. Bianca was very low maintenance.

Bianca got along well with most of the other cats but didn't care for the dogs. By that I mean she was uninvolved with them. She didn't hiss at them or swipe at them. Nor did she seek out their favor. Except for one. Oliver was the chosen object of her affection. Why? Absolutely no idea. Oliver incurred the wrath of all the other dogs and most of the cats. Not Bianca. Maybe she felt sorry for him. Maybe she "felt his pain". Whatever the reason, Bianca loved that Schnauzer. Gail has a picture somewhere of Bianca sitting close to Oliver with her head resting on his shoulder. It was from behind and it's such a touching silhouette. Oliver was always gracious and accepting of her attention, even when he'd gone blind. What an odd couple they were.

Bianca was quite old when she got sick. We were never quite sure but we guessed she was around eighteen, which is ancient for a cat. She had gotten cancer and was starting to become frail. She took regular trips to the doctor for fluids. Bianca's world changed one final time when she became an indoor cat for the first time in her life. She LOVED it! She had never shown any interest in coming in the house before. Not once. But now that she was indoors, she was making the most of it. She'd would sit in the center of the kitchen table and announce to anyone within earshot, that she wanted food or a treat. It made us so happy that she was in her glory. She got lots of focused attention and anything she wanted to eat. She wasn't picky and she ate like a little piggy.

Eventually her appetite waned and her physical strength floundered. The time had come to finally say good-bye. It was fitting that the person who saved her all those years ago, would take her for her final ride. Gail said Bianca slipped quietly away. Peaceful and pain free at long last. She had a wonderful life. Even her last days were happy and filled with love. And she deserved every second of it.

. . .

PEPPER

aka
[Peeper; Peeps; Pepper Potsie]

In the litter that was Salt, Pepper and Oregano, Pepper was definitely the runt. She was always much, much smaller than her sisters. She was more skittish and human-shy than they were, as well. It was only when she got very sick that I was able to catch her. Without medical attention she surely would have died. We kept her in a recovery cage downstairs with Sonny, Bunny, Carmen, Romeo, Domino and Mittens. No matter how hard I tried, I couldn't seem to tame her. I couldn't get her used to human touch. It was always so frustrating. When I came into the room, she'd either run and hide or dive out the cat door in the window and stay in the outside enclosure until I was gone. It made me so crazy.

She was such a pretty little girl. A diluted grey calico with big eyes. I worked my ass off being nice to her. I always spoke gently to her and did my best to make eye contact but she was just not having it. For years, day in and day out, this was the case. I just had to accept it. Pepper was never going to be my buddy. But she was safe and got along with her adopted brothers and sisters. But things were about to change. For better...and for worse.

I began to notice that something was going on with Pepper's mouth. She was drooling a bit and her tongue stuck out to the left sometimes. I felt sort of helpless because there was no way I could catch her. Then something strange happened. She started to court my attention. One day, she walked up to me while I was petting another cat and turned sideways, arched her back and rubbed against my leg. I let her do that a couple times before I finally just put my hand down and ran my fingers down her back. She didn't run away. It was an encouraging sign, to be sure, but it was just a first step. After all these years, she was reaching out to me.

I worked hard on gaining her trust. I'd sit on the floor and she'd come over and throw herself down on her side and lay against my leg. She'd purr and purr and let me pet her. But then there were times she'd go back to her old ways and stay away from me. I had to get her to a vet and find out what was going on with her mouth. I finally took the plunge and grabbed her and stuck her in a carrier. I was on pins and needles and a nervous wreck, anticipating how she'd react. She was remarkably amenable to the entire thing. The news, however, was not good. Pepper had a cancerous tumor in her throat and there was not much that could be done. The doc gave me some holistic supplements to slow the growth but that was about all that could be done. I was crushed because it seemed that we were just beginning a friendship. But I was determined to make these days count.

I'd go in the cat's room and sit on the floor. She'd run over and lay beside me. She purred so loudly even the other cats noticed. I sang to her and she eventually crawled up on my legs and then lie down and twitch her tail. It was as if she knew her days were numbered and wanted to make up for lost time. I'd sit there and look at the little cat and I had to work hard not to hate myself for not doing something sooner. It was little comfort that the vet said these sorts of things don't usually respond to treatment. I still was eaten up with guilt. I put everything aside to make sure she was happy.

I brought her into the office. Most cats are terrified at new surroundings. Not Pepper. I'd sit in my old chair, put my feet on the foot stool and watch an old movie while Pepper would circle my head over and over again and then settle down and happily nap on my shoulder. Even my baby, Speck, normally jealous to a fault, helped care for Pepper. She'd clean her face and lay close to her. Speck didn't care for other cats, or any other animal, for that matter. She was devoted to me. It brought a tear to my eye to see her care for sick little Pepper.

Sometimes I would lie on the floor and Pepper would snuggle next to my warm belly or lay on my side. Pepper was very attached to me and Speck gave her space to be with me. I'd give Pepper her special holistic drinks in the office and she'd drink a little and then come over and love on me and go back and drink a little and then come back and love on me some more. I made her food into a very thin gruel because the tumor in her throat made it hard to swallow anything. Some days she'd eat like a pig. Other days, not. Day by day I could see her struggle, but as long as she was with her dad, she seemed happy. At night, I cried myself to sleep thinking about her and what was to come.

Towards the end, she was getting weak. She was now so happy to be held and kissed and cuddled. I tried not to think about how wonderful it would be if she wasn't terminal. How much closer we could become if only cancer wasn't in the picture. All the years she spent so terrified of me. All the time she was getting sicker and I didn't know. I tried not to cry in front of her. Animals can tell when you're distressed and I didn't want to burden her with that vibe. So, I'd pick her up and baby talk her and rub her skinny belly and scratch her head. All the things she loved best.

I knew the time had come to say good-bye. The night before, I let her out into the living area to walk on her own to the office to spend one last night with her dad. She'd never really had contact with anyone but me, so when she went up to Haley and rubbed around her legs and arched her back when she was being pet. At long last, Pepper was a domesticated cat.

The next morning, I didn't want to get up. I put Pepper in a carrier and headed to Atrium. Once we were in the car, I opened it and she happily hopped out and went immediately to my shoulder where she rode the entire way, purring in my ear every time I said her name. I carried her inside and we were immediately shown into a room. Dr. Kerns came in. She'd been Peppers doctor for the last three months of her life. Her eyes were tearing up as she gave Pepper some loving. She put a big comfortable blanket on the table and without prompting, Pepper laid down right in front of me and she never got up again. I stroked her and kissed her and sang to her and she twitched her tail and purred. Before Dr. Kerns gave her the final injection, I turned her head towards me and looked in her eyes. "I love you, Peeps. I hope you know that. Poppy loves you." She did something she'd never done before. She licked the end of my nose and then lay back down. She was ready. She was gone before the injection was finished.

I had Pepper in my life for many years, but I only had her in my heart for a short time. Now she'll be there forever. We didn't get much time together, but what we had was wonderful. Most importantly, it was wonderful for her. Although I still feel enormous guilt for how her life ended, I will be eternally grateful that she got to know closeness and love before she left this world because I know there are so many animals out there that never, ever get to experience those things. I still think of her every day. I keep her box of ashes in my office next to Speck's so we can all still be together.

...

SWEETIE

aka
[Sweet Pea; Sweets]

A friend of a friend saw someone throw a cat out of a moving car in front of where they worked. She ran off, but in the next few days they saw her hanging around in front of one of their buildings. Funny thing was, she never left the cement pad. So they would bring the poor thing food and water every day. One morning she wasn't on the pad. They looked and found her not far away, walking in circles. They realized she couldn't see. She may have been run off the pad by a dog or another cat and then couldn't figure out how to get back.

Gail heard the story and wanted to do something. She got her a box and put her food and water next to it. That's where the

The House of Goodbyes

cat stayed. But it was the beginning of winter and the weather was turning bitter cold, with below freezing temperatures that coming weekend. Gail called her friend, Alan, to see if he could catch her. Armed with heavy gloves and a cat carrier, he managed to capture the terrified and confused cat. Gail had set up a rehab cage in the house and the newly christened Sweetie took up residence with us. Gail took time to gain her confidence, making sure she knew where her food and water was coming from. In time, she was able to pet her. When she got to that point it was time for a long overdue vet appointment.

The vet confirmed what we had feared. Being thrown from the car window and the ensuing fall likely caused neurological damage. The blood work and other tests showed that she was basically healthy, otherwise. In time, her eye sight started to come back, but she was never, ever what you would call normal. She had no depth perception and never in her time with us, did she ever jump up on a chair or bench. That handicap did not keep her from being oh, so sweet. She would rub around your legs and purr up a storm. She bonded strongly with Gail and loved it when Gail would spend time in the sunroom with her, which was quite often. I would go out there and sit in a chair and call her name. She'd make her way over to me and lay against my leg. She couldn't really look up at you but she connected, nonetheless.

Who in the world could treat an animal like that? There is nothing she could have done that warranted such an abominable act. I could never really look at Sweetie without secretly wishing I could find the person that did this to her. As God is my witness, I would find a way to throw them from a speeding car without a blemish on my conscience. People like that make the world a cold and ugly place. If they all disappeared tomorrow, I would not shed a tear. In fact, I'd throw a celebration.

Sweetie had serious challenges but handled them as best she could. Gail was a good mom to her and saw to her every need. But we knew deep down that her condition would probably lead to her demise. Gail went to feed the sunroom cats one night and found Sweetie lying in the middle of the floor and she wasn't moving. Gail called me to help. I picked Sweetie up and she was in very bad shape. She was clearly struggling. I put her in a carrier and Gail sped off to the ER. The news was not good. Their diagnosis was that it was likely some sort of aneurism. When they learned her back story, they were even more certain. There was no saving poor little Sweetie. Gail agreed it was time to say farewell.

Sweetie was a hard luck case that got a second chance. Her tormentors failed in their mission to discard her. She beat the odds and then some. We didn't have her for very many years. Her quality of life wasn't perfect, but she lived out her days with love and warmth and safety. Thank God for that.

. . .

PO PO

aka
[Po Cat; Polecat; Po Po Kitty]

We were in the little house in Mint Hill. We'd put a doggie door in the laundry room door that led to the back yard so the hounds could come and go. One day, while Gail was working in the kitchen, she heard a meow. She spun around to see a young Calico cat rubbing her face on the baby gate that kept the dogs out of the house. Apparently, she just pushed her way through the doggie door and decided this is where she wanted to live. She was friendly, liked the dogs and was just the most gentle cat we'd ever seen. This is one of the rare times that the animal picked us instead of the other way around.

I named her Po Po and I can't tell you why. I just started calling her Po Po Kitty. To me, she looked a little cross-eyed but she really wasn't. It was just the way she would intently look at you. We introduced her to the outside enclosure with Timmy and Bianca and she was a perfect roommate. She got along famously with them. Gail went out to feed them one day and Po Po was gone. She had managed to get through a small opening and had escaped. We were sad because even in the short time she was there we'd gotten very attached to her. The popular consensus was that she just went back to the home she'd come from. Oh, well. But then, less than a week later, Po Po let herself in the back door again! "I'm home!" she seemed to say as she talked and talked to Gail and walked among the confused dogs, saying hello. Po Po had come into season and went off whoring around the neighborhood and got herself knocked up. As Donna Summer once said "Bad Girl". We secured her in the big cage in the carport until we could make the other enclosure escape proof. Once Po Po was fixed, she was no longer interested in roaming.

Po Po loved the freedom the move to Mineral Springs offered. She never went too far but she got around. Po Po was an indoor/outdoor cat and loved the luxuries of both, equally. When she was outside, she lounged on the porch or the swing. Sometimes she'd set up camp on the back patio, either on the deck or somewhere in the garden. She was always quick to greet you, even if she'd seen you only moments before. If you drove up, she'd come out to welcome you home. All she wanted was a rub on the head and a chuff under the chin. She was very easy to please. In the house, she'd find a spot on the kitchen table to soak up the sun coming in the bay window or she'd cuddle up on her mom in the chair or on the couch. Like all our cats, she loved treats but was never so selfish that she tried to keep the other cats from getting them. She would always share. Probably the most polite cat that we ever had.

I noticed a bump over Po Po's right eye one day. For the world, it looked like a she'd gotten into a tussle with another cat and took a toenail to the forehead. But it didn't go away. Off to the vet she went and the news was devastating. Cancer. We talked about our options and decided we would try to remove it. The doctor warned us that it would likely alter her appearance. We didn't care if it made a difference. No matter what she looked like, we would always love her. The results were startling.

Poor Po Po's right eye lid was pulled up, making it hard for her to blink. We had to put drops in her eyes to keep them moist. Despite her situation, Po Po was an excellent patient. Unlike most cats, she wore the "cone of shame" with grace and ease. After a while, we felt bad about keeping her locked up in a recovery cage. The hard truth was that her future was uncertain and we wanted her to be as happy as possible. Her habits and behavior didn't really change. She still looked forward to dinner time. She sat patiently for treats. The cancer may have altered her appearance but it didn't change who Po Po was.

The cancer progressed, taking over more and more of her face. She lost her right eye and her face was a grotesque mask, the flesh raw as the cancer consumed her face. You could smell the rot. It was horrible. But Po Po was still being Po Po. She came to get loved up and how could you not give her all the affection she wanted. She wasn't supposed to go outside, but dear God, what's the worst that could happen? She enjoyed the sunshine and fresh air. She was a good girl when it came time to go to the doctor for fluids and pain meds. Po Po was never, ever a problem.

At long last, when the ravages of the cancer had taken its toll on her, she changed. She stopped eating. She got weak. Po Po was telling us that her run was over. She had a good, long, uneventful life until the cancer struck. Po Po was likely seventeen or so. That's a pretty solid accomplishment. Gail took her on her final ride. As always, she was a good girl. Right to the end. Po Po was a glorious example of bravery in the face of the inevitable. Her stoic determination was, at the very least, inspirational. She appreciated every day, no matter what it held, and we made sure she enjoyed them as much as we could.

...

SPECK

aka
[Chip; Chip Chip; Cheddar Cheese; Pecky-O; Chubs; The Turd]

She was just another barn cat. A tiny, angry looking, feral orange tabby. I named her Speck after Pee Wee Herman's dog in "Pee Wee's Big Adventure". She stood out from the rest because every morning she would always wait for me down by the barn. "Good morning, Speck!" She'd stand up and follow me to the barn for breakfast. She wasn't bossy like some of the other cats. She didn't run in a "kitty clique". Speck just kind of did her own thing.

She had a run in with the one of the dogs early on and wound up dragging herself around for a while. She was obviously injured but could never seem to catch her. Eventually she was back up to full speed. For a while, anyway. It was a year or so later that I noticed Speck was limping. Her right hind leg was a bloody mess. It looked like she into a brawl with another cat or some other animal. One of the things we have to accept here at The Compound is that you can't always help a feral cat. You just can't. Some are too wild and some just won't let you near enough to catch them. We finally decided we'd try to help Speck. I took a pet carrier to the barn and left it for a couple days. A few mornings later I decided to go for it. I grabbed her while she was eating and stuffed her in the crate. She wasn't happy and she let me know it.

The vet said she might lose the leg. Might. The leg was badly infected and full of maggots. She stayed in the hospital for three days or so. I prepared a large cage for her in the downstairs cat room. They were, of course, less than welcoming.

Every day; twice a day; I'd go down and give her food and clean water and make sure her wound looked okay and her litter was clean. I really couldn't do much to her because she was still very feral and would stay in the back of her cage, either in her box or on top of it and just scowl at me. After about ten days, she ventured down to the cage floor. I have learned when dealing with ferals, you let them initiate first contact. She looked up at me and her grouchy orange face seemed to soften. I offered my hand. She sniffed it. Then rubbed her face on it. I didn't know it, but at that moment, she became my cat.

Every day she got more comfortable with me. About a week after first contact, I was on the floor on my hands and knees cleaning her cage. She came right over to me and reached up and rubbed her face against mine. It was instant love. I reached down and put my arms around her. She purred loudly. For the first time in her life, she knew love. Whenever I fed her, I sat on the floor and she'd come out and sit in my lap to get loved up. She was content and joyful.

Her leg wasn't getting better. In fact, it was getting worse. Her cage was always a bloody mess. She begrudgingly let me clean her wound. I was careful because I didn't want to betray her trust. I started carrying her from the cat's room to my office at night. She would sit in the old chair or ask to come up on the desk. As I was sitting in my office chair, writing, I was startled by her growling and thrashing around. I thought I'd rolled over her leg or tail with my office chair. I spun around to find her in some sort of seizure. She had her injured leg in her mouth and biting it. She was peeing all over my chair pad and bleeding profusely. What the hell was going on? It kept happening and it seemed there was nothing I could do about it. One night, it happened while she was sitting on my desk. I grabbed her to keep her from falling and instead of biting her leg, she bit me. All four fangs right into the meaty part of my left hand. It hurt like hell but I didn't let go of her. Afterwards, she was always in a daze. She'd go off and just sit a spell. But not long after she was back to normal. This was a real puzzle and I needed to solve it for her.

I went to a couple different vets looking for answers. Nobody offered anything of substance. All this time, Speck was having episodes. I felt helpless. I went to see Katie Smithson at Atrium Animal Hospital. She was sort of flummoxed, too. She suggested I take Speck to a neurologist at a certain veterinary specialist clinic in the Carolina's. As luck would have it, they actually got to see her have one of her episodes. Well, a thousand dollars later, they could offer no answers. But that was sort of their "modus operandi". This chain of clinics had a bad rep for using pet owners as an ATM. So, I hit the Google. I spent a couple days comparing symptoms. Now, keep in mind, I'm not the smartest guy in the world. I write song parodies and fart jokes for a living. And while that is a skill, or so I tell myself, it doesn't require much deep thought. I felt like I was in over my head. But finally, I landed on what I thought was the answer. I thought Speck might have Feline Hyperesthesia.

> "**Feline hyperesthesia syndrome**, also known as rolling skin disease, is a rare illness in domestic cats that causes episodes of agitation, self-mutilation, and a characteristic rippling of the skin when touched. It is often described as a seizure disorder but the cause is unknown."

Now, I found this on Google. I didn't go to veterinary school. I paid a lot of people a lot of money for answers and no one could tell me anything. I was pissed. I went back to Katie Smithson at Atrium and told her what I thought. It was like a light went off over her head. Fleas. Speck had a flea allergy that exacerbated her condition. It worked. I had to keep flea meds on her but she was 99% episode free. We were so happy. Speck was finally healing and soon her leg looked back to normal. She had many health issues. She had chronic cystitis, which made her prone to urinary tract infections and bladder issues. She tended to pee wherever she felt like it. It wasn't spiteful. She just had problems. And I dealt with them, gladly.

If a pet can be a soul mate, Speck was mine. During the ordeal of her illness, we bonded very closely. A little feral cat had learned to love and trust. At the end of a long day, I looked forward to sitting in the chair and cuddling with my chubby cat. There was no more carrying her to the office. I opened the door and called her and she came running, chirping the whole way, and running right to the office. She would sit on my lap or the crook of my arm and snooze. But what she loved best was sitting on my chest, closing her eyes and rubbing her face against mine. She would rub her nose against mine so hard that sometimes it actually hurt. But she was giving me all the love she could give me. I'd sing the "Pot-O Pot-O" song for her. A silly song I made up. Sometimes she liked it. Other times she'd just look at me and put her paw on my mouth. Everyone's a critic.

She was a funny cat. She went through a phase where she'd go out into the downstairs rumpus room and collect Haley's shoes. No joke. I'd look up from my desk and she'd be carrying a shoe which she'd hide in her cubby on her cat tree. She loved her toy mice. She would wear those things out, man. Slap them around the floor. Toss them up in the air and attack them. When she felt like she'd really made a "good kill", she'd bring it over and drop it on my desk. She also had a way of telling me I was working too much. She'd jump up on the desk, sit between me and the keyboard and stare at me. I'd lean back and she'd climb up on my chest, content that she got her way.

One of her little roommates, Pepper, had a cancerous tumor in her throat. She only had a month or so to live. I was determined to spend as much time with her as I could. Speck was definitely the jealous type. I was HER boy. No one else's. But to my surprise, she gladly shared me with Pepper. Pepper, who had also been a feral, was never really socialized. But in her final weeks, she became a lover cat. Speck would hover over her, licking her face and grooming her. I would sit in the old green chair in my office and Pepper would curl up on my shoulders. Speck would sit on my chest and love her up. It touched my heart that Speck would not only share me, but go out of her way to show love and respect to another cat.

I noticed a hard lump on Speck's right shoulder. Dr. Johnson did a biopsy and decided we should remove it. The incision was quite long. But Speck was always a good patient. She was a good sport and took confinement in stride. Just as long as I would spend some time with her each day. Then we got the results. It was cancer. Fibrosarcoma. My heart sank, but I didn't give up. They sent me to the oncologist at that veterinary specialist clinic. The doctor was a dick. Cold and unsympathetic. Sort of what I expected from them. He wasn't optimistic and didn't mince words. I had to find something else.

A new clinic had opened in town. CARE, which stood for Charlotte Animal Referral and Emergency. They'd just hired a new oncologist. Dr. Wesley Campbell. In this book, I only name vets that deserved to be recognized. She was my angel. I took Speck to see her. Her bedside manner was what I needed. Honest, but sympathetic. The type of cancer she had was not the most aggressive. Dr. Campbell mapped out a treatment plan for chemotherapy.

Speck didn't like going to the doctor. She fought like a rabid badger when I had to put her in the carrier. But when she got to see Dr. Campbell, she'd stroll out of the carrier, purring and rubbing around her legs. She just loved her. That's when she got the nickname "The Turd". "No, she's so good!" she'd say and I'd just look at the dopey cat and shake my head. I scolded her on the way home and Speck just sat satisfied she'd put her old man through the wringer.

The first series of chemo was a success. Speck had no ill effects. Her appetite was very good. She ate like a piggy. I splurged on a new recliner for the office. Our chair. Every single night after chores, I'd let Speck out and she'd run to the office and wait for me to sit down. She'd tap on her treat jar to let me know it was time for a snack. We'd watch "Impractical Jokers" on Tru TV. Speck loved it when I was laughing and that show makes me laugh. Periodic check ups showed no recurrence of her cancer. But that would be short lived.

I noticed an irregular lump on Speck's shoulder, near her original incision. A trip to see Dr. Campbell revealed the cancer had returned in a more aggressive form. In fact, it had spread to her chest and was in her lungs. We tried a new chemo, but it didn't seem to work. It would only be months before I had to let her go. I spent a lot of time crying. We watched "Impractical Jokers", but it was getting harder and harder to laugh. Speck stayed with me on the chair but I could see her getting weaker. Her appetite waned and my chubby little cat; the Flabby Tabby; was getting thin. She'd never spent any time around dogs but I brought my Pitbull, Daisy, to the office. Speck loved her. Little did we know that Daisy had cancer, too. Maybe Speck sensed that. She left me and sought out Daisy's company on the floor. It made poor Daisy uncomfortable but she tolerated it for her dad. But there came a point where Speck even abandoned Daisy and would go sit in the corner of the office. She withdrew. I decided that the next day, I would let her go.

I emailed Dr. Campbell of my decision and she said she'd be there waiting for us. Putting my precious Speck, my beautiful Chip Chip, in that crate for the last time was horrible. She was my baby. We'd been through so much. Just a couple hours a night of cat love got me through many long, tough days. When we arrived at CARE, they took us to "the room". The room I've been in too many times. Speck was out of her carrier and investigating the room. She was weak. She tried to jump up on the couch and couldn't. Dr. Campbell came in with the syringes. I put Speck up on the table. She lay down in front of me on the big soft blanket. I held her for the last time, crying uncontrollably. Dr. Campbell gave her the shot to sedate her and she immediately passed out. Then the final injection. I held her as she passed. When Dr. Campbell confirmed she was gone, I just erupted in wailing sobs. How could this little cat be taken from me? I looked up and Dr. Campbell was crying, too. I hugged her and took the empty carrier and left. I cried all the way home. The rest of the day. All night. In the days that followed, I discovered that Dr. Campbell never charged me for Speck's final visit. Nor for her private cremation. And she made a donation in Speck's name to a feline cancer research foundation. I have never been so touched by a gesture in all my years as a pet owner. I will never forget her and always love her.

Speck's ashes now sit on my desk, right in front of my monitor. There are nights that I can still feel her here with me. I'll feel a brush against my leg. A whisker on my cheek. I'll see an orange blur out of the corner of my eye. And that chair that I bought just for us? As I write this, it's been over a year and I still haven't sat in it. It was our chair. Not my chair.

...

TINA

aka
[Tiny Tina; Teeny; Teener]

Tina was, indeed, quite tiny. She fit in the palm of little Haley Pillars' hand. So, they brought the entire litter (with Blackie and Dusty) from the dusty confines of the hay barn to the house. Gail was on the fence about Tina making it. The whole litter was smaller than normal, but Tina was so small, it seemed unlikely that this mewling runt would survive. But she was determined to make it. Tina and the rest of the litter was not bottle fed. They were old enough to eat from a dish despite their miniature size and thankfully they were all good eaters.

From that tiny little nugget, Tina grew to a pretty decent sized cat. She was black, like her brother, Blackie, but not quite as long haired. She was a real lover. She always wanted to be held, not just pet. She spent a great deal of time curled up on Gail's chest or as close as she could possibly be. Tina's major quirk was tricking an unsuspecting human into thinking she actually wanted her belly rubbed. She would roll over on her back, tempting you with her sleek, soft underbelly and the minute you took the bait, she'd lay into you. I fell for it a few times but eventually I'd just say "Yeah, right, Tina". She'd wiggle and meow and keep trying. Many years later, she was still doing it. I wondered if she'd outgrown her foolishness, so I reached down to pet her tummy. Once a sucker, always a sucker.

Tina staked her claim for territory. She hung out on the back patio, the deck, the garden and later on, the pool deck. You couldn't take a step anywhere in that area without Tina underfoot. She loved the garden especially. As soon as Gail would plant in the spring, Tina would be caught lounging in the planters. No matter how many times you chased her out, she'd be back the second you turned your back. I shudder to think of the produce we were deprived of because of casual cats sleeping on seedlings.

Tina's best friend was CeeCee. They were inseparable. Where one was, the other was not far behind. They'd hang out like a couple of BFF's on the pool deck in the cool spring and fall weather. In the summer, they'd relax in the flower beds under the Weeping Willow on the back patio. They dined in the sunroom. That is, when their best friends, the raccoons weren't eating out of their dishes.

Yes, the raccoons. Gail put a cat door in the wall between the sunroom and the deck so Tina and CeeCee could come and go as they pleased. But the raccoons used it, too. Tina and CeeCee would sit to one side as the raccoons ate. They seemed to be enthralled as they watched the fat raccoons sit on their big asses, both hands FULL of cat food, munching away. It was quite funny. The raccoons got used to us, as well. At one time, when we turned on the lights, they'd scatter. After a while, they'd just look over, give us a nod and keep eating. And there sat Tina and CeeCee watching them like it was the series finale of their favorite TV show.

Gail asked me one day if I'd seen Tina recently. I had to think about it for a second because you get to a point where you simply don't notice. I couldn't remember, so I went looking. There was a small dog house under the pool deck that was heated and Tina was in there. She wouldn't come out when called and that was very unlike her. So, with a lot of work and effort, I finally got her out. Something was clearly wrong, so I took her inside. Gail found a pretty significant wound on her hind leg. It was profoundly swollen and hot. Gail rushed Tina to the ER and blood work showed that her liver was severely compromised, among other things. Everything was failing and very quickly. They never got to examine the wound but I can only guess one of the dogs got her or maybe a raccoon or possum. Gail stayed with Tina as she left this world. I wish I had been there. I would have loved to rub her belly before she left.

...

LULU

aka
[Miss Lou; Loubotski]

It was the same day Gail rescued little Clark that she found another white kitten in distress. She seemed disoriented and unsure of what was going on around her. She wasn't playing with anyone and seemed to be lost. Gail and Haley walked up behind her and she didn't respond. They assumed she was deaf and clearly, left to her own devices, she would likely not survive for long. So, they gathered up the little kitten and brought her to the house. They put her in one of those collapsible, foldable cages so she could acclimate to her surroundings. To their shock and surprise, she went absolutely insane! She was the living, breathing embodiment of the Tasmanian Devil in the Bugs Bunny cartoons! Gail had never seen anything like it before. There was a distinct possibility that this frantic kitten might not be suitable for indoor life. But in fifteen minutes or so, she calmed down. It was like it never happened. In direct contrast to her terrifying introduction, she became surprisingly domesticated and very loving and sweet. Gail named her Lulu.

Lulu had one green eye and one blue eye. Something common in white cats more than others. White cats are also born deaf more often than other cats, which I didn't know. The vet confirmed that was the case as well as the possibility that she was blind in one eye. Lulu was starting out life in a deficit. But she was safe in the house and she adapted to her new world with grace. Lulu loved sleeping on Gail. She'd curl up either on her head or very near it. When she developed a respiratory infection, Gail brought her into the den and Lulu would sleep on the back of her chair while she read in front of the fireplace, happy and content. She got along nicely with the other cats in her block. She might not have been able to hear, but she damn sure knew when the treats were being handed out! I'd get the treats out of the cabinet and in a flash I was surrounded by cats. Right there, on her special little corner of the bathroom counter was Lulu, patiently waiting. I had a soft spot for her and I always made sure she got a few extra. I'd stand guard until she finished in case the other cats got it in their head that they were going to hoark her stash. As she nibbled away, I'd pet her head and back and she'd purr and settle in, knowing she was protected.

I had done the litter boxes in the outdoor towers one morning and got distracted. I accidentally left the doors unlocked. Gail called me at the radio station and told me the cats had gotten out. I wasn't worried about anyone but Lulu. She was unprepared to deal with life outside the safety of the house. I raced home and found Gail seated in the glaring, hot sun waiting for the remaining cats to go back in the tower. She'd collected most of them, but Lulu, afraid and confused, was a hold out. I tried to catch her with my bare hands and she reacted with such fury and madness that she left my hands shredded from her teeth and claws. I was bleeding profusely. Gail was patient and waited a while and sure enough, she was right again. Lulu came from hiding and went right back in the tower and into the house. I waited a while and went in to see her. She purred and came in the bathroom for treats. She was just fine. I took a while to heal but she was back to normal and that's all that mattered.

The House of Goodbyes

It was time to feed and water the Green Room cats. As I opened the door, it bumped against something. I had a very sick feeling in my stomach. I poked my head around the door and looked down to see Lulu, curled into a ball. Her eyes were closed and she wasn't moving. Even though I knew, I reached down to check. "Loubot, baby?" She was dead. She wasn't completely cold yet so it must have happened sometime in the previous few hours. I just kneeled by her for minute and stroked her soft fur. "Oh, Lou. Poppy is so sorry." She hadn't shown any signs of anything wrong. She didn't look like she died in any sort of trauma. She looked like she was sleeping. I went out to tell Gail. "Lulu passed away, Mommy. Lulu's gone." Gail just sat down for a minute. I went and got a soft towel, wrapped her up gently and took her to the car. Gail drove her to the vet for cremation. A trip we've taken too many times. Lulu's story is not an unhappy one. She was saved from certain doom and given a life she would never have known under any other circumstances. She had a good long life and she passed quietly with little or no pain. In so many ways, it was the perfect ending.

. . .

DULCIE

aka
[Dulce; Bunny Fur; Bun Bun; Baby Bun]

Turtle was giving birth in the barn. In fact, she was running down the barn aisle with a kitten hanging out of her! When it finally plopped out, she didn't attend to it. Or any of them. She ran up into the paddock and lay down in the grass to clean herself, unconcerned about her babies. She didn't return to her new born kittens. Turtle is a sweet cat but a terrible mother. Gail and Haley quickly collected the kittens, still wet, the umbilical cords dangling, and rushed them to the house. They named them Sam, Mary and Pippin. After the best possible care they could provide, Sam passed away. Five weeks later, little Mary joined him. That left Pippin, the diluted Calico. She started showing signs of the illness that claimed her two siblings so Gail took her to an ER in Matthews, NC. What a shit hole that place was. They started running down everything they wanted to do to save the kitten. It totaled over one thousand dollars. "I'm not going to spend that much. This is just a barn kitten." The vet showed his true colors with his next comment. "How much would you be willing to spend?" If I'd been there, I'd have strangled him with his stethoscope. Gail told him "Three hundred dollars", and that's what they charged her. No itemized list, just a bill for three large. For that, the kitten got fluids and antibiotics. She was already feeling better before they left. So basically, the other seven hundred bucks they wanted to charge was just tacked on bullshit. This is why I hate so many vets. Scammers. But the kitten was feeling better, so mission accomplished.

The kitten had such a rough start in life that Gail changed her name to Dulcie, after "Aldonza/Dulcinea" in "Man of La Mancha". As the song from the musical says...

"I was spawned in a ditch
By a mother who left me there,
Naked and cold and too hungry to cry;
I never blamed her.
I'm sure she left hoping
That I'd have the good sense to die!"

But no one ever accused Dulcie of having any sense. She survived. She was a little fighter. One of her favorite things to fight was her bottle. Gail still remembers what a little shit Dulcie was when it came time to eat. She'd slap her little paws at the baby bottle and fuss like she was being fed poison. It frustrated Gail, but to everyone else it was hilarious. Dulcie came away from most meals caked and matted with formula, looking like she just came from a pie fight!

Dulcie had an unusual physical deformity. Her left rear leg never fully descended. The leg was fully formed, but it was always like it was in the seated position. Did that stop her or slow her down? Please. She'd fly around the house and act the fool with the best of them. When you let her outside, she'd scoot right along down the sidewalk. Gail called her "The Sidewinder." We had talked about seeing if surgery might be able to correct it, but no one really seemed to think it was worth it. It really didn't affect her life with any degree of negativity, so we just left well enough alone. To me, it just added to her personality.

While we're on the subject of personality, Dulcie had a big one. She was, in a word, kooky. You had to be careful opening doors because nine times out of ten, Dulcie was on the other side, getting ready to bolt past you. Especially the door between the living room and the den. Dulcie would explode past you, run into the living room and to the front door to go outside.

She wasn't doing it to be a brat, that's just where she liked to go outside. I always tried to be patient and accommodate her. Gail would say "Dulcie, you little shit!" Dulcie didn't care. She'd wait by the door, looking and acting so innocent, until you let her out. I'd reach down and pet that soft head. "Hey, Bun Bun." She'd meow and look up sweetly. I'd open the door and off she'd go down the sidewalk in a manic scamper. I knew where this was going. I'd walk back into the house, through the living room, to the den and into the kitchen and to the door to the garage and there Dulcie would be waiting, asking to come back inside. Like I said, kooky. I gave up trying to figure out what she was thinking and just accepted Dulcie as Dulcie. Lunatic.

I never really called her anything but "Bunny Fur". She came by that nickname honestly. She had the softest fur of any cat we've ever had. It was luxurious. Soft, like a bunny rabbit, hence the name. It always amazed me when I'd pet her. The tactile sensation was remarkable. Anyone who would pet her remarked about how "touchably soft" her fur was. You wanted to just hold her. Sometimes she was down with that. Other times not. But she was always sweet with people. And dogs. Especially dogs. Almost exclusively dogs.

Dulcie loved dogs. Sometimes that feeling wasn't completely mutual. When she was little, she'd sit on our Boxer, Rosie, take her ear gently in her mouth and nurse on it and with her little paws, she'd knead the side of her head. Rosie would just sigh and lay there and take it. Dulcie was very fond of Rosie. She'd snuggle and nap with her, curling up against her belly or just lay across her. If she was in any proximity to Rosie she'd rub all around her and try to get her attention. Rosie always looked at you with an expression that said "Why me?" But the only one who could answer that was Dulcie and she was too busy loving her up to answer.

Dulcie hadn't been feeling well. It appeared that there was something wrong with her bottom. Either her stool was very soft or she was suffering from some sort of infection. Either way, it was time for her to go to the doctor. Gail took her to the vet. He wanted to put her on antibiotics and fluids and keep her for a couple days. I thought it was a good idea. A couple days turned into five days. Gail was told she was doing much better and went to get her on a Monday afternoon. I was sitting in my office and I texted Gail to ask how Bunny Fur was doing. She texted back that she just got home and Dulcie couldn't stand up.

I ran upstairs to find Dulcie struggling to try and stay on her feet, her abdomen distended and clearly full of fluid. Something was horribly, horribly wrong. How in hell could her condition be interpreted as "doing much better"?! Apparently, Gail never got a chance to see her before they put her in the carrier. She had no reason to be suspicious. Dulcie groaned in pain. We put her in a carrier and raced to CARE and the ER. I was furious. How could a vet send a cat home in that condition? HOW? This was inexcusable. "Dulcie isn't going to make it, Gail". "I know". That was the extent of the conversation. We were about three miles from the ER and suddenly smoke started to erupt from under the vans hood. "Son of a bitch!" We crossed our fingers and prayed. It's always infuriating being behind stupid people in traffic. It's worse when you're on the verge of a breakdown, mental and vehicular, and have a pet in dire straits on top of it. But we made it and while Gail called someone about the car, I rushed Dulcie inside.

The news was not good. Dulcie's vitals were declining. I turned to the doctor and asked "Would you send a pet home in that condition?" She stared at me blankly. "No, of course not." I vacillated between profound sadness and blinding fury. The consensus was that poor Dulcie was not going to recover. It was time to let her go. We were escorted to the "quiet room" and they wheeled Dulcie in on a cart. Gail and I both started crying. Dulcie was weak but when Gail reached for her, Dulcie summoned what little strength she had left and crawled onto Gail's chest. And that's where Dulcie passed away. Our little Bunny Fur was gone.

My first instinct was to find the vet and beat him to a pulp, but I let Gail deal with it. This is a perfect example of why there should be "veterinary malpractice". I don't know if it was a misdiagnosis or just pure laziness, but someone dropped the goddamn ball. Dulcie spent her final days surrounded by people she didn't know. Afraid and alone. She deserved better. Much, much better. The only consolation is that she left this world in the arms of the woman who brought her into it. The only mother she ever knew.

...

LEWIS

aka

[Mr. Maloosh; Malooshavic]

We used to have an old shed behind the barn to keep things out of the rain. One day, Haley's boyfriend, Josh, went to get something for Gail and found four kittens in there. Two were dead. The two white kittens were still alive. Gail had Josh put some water in the shed for the two survivors and bury the two deceased kittens. That evening, when Gail went to the barn to bring in the horses, she checked on them. Only one white kitten remained and Gail brought him to the house. He was such a dopey, nerdy cat, that I named him Lewis after "Lewis Skolnick" from "Revenge of the Nerds".

Lewis was Haley's first experience bottle feeding a kitten. Lewis was wild. It seemed to Haley that Lewis would never break the "baby bottle habit" and learn to eat like a normal cat. Poor Haley. Lewis exhausted her, but she loved him. Of course, he finally got the hang of eating, but for a time we were afraid that he might be mentally challenged.

In his adolescence, Lewis was a tad unpredictable and I loved him for it. You'd pick him up and he'd be so sweet and adorable…and then…a switch flipped. His pupils would get big, his tail would start to flick, his ears would go back and he'd slowly extend his talons, clutch your flesh and then start to bite. He was playing, of course, but he was rough. Gail and Haley scolded him but I let him rough house. He was a growing boy and needed his wrestling time. Even though it was years ago, I can still see a pretty visible scar on my right hand!

Lewis became a member of the Green Room clan. He was miserable. He didn't like, what I'm certain he interpreted as, being confined. He didn't get along particularly well with the other cats. So we finally moved him into general house population. Lewis had outgrown his youthful temperament and was much more laid back. He'd lay all stretched out on the glass shelves in the big kitchen window and sleep for hours. He was in his glory. At night, he'd sleep on Gail. He even worked hard at getting along with the other cats. For four years, Lewis was finally happy. He was with his family.

Lewis was regal looking. Long pure snow white hair with a big white ruff on his chest. But despite his long coat, it was apparent Lewis had lost weight. He was thin, but not sickly. That changed very, very quickly. Gail took him to the vet for an exam and some blood work. The vet couldn't feel any palpable masses so he didn't think it was cancer, but Lewis was quite anemic. The blood work showed that not much was out of whack but it might be an immune disorder. Lewis wasn't very active. Not that he ever was, but he didn't come running for treats now. He ate them if you put them in front of him but wasn't interested in food. It was very disconcerting.

The next morning, I opened the door to the den and Lewis was lying on the rug in front of the door. He hadn't done that before, but I didn't put much stock in it. I reached down and loved him up. I rubbed his boney back and he rolled over and let me rub his belly. When I got back from doing chores, Gail had finally gotten up. I passed Lewis laying on the floor and it was quite noticeable that his breathing was labored. Gail called the vet and they said to come in. "No. We have to go to the ER. NOW!" I put Lewis in a carrier and we left. On the way, he was moaning. I couldn't bare it. I opened the door to the carrier and he crawled out. I held him the rest of the way. He was clearly struggling, but I hoped I gave him some comfort.

We got to CARE and they took him back immediately. The vet tech came back in less than a minute and asked us if we wanted to the doctor to perform CPR if necessary? What the hell?! They got us into a room pretty quickly. The vet told us Lewis was in heart failure. He had significant thickening of the heart muscles and he was very anemic. She explained that they could try and treat it but there was a good chance he wouldn't survive. I didn't want him to linger in agony and pass away without his family near. We decided, as much as it hurt, to let Lewis go.

We texted Haley with the grim news and she was understandably upset. Lewis was her first cat. And just the day before, she'd lost her first pony, Kita. It was a double gut punch for my poor kid. I told her not to come, Lewis wasn't going to last that long. The doctor came in carrying Lewis in a blanket. She didn't think it was prudent to wait very long. Gail and I kissed and hugged Lewis. We told him how much we loved him, what a beautiful boy he was and how very sorry we were. He was in such dire condition that we told the vet to go ahead. Lewis passed almost instantly. Gail and I sat with him for several minutes. We stroked his oh, so soft fur and quietly cried. Such a tragic end for such a wonderful cat. We will all miss him every single day. But at least I still have that scar to remember him by.

...

EQUINE

GYPSY
aka
[Mipsy; Miss Gyp; Gypsy Pony]

In the early days, when I didn't have much interaction with the horses, I did fall in love with a little fat, black pony named Gypsy. What a ridiculous, comical cartoon she was. Gail's friend Kathy knew someone in Raleigh who owned Gypsy. They were going to donate her to a research facility, so Kathy took her in and had her transported down here. One look at this chubby equine cherub left you to wonder who in the world would sentence her to such a fate.

Shortly after we moved to Mineral Springs and we had all the fences up, we brought Gypsy to be with us. She was Kita's best friend but the other horses didn't want her in the pasture with them. So, for one whole year, Gail and Haley had to walk Gypsy, with Kita close behind, all the way over to the two acre pasture. In the evenings, Haley would just put a rope on her and jump on her back and ride her to the barn. Gypsy was so sweet and patient. One day, Gail was leading her to the two acre pasture when she just decided to stop. The other horses came around and sniffed. They didn't chase Gypsy or nip at her. They just turned around and wandered off to graze. And that was it. Gail took Gypsy's halter off and she was officially part of the herd. She was pretty pleased with herself.

Haley was in the fifth grade and an injury to her foot forced her into a cast. During that time she took Gypsy to a couple of small dressage competitions and even won a blue ribbon! Gypsy was so much fun to watch. She did all the typical silly pony stuff, romping around the pasture on her fat little legs. In the evening, when it was time to come in for dinner, you could stand by the gate to the barn and call her. Then you'd wait. Soon, you'd hear the thunder of tiny hooves and moments later, appearing out of the darkness like a fat ninja, she'd burst through the gate and head to her stall for chow time. She did it hundreds of times and there wasn't a single time it wasn't hysterical comedy gold. Even better. Comedy platinum!

We had only had Gypsy for a few years when she got sick. She started slowing down. She looked awful and was no longer her jolly self. It was heartbreaking. What was once a pudgy ball of goofy energy was now frail and listless. So much so, that I couldn't bear to look at her and I avoided going to the barn. I still regret that decision to this day. I should have been with her. I should have given her my time. Gail checked on her often. Towards the end, Gail would go down to the barn several times a day, even over night. One night, she went down at 2:30am to find that Gypsy had passed away. The vets never figured out what happened to her, but decided, ultimately, it was probably some sort of cancer. Maybe that's why the previous owner wanted to give her to research and they never told us. Regardless, I'm glad she spent her last couple of years with us. She was happy and she was loved. Just as God intended when he sent her to us.

...

ZOE

aka
[Zoey Big Toey; Zo Berry]

Zoe was a beautiful silver Appaloosa. The girl who owned her went off to college and sold her to a lady that worked at the barn whose horse had just passed away. It was shortly after that that Haley's horse, Kita, went lame with frozen stifles and couldn't be ridden. We couldn't afford to board her there but the owner agreed to pasture board her with Zoe. They spent an entire year together and became the best of friends. When Kita finally recovered, Haley would go to the stables to ride her and right along behind was Zoe. Haley rode Kita all over those twenty five acres and Zoe trotted in tow like a young foal. Kita loved it.

. Gail's friend wound up going through a very tough divorce and lost her farm. Gail agreed to take Zoe and Kita. Zoe stayed with Gail's friend, Kathy until all the fences were up and the pastures were secure. By this time, Gail had fallen in love with Zoe. She was the sweetest, easiest going horse she'd ever met. She always talked about how great she was to ride during lessons. Zoe was low and no maintenance. She went in and out of the trailer like a champ. You almost didn't have to ask her. She stood silently when saddled and tacked. You couldn't tell if she was so good because she liked it, or out of gratitude.

There came a time when we had so many horses that we decided to try a twenty four hour turnout. We fed them along the fence line and everything seemed to be going along smoothly. We're not exactly sure what happened, but the vet said that Zoe and Jessie must have gotten into some sort of weed or vegetation. They both came down with some sort of illness that we treated as "The Heaves", which is a chronic, non-infectious airway infection. Jessie responded to the treatment. Zoe did not.

Zoe's symptoms would ebb and then return, but never completely went away. In a short time, her condition worsened. There was nothing else we could do. But before the vet could get here, things went from bad to worse. Gail let Zoe out of her stall. She was struggling to breathe. Finally, she just let out a loud, long neigh and collapsed. She was dead. Right in front of Gail and Haley.

This was the first time I was present for the disposal process. A kindly older black man came out with a dump truck. The bed of the truck tipped up and he placed a cord around her neck and turned on the wench. Zoe's body slid up the ramp and onto the truck. I cried and cried at the sight. It was horrible and a farewell unbefitting to such a wonderful old girl. I never watched the process again.

...

JESSE

aka
[Jess; Jester; Jester Bean; Jester Belle]

Jesse was a rescue Mustang. She had a brand on her neck still showing her "number". She was literally headed to the glue factory when Gail's friend, Kathy, took pity on her and bought her…for a dollar. Jesse was not in good shape. She had been, what they call, "cowboyed", which means she was caught as a wild mustang. From everything we knew, she was treated horribly. Brutal bridle abuse left her tongue almost cut in half. She had scars on her legs where she'd been tied down. Even after all that vicious treatment from humans, she was still willing to trust again. It took some doing, but Kathy got her back to feeling good. She was used as a school horse for a while, but that mustang spirit still burned bright and you could never quite be sure if she'd run away with her rider. Haley rode her several times and said what a dream she was. Kathy sold Jesse to the family of a young girl who rode her as a student. We were all happy that Jesse had gone to a good home. Or so we thought. A few months later, they brought her back. Kathy's herd was getting too big and someone had to be moved. We were happy to bring her to what would be her forever home. This time forever, for real.

Jesse was quite on in years when she came to us. No one knew for sure but she was estimated at close to thirty. For a horse, and some people, that's ancient. We knew that her time was short, so we took extra special care of her. But in a way, we sort of let her down. When we tried to do twenty four hour turnout, she and Zoe got into something and they both came down with the heaves, which is a chronic respiratory condition. Zoe didn't survive, but Jesse did. It would not be the last time she beat the odds.

I always liked Jesse because she was such a joker. I can't tell you the number of times I'd be in the barn with her, cleaning stalls or filling water buckets, and when my back was turned, she quick reach over and pull my gym shorts down. I'd turn around and she'd be looking the other direction and acting innocent. It made my heart happy that she was so good at physical comedy. Another thing that always cracked me up was her water trough antics. Jesse wouldn't just take a drink like a normal horse. She'd take a nice, long sip and then, all of a sudden, plunge her face into the water. She'd blow bubbles through her nose and bob her head up and down, splashing water everywhere! You could see the joy in her face. That's why she loved the pond so much. I'd stand at the fence looking for Jesse and I'd see her lying in the pond with just her head above water like a big, dopey Loch Ness Monster. Many nights, she'd return to the barn to eat, caked in mud and smelling like the pond. If horses could smile, she'd have been grinning ear to ear.

Jesse had terrible problems when she went to founder. Foundering is the extremely painful inflammation of folds of tissue connecting the pedal bone to the hoof. To compound it, she also got a huge abcess in her hoof. All she could do was lie in her small paddock. It was horrible. She looked so sad. I'd go down to spend time with her. I'd just sit close by and talk to her, rubbing her head and scratching her neck. Sometimes I'd read to her or sing her a song. Jimmy, our farrier, came out to try to trim her hooves and drain the abscess in her hoof and trim them. He said "She's about done. I'll be surprised if she's here when I come back." About a month later, Jimmy came back. Standing in the paddock to greet him was Jesse. Jimmy just laughed. He couldn't believe it. Jesse was always full of surprises.

Jesse's health problems seemed to come and go. One day, Gail was with her in the side yard beside the house. We'd been letting her graze there. Gail put a lead on her halter and was leading Jesse back to the barn when she reared up on her hind legs and fell over. It almost appeared to be a seizure. Gail finally got her up and back to her stall. I went down later to check on her. I put a lead rope on her to see if wanted to go back and graze. There was a big trough just outside her paddock and, as usual, she stopped to get a drink. In went her head and the bubbles erupted around her face. She started splashing her face in the water. I was laughing at her, when all at once she stopped. There was a look in her eye I can't describe. Confusion? Fear? She suddenly staggered backwards and then reared up on her hind legs and fell right in front of me. She was alive but she wasn't moving. I tried to get her up with no luck. I called Gail and she called the vet.

When the doc got there, the first thing he did was try to get her up. No dice. Jesse was all done. Gail and Haley came and said their good-byes, but I stayed. She was my buddy. I got on my knees and kissed her face. "I love you, so much, pony. I'm sorry, Jess. I'm so, so sorry." The vet gave her the injection and she was gone. I could not hold back the tears, but I also was so grateful that the last thing she did was something that always made her so happy. The trough. If only they could all go that way. There isn't a day goes by that I don't think of that old horse. We made her last years happy and she did the same for us.

One of the last pictures we have of Jesse was one we took for a Christmas card. She and Haley were wearing big, feathery Steeplechase hats that Gail had made. She was perfectly patient and a very good sport. I'd like to think it wasn't only the trust that we'd cultivated in her, but her way of showing gratitude for all the kindness we'd shown her.

...

RANGER

aka
[Big Head; Muley; Danger]

An equestrian friend of Gail's knew she was looking for a horse. She finally called about a quarter horse someone wanted to sell. He was underweight and kind of just generally sad. He had been turned over to the horse dealer to try and sell because he'd gotten the reputation for being "unrideable". Gail spent the next six months babying him, grooming him, walking him around and teaching him ground manners, but very seldom sitting on him. He had the nickname of "King of the Crossties". Crossties are the chains that are connected to either side of the halter in the grooming bay and Ranger would always break them by lunging, probably out of fear from an unpleasant previous experience. What reinforced that idea is that he wouldn't let Gail touch his face for a very long time. So, she just put a lead rope gently around his neck and let him stand there while she groomed him and treated him sweetly. Gail did find out who his previous owner was. Indeed, he was an asshole of gargantuan proportions. I pity the poor horse that falls under his ownership. Someday, there will be a special place in hell for this prick.

Ranger had some issues, health and pain wise. We had an equine chiropractor, Susan Chandler, come out and work on him. Ranger was completely out of alignment. This probably contributed to his bad behavior due to the pain. Quarter horses are known for what they can endure in regards to pain, so he was likely hurting pretty bad. He also had the equivalent of a pelvic bone broken off and a burn mark across his lower back. The vets wondered if he hadn't been in a fire and a timber came down across his back because the hair never grew back. Ranger had a long road ahead of him. He was going to be a real project for Gail. For example, she couldn't ride him out of the barn. He'd spin and spin and run back into the barn. Again, he must have associated being outside the barn with some sort of abuse. But once he trusted her, she could take him out into the pasture. She'd sit on the ground and he'd graze all around her. He'd trot around and learned to follow stop and start directions. He was learning that he didn't have to be afraid anymore. And Gail was learning too. Sometimes, the hard way.

She was riding Ranger out in the pasture one day. She was on a flat "pancake saddle" and her feet weren't in the stirrups, the reins lying across his neck. Another horse galloped past them and nicked Ranger. He spooked, spun and Gail, who was unprepared, went down hard and broke her tail bone. On another occasion, she learned about "pawing". They were on a trail ride and after a long climb everyone was enjoying the view from a big, sandy area. After a moment, Ranger started pawing the ground and then down he went, taking Gail with him. She managed an emergency dismount and watched as he gleefully rolled and rolled in the soft sand. He stood up, shook off like a dog and then everyone waited while Gail took the blanket and saddle off and brushed all the sand away so there wasn't any irritations between Ranger and the saddle. She was ready the next time. They were crossing a stream and he stopped and started pawing the water. Gail knew what was going on and got her heels into his side. They got across without anyone taking a dunking.

Once he knew he was safe and happy, his silly side came out. His very first Christmas at the barn, all the barn kids put on a show. Ranger got to be a reindeer and was such a good sport when he had to wear a big set of antlers. I think he actually enjoyed it. He was notorious for biting buttons off of shirts and jackets. We know he did it but he was so stealthy you could never catch him. I didn't have a lot of interaction with Ranger, early on. But once, I was out in the pasture at the pond. I liked to go down and watch the turtles and the snakes. I don't know exactly why but I was bent over at the edge of the pond, probably catching a frog, and I thought I felt something on my butt. Before I could check, or even react, into the pond I went, courtesy of a push from an all-too-pleased with himself, Ranger. I wanted to be furious, but how could I be. I stood up and Ranger just looked at me and walked away. From that point forward I never turned my back on him at the pond. Jerk. But he also had a loving side. Often, when I was either letting him in at night or feeding or doing stalls in the morning, he'd give me, what I called, "snuffles". He'd put his huge moose nose in my face and blow and inhale. I learned to do the same. Gail told me once what it meant, but I don't remember exactly. In a nutshell, it was his way of accepting me. Such a brave boy for one so mistreated in the past.

Gail was having a rough time. I don't remember which birthday it was, but that night there was no celebration. We lost our Buddy the Beagle to heart failure. It was horrible, but it was about to get worse. Much, much worse. The next morning, Gail came up from the barn. Ranger was down and he didn't want to get up. Gail called the emergency vet, fearing colic. Colic is a general term for abdominal pain but can take many forms, from simple gas to a twisted gut. After an examination, her worst fears were realized. Ranger's intestines had somehow gotten twisted. The vet tried everything he could including reaching into his rectum to try to manually undo the twist. He worked with Ranger for almost seven hours. There was nothing he could do. We had two choices. If we did nothing, Ranger would die a horribly painful, prolonged death. Or we could let him go. We chose the most humane way. He had earned that much.

The vet lead Ranger to spot in the pasture where his remains could be most easily collected. Gail's friend, Kathy, came over to comfort her as she was teetering on collapse. This was her baby. Ranger was, in many ways, another child. An abused foster child who was shown love and learned that the world wasn't an ugly, terrifying place after all. Gail gave him a better life than he would likely have ever known and their bond was deep because of it. Now, in such a horrible circumstance, she was forced to say goodbye. She held his face and tried to speak comfort to him but she was crying so hard, he must have known something was up. Kathy took her towards the house. I put my hands on his face and leaned close and gave him one last snuffle. I did my best to hide my tears. I went to take Gail back to the house and Kathy stayed with the vet to ease Ranger on his way. I was terrified Gail would have a heart attack.

Minutes later, Kathy and the vet came back to the house. It was done. Ranger was gone. Even the vet was choked up. He brought Gail a beautiful braid of Rangers hair, which she still has. The worst part was the couple days it took for them to retrieve his remains. He lay in the pasture, covered in a blue tarp. Gail had to drive right past him when she came and went from the house. My heart broke, and still breaks for her. It was hard on Abby, too. She took her lead from Ranger. He was her "boyfriend". We kept Abby and Kita down at the barn until Ranger was gone. When she was released into the pasture, I watched her. She sniffed all over and she found where he had laid. Her look was not sadness, but confusion. For the next several days, she looked for him, finally resigning herself to his absence.

...

KITA

aka
[Stinkita; Stinkita Blanqita Pinqita; Kita Belle; Kita Beans]

Kita was a pretty horse. A white and brown Paint. She was a real baby maker for whoever had her originally. When she completely rejected her last foal, the owner was done with her. They sent her to the barn to see if someone would buy her. She and Haley really hit it off. We'd been looking for a horse that was just Haley's size and little Kita was a perfect fit. Haley loved her and it seemed she loved Haley, too. This was illustrated perfectly when Haley was riding Kita in a synchronized riding group with five other riders and horses. During a practice session, one of the horses a bit higher up on the totem pole pushed into Kita and Haley during one of the turns, knocking them right over one of the railings! Down they went among all those horses and riders! Kita scrambled to her feet and stood beside Haley who was lying on the ground and she stayed next to her until she knew everything was OK.

Kita's only downside was her stubborn streak. She was a text book brat. But one of the reasons of her stubbornness was the pain in her fetlocks. They were freezing up and making it painful for her to move. Her tenure as a school horse was short lived. She didn't have the temperament for it. It was expensive to board the horses because they weren't earning their keep as school horses. It was time to find a place they could call home.

The move to Mineral Springs meant room for ponies. Kita was so happy. She was content in her position in the pecking order. Go along to get along was her motto. But that didn't always matter to Abby, who, more than once would kick her or nip her on the rear. But once Ranger was gone, that behavior sort of went away and their relationship strengthened. They were like a couple of sisters. They'd bicker occasionally, but nothing ever came of it.

One of my favorite things about Kita was her mouth. Big, soft, wiggly lips! When she was sad or upset or begging for a treat, that huge lower lip wiggled and twitched like a plate of Jello Jigglers. If Kita had a poker face, it would be her "tell". What a character. Like Jesse before her, she loved taking treats out of my pockets. I guess it didn't help that I'd leave an extra carrot in easy grabbing distance. When I was doing pony dishes in the morning, she'd raise her head and put her chin on my shoulder. I'd look out of the corner of my eye and see those giant lips. "Do you want a treat, pony?" Wiggle, wiggle, wiggle. That was a definite "yes". And she always got it.

Kita's arthritis had gotten much worse in her later years. But it wasn't so bad that she couldn't trot around the pasture, doing her best to keep up with Abby, and kick up her little fat legs. But it wasn't always fun and games. The Sunday morning after my fifty ninth birthday, I got to the barn that morning to find Kita down. I didn't know for how long. She was in her hay stall, which was smaller than her regular stall. Apparently she had lain down to roll and got stuck with her head and front legs in the corner. Not good. She was cut up and bloody from struggling. I went to the house to get Gail. We tried to move her but Kita was out of gas. Gail called the Equine ER Vet but it would be an hour or more before they could get there. It looked like the end. Gail went back to the house for something and didn't want to wait.

I put a big soft lead rope around her front legs and a halter and lead rope on her head. I dug my heels in and pulled. She moved. I reset my feet and pulled again. And again. And again. I knew that what I was doing would send me to the chiropractor but so be it. I finally got her turned around. Now I was out of gas. I went around outside the barn and opened the door to the paddock. I went back in the stall with Kita. "Don't go out like this, pony. Don't give up on your dad." I reached down and grabbed her halter and pulled. Up she came. She took a moment to steady herself, then she noticed all the tall, luscious green grass in the paddock. She stepped out and started grazing as if nothing happened. Whew. The vet finally came and stapled her wounds shut and doctored her up. Her gut sounds were good and she came through with flying colors. I was not so lucky.

I spent the rest of the day in bed. The chiropractor wouldn't touch me without an x-ray, so I went to the doctor to get one. They revealed that two of my vertebrae cracked under the pressure of pulling Kita to safety. Would I do it all over again? You bet. And I got to prove it three months later. On November 1, 2017, I went to the barn as usual. As I was walking through the pasture to the barn, I heard the unmistakable sound of hooves on the barn wall. I opened the gate and I could see Kita lying crossways in the barn aisle! The sight took my breath away. "Not again." I rushed to her and she was very tired. How the hell did she get in this position? I knew what I had to do. I went to get Gail and then returned to get the ropes. I was able to pull her around so she had more room. The pain in my back was instantaneous, but it didn't matter. I pulled and pulled until I couldn't pull anymore. Gail called the vet and then she called our neighbor, Dave. In the meantime, Kita would thrash and struggle, never quite able to get her footing. She was slipping on the mat in the barn aisle. I managed to wiggle it out from under her and Dave helped get it out of the way. Kita flailed and flopped. I leaned over her and she looked me right in the eye. A pleading, plaintive look that made me so sad. "Don't give up, pony. Rest a bit. Doctor's coming." She struggled but couldn't get up. Her spirit was powerful but she was betrayed by her weakened body. I knew my time was limited until I couldn't walk so I went to finish chores. When I returned, there was that damn Kita, eating hay and getting a drink. She ambled over to her "Potty Corner" of the paddock and dropped a big deuce. A very good sign that her tummy was still working. The vet came out and they discussed some additional treatment and meds. But the bottom line is that she's lost so much muscle mass due to her worsening arthritis that there would come a time when she won't be able to get up. And that time came on the morning of November 13, 2017.

"Pony! Pooooooony!" That's what I'd always call to her as I made my way to the barn in the morning. She'd poke her big, dopey mug over the stall door and wiggle her ears. She was ready for her "crunchies" which was the first bite out of the cat food bucket. But this morning, Kita didn't appear. I knew. It had been terribly cold the night before and I was already worried for her all that night. I looked over the stall door and my worst fears were confirmed. I knelt by her side and she craned her head towards me. She looked tired and very sad. "Oh, pony. Let's try to get up, OK?" I put the ropes around her front legs and tried to get her into a position to better attempt a stand. She gave a few half hearted attempts. I offered her a hunk of carrot and she gobbled it up. "Good old girl." Gail and Haley finally got to the barn and Haley was beside herself. Kita was her baby. We let Kita rest a while. We covered her with a horse blanket to warm her up. She tried a few more times but it was clear Kita would not be getting up again. I walked over and looked at her. "It's time, isn't it, pony?" The look in her eyes told me it was so.

The vet got there and explained that if she'd been down a while, with the withered condition of her hind quarters, there is likely a degree of nerve damage. Kita's legs had been drawing up and twitching, which was a good indication that was, indeed, the case. I told Haley to say her good-byes. Tears rolled down her cheeks. She kissed her big cheek again and again and hugged her neck. Gail was next and stroked her face over and over. I asked the vet to step in and I knelt next to her and kissed her and rubbed her ears and cheeks. When the vet inserted the needle, she didn't flinch or fight it at all. I put my face close to her. "Good-bye, pony. Good-bye, Kita Belle. It's OK. You can go now." The vet pushed the plunger. He said her heart would beat for another minute. Kita's beat for over two. Her spirit was so strong. Her vessel was just worn out. I leaned over her and whispered in her ear. "Go on now, pony." And she was gone.

    Haley had said that Kita saved her life that day in the arena all those years ago but today she couldn't save hers. That's not true. Haley saved Kita the day she brought her home. Until that day, Kita's future was uncertain. She lead a good, long life because of that decision. Kita did her job. She had nothing left to prove. I will miss her every single day.

. . .

FERAL FELINE

THE BARN CATS

There have been many over the years that we barely knew. Momma Cat, Toaster, Bing, Spooky and many others had limited tenure at the barn. In the early days we lost a lot of kittens to predators and the dogs. I have to state here that I was late to the dance with the barn cats. There were many that came and went before I started doing barn chores. So, the ones mentioned here are the ones I directly interacted with. There are many, many, many not listed here. While all of them touched my heart and my life in some way, a few stood out because they endured or affected me personally.

BOOGER

aka
[Boog]

Booger was at the Mineral Spring property when we arrived. Bless his heart, he was in pretty rough shape. Beat up and ragged, we mostly saw him at a distance, usually walking across the pasture. He was a faded grey tiger, well worn with his share of scars and battle damage. We never had a clue how old he was but I'd say he was at least ten years old. After about four or five months we didn't see him anymore. But this is proof that he spent time on this planet. Unlike so many, he at least has someone who remembers him.

· · ·

BRUCE
aka
[Brewster; Sissy Bruce; Beautiful Bruce]

We think Bruce was Booger's son. He looked a lot like him. Bruce had the big, thick tomcat head, but it was proportionately bigger than the rest of him. So he looked sort of like a grapefruit on a stick! He was also sort of a coward. That just made me love him more. He was so laid back and sweet. Unfortunately, he managed to find himself in the yard with Daisy one day and she killed him. Shook him and broke his neck. I never really forgave her for that. Bruce met an end that he truly didn't deserve.

. . .

BLONDIE
aka
[Mr. Blonde; Boss]

Blondie was one of our first home grown barn toms. He was a big, easy going light yellow faded tiger. He was quite the Casanova and sired many kittens during his tenure. Not that we didn't try to trap him and have him neutered. He was just too damn smart. We almost got him once. We had a drop trap built because he wouldn't go into a regular trap. The drop trap had a small door on it and the plan was to put the trap in front of the door and then lift the sliding door and hope he'd run into it. Well, Blondie wasn't the only one who went in. So did his girlfriend, Baby. We caught Baby but I wasn't fast enough with the trap and Blondie tore through the side of the trap. After that, it was no dice.

Blondie always came strolling up the paddock when I'd go down in the morning. He was very casual. He never avoided me but he wasn't keen on being pet, either. "Good morning, Mr. Blonde!" Up went his tail and he walked alongside me to the barn for his breakfast. He was never a trouble maker at meal time like some toms. He didn't fuss with the other cats and always made sure the kittens got to eat. It was that way every day. Some days he was a no show but I never worried about it. I knew he was just out there somewhere being a "boy cat".

One morning I walked into the paddock. I saw Blondie lying over in the weeds. "Good morning, Mr. Blonde." He didn't move. "Come on, lazy bones. Come have breakfast." He got up slowly and walked to the barn. It was then I saw the wound. On the right side of his face and neck were big bloody marks and he was swollen. Of course he wouldn't let me get close enough to see what was wrong. He was staying away from me. He went over to a dish and ate a few bites and then just lay down. I couldn't tell if it was from a dog or he got into a scrape with a raccoon. One thing was certain. He was in rough, rough shape. After a few days of watching him linger on the periphery, I was determined to try to catch him but he would have none of it. Blondie did things his way. Always. And this would be no exception. From a distance I spoke to him. "Pa loves you, Blonde. I'm so sorry you won't let me help you but I understand. I hope you'll be alright. But if not, Pa will never forget you." I never saw him again. But I didn't lie to him. I'll never forget him.

...

WHITEY

aka
[Mr. White; Wonder White; White Boy]

Whitey was one of three white cats from a single barn litter. His sibling, Powder, was attacked by BJ and ran off and never came back. I assume his remains are somewhere beyond the fence line. Snowy just disappeared one day. But Whitey was my boy. He made friends with me right away. He was very social. He was trapped when he was young and we had him neutered, but in a bizarre turn of events, his cojones grew back! I didn't know such a thing was possible! One day, he scampered ahead of me and there they were! We tried to catch him again, but he was not having any of that.

When he was young, Whitey was bright white and silky and soft. As he got older, his fur began to mat. He began to drool. I'm sure there was something wrong with his mouth but it never stopped him from gobbling up his food. He looked like a mess, but his personality never changed. I'd walk into the pasture and call "Whiiiiiiiiiiiiteeeeeeey!" Here he'd come, tail in the air and ready for his neck massage. He loved his neck massage and back rubs. I rubbed his back like a masseur and he'd stay right there for as long as I'd do it.

There was no warning that Whitey was going away. He just walked into the back paddock one night and that was the last time I saw him. I always made sure I told him I loved him every single time I saw him. Just in case. I assume something got him. Or one of the rednecks shot him. However he went, I always prayed that he went quickly. He didn't have a perfect life, but he was loved.

...

BOOTS

aka
[Mr. Boots; Bootsy; Booter Boy]

Boots was from the litter that included Socks and Mittens. Boots was steely grey with little white feet. Boots was always cool. Even as a kitten. He was quick to make friends with the family. He loved, loved, loved getting pet and getting his thick neck rubbed. In his youth, he got into a good scrap with someone and wound up blind in his right eye. Didn't matter to Boots. He was tough as nails with other toms, but around us, he was a lover. Many times during his years with us, he'd show up to eat showing evidence of another war fought. "You should see the other guy, huh, Bootsy?"

Boots would often be gone for several days. Or rather, I didn't see him for several days. I always had to keep in mind that I was only at the barn a couple hours a day. Chances are our paths just didn't cross some days. That was just Boots. He wasn't on YOUR schedule. You were on his. He'd wander in after I hadn't seen him in a while and rub against my legs as if to say, "I'm still here, Pop. Been busy. Where's my food?"

Boots had been with us for over ten years. Because of that, I worried more when I didn't see him. When I didn't see him for ten days, or so, I started to worry. I'd step out of the back of the barn and call to him. After three weeks I declared him missing in action. I never saw him again. But that doesn't mean he's not out there somewhere. That's just Boots.

...

OREGANO

aka
[Big O; Grouchy Oregano; Reggy]

Oregano was the largest of the litter that included Salt and Pepper. They were all grey diluted calicos. Oregano was the bossy one. Not just with her litter mates, but with all the other cats. It was very common for her to bum rush another unsuspecting cat and give them a smack. She was also a bit of phony. She'd go up to some poor gullible cat, or especially kittens, and pretend to be all loving and the second they fell for her come-on, she'd light into them. Nothing vicious, just intimidating. Lord, she was a pain in the ass. I don't think I've ever cussed any other barn cat the way I did Oregano.

It wasn't always that way. When she was a kitten she was cute and sweet. A happy little grey bundle of mischief. But as she got older and had to, in her mind, compete for her place on the totem pole, she developed an edge. She never crossed the line with humans. In fact, she practically avoided us. She was cordial with me. When I went to the barn, she was always in the upper paddock near the gate. Her tail would go up but she always regarded me with caution. In all the years, I never gave her any reason not to trust me, other than cursing at her, but that was usually under my breath. She didn't seem to be affected by it. Still, she kept her distance.

In the fall of 2016, I noticed a change in Oregano. She seemed to be unsteady. Her gait was crooked. She still came to the barn for mealtime but something was off-kilter. A few days later, I detected her head taking a noticeable tilt to the right and her wobble was becoming more pronounced. In the ensuing days, her condition worsened. I tried to catch her, but she'd frantically try to get away and it was difficult to watch. I could see the writing on the wall. Oregano had some sort of neurological situation happening. Probably a tumor of some sort. The last time I saw her, she was trying to navigate a hole in the fence. I watched her, heartbroken. "Oregano!" She stopped and looked back at me. "Dad loves you. OK? It's OK if you want to go be with Pepper. It's OK." Pepper was her littermate who had passed away a few years prior. She looked at me. Her expression was one of confusion and frustration. She turned back and made it through the fence. And that was our goodbye. I'd never see Oregano again. I want to say that I hoped her passing was peaceful, but that's likely a false hope. No matter. She's at peace now.

...

BUNKY

aka
[Bunk; Hunk-a-bunk; Bunk Hogan; Bunkers]

Bunky was a big, hulking tomcat. Not surprising since he was a big kitten. He was a very human compatible cat from the start. When I put food down, he was always underfoot. I was petting him from the time he wandered into the barn. He grew up fast. It was so nice to have a big friendly tom around again. He was always happy to see me and always ready for attention. It makes what happened even more tragic. One morning I noticed Bunky was lame on his rear left leg. Upon closer inspection, I could see the leg was just hanging there! I quickly trapped him and we got him to the vet. His leg was severely broken. So badly, in fact, that it couldn't be repaired and would have to be amputated. The reality was that he was still feral. His recuperation would necessitate constant care for the incision and then rehab. Getting him in and out of the carrier for the needed doctor visits was an x-factor. As much as it broke my heart, I decided, as long as he was under anesthesia for the x-ray, to simply let him go. I regretted, and still regret, my decision. I just did what I thought would be best. I can look into the pasture and still see him there. And I'm sure he is, in spirit. I miss you, Bunk. Every damn day.

. . .

PUNKY

aka
[Punkin'; Punkers; Punky Mewster]

Punky was sister to Bunky. She was mostly white with a grey patch on her head. She was always so pleasant but just so scared of people. Once Bunky was gone, Punky didn't stay long. I don't know if something happened to her or she just moved on. I hate that I could never get close to her.

. . .

HALLOWEEN

aka
[Weenie; Halloween Cat]

What a remarkably beautiful cat. I called her Halloween because of her coloration. She was black with orange dots. Not spots. Dots. Small orange flecks all over her body. She was short legged with a shorter than normal tail. Big eyes. She was kindly roly-poly and quite precious. She wasn't overly social but would always be around. Gail didn't like the name "Halloween" so she called her "Haleigh". Whatever. She was Halloween.

Her stay was unremarkable. One day, she was just gone. Over a year later, she reappeared alongside Boots! "Halloween! What the hell? Where have you been?" She ambled up to the feeding dishes like she'd never been gone. "Don't be a stranger, kid!" That was the last thing I said to her. I can't say that she definitely has passed away. For all I know, she's found a home nearby. If so, good for her. I just hope she's well and happy. Even if it is on the other side of the rainbow.

...

PEACHES

aka
[The Peach]

Peach was a little yellow boy cat. He would romp and cavort with his twin brother, Bing. They were the text book definition of barn kittens. One day, our farm hand, Jeremy, found Bing in the hay barn. He was unconscious and dying, of what we don't know. It wasn't long after that, that Peaches started to show signs of illness. The weather was cold and in the mornings he'd sit in the paddock in front of the barn and soak up the sun. I knew I didn't have much time, so I tried petting him. He let me. I went to the house and got a carrier. I went back down the barn and found Peach sitting in the back paddock soaking up the sun. Boots was sitting with him, seeming to watch over him. I put the carrier down and unhooked the door. Peach didn't try to get away. I pet him a couple times and then just grabbed him and put him in the carrier. Dr. Johnson, at Atrium, took him on. He was very, very sick.

Peach won everyone's heart. They all took turns loving on him. He was in an oxygen room and he responded to some meds and was eating a little. Dr. Johnson said that, if he pulled through, she was taking him. I stopped in to see how Peach was doing. Dr. Johnson brought him out. He was laying in her arms and purring like a buzzsaw. He seemed quite content. The next morning, during chores, my phone rang. I looked at caller ID and saw it was Atrium. I had a bad feeling. Dr. Johnson calmly told me that Peach had passed away overnight. My heart sank. I could tell in her voice that she was upset as well. I consoled myself in the knowledge he didn't die cold and alone in the barn. The Peach wasn't here for long, but he captured many hearts in his brief time. I still think of him when the warm sun hits my face during cool barn mornings.

...

NINJA

aka
[Ninj; Ja Bird]

Ninja, and her sibling, Spooky, were two grey females. The only distinguishing mark to tell them apart was a white mark on her chest that resembled a throwing star, hence the name. Spooky and Ninja were inseparable. They played together, ate together and I even saw them napping together several times. One day Spooky was gone. Ninja just seemed lost. She didn't even know what dish to eat out of without Spooky. I began to notice her eyes were wet a lot. She spent a lot of time sleeping in the heated beds. I could tell she was sick. It could have been that Spooky succumbed to some illness and now Ninja was on the same path. As I predicted, Ninja went missing. Later, our farm hand, Jeremy, found her. She had chosen the subfloor of the hay barn to crawl off and die. The saddest part of all was that she was found next to three newborns kittens that we immediately rescued. We buried her out behind the barn where she and Spooky played tag in the tall grass.

KIBBY

aka
[Kibbible; Kibby the Cougar; Kibby Cougar Melloncat]

Kibby was a high strung, playful young barn tom. A pale yellow tiger cat who is one of the rare instances of having instant rapport with old dad. I don't recall when it started but one day he just matter- of-factly sauntered up to me, tail in the air, and started rubbing around my legs. That was it. We were buds. In fact, when Clover and I used to take our walks over to the Church Lot, Kibby and Pokey would cut across the goat pasture and walk with us. If they didn't come along for some reason, I'd holler, "Kibby!" In a few seconds, you'd hear the crack and crunch of leaves and sticks as they bundled through the underbrush! Every morning, Kibby would walk with me down to give the goats their feed or treats. Then one day, he was gone. He was there for dinner one night and that was the last time I ever saw him. But every night, I still call to him. Maybe someday, he'll pop in. I hope so.

. . .

BOB

aka
[Bobb-O; Little Bob; Bobtail]

Bob was a jet black slab of mischief with a stumpy bob tail. Before he went missing, Bob and I established trust and a routine. He would always take his food on the big condo porch. When I'd put his dish down, he'd let me pet and pet and pet him. Bob had all the makings of a good friend. But like so many of them, one morning he just wasn't there anymore.

SMOKEY

aka
[Smokey Jones; Big Smoke]

Smokey was almost a mirror image of his mom, Pinky, with the exception of his half tail. Without fail, Smokey was always the first kitten to come running to me when I came up from the barn to feed them. He'd run right to me and then walks alongside me up the condos. When I come back with their dishes, Smokey always waited by the gate and trotted beside me to get his food. He disappeared at the same time as Bob. I sure do miss that friendly greeting in the morning.

...

BLINKY

aka
[Little Blink]

Blinky actually got her name the day before she died. I noticed one of the little dark calico barn kittens had a gunky eye. Kittens get scratches on their eyes during play time so I really thought nothing of it. I put some Terramycin on it and moved on. The next morning, I noticed Blinky laying flat out in one of the heated houses. It had been cold the night before and kittens usually ball up to stay warm. I reached in the grab Blinky and she was very disoriented. I could tell that she was likely close to death. I dropped everything and bundled her to the house. She passed away in my arms not long after. Brutal evidence that you can't save them all.

...

SHARPIE

aka
[Sharpshooter]

This one hurt. Sharpie's story is told in length in the "Personal Thoughts and Reflections" section.

...

MISS BABY

aka
[Momma Baby; Baby Cat; Miss Meany]

Miss Baby was always sort of a loner, too. She was a pretty, big, black and white cat with a mysterious and cantankerous disposition. She arrived at the Barn as Mr. Blonde's girlfriend. But after a few litters, he abandoned her. You could tell it hurt her feelings. She was just never the same after that. She was never really a "people cat" but she became even more distant. She got sick one time and I'd always bring her some wet food with some antibiotic in it. She would let me put the dish down and back away before she'd eat. But she ate. And when I came down every morning for two weeks, it was like we had an appointment. She was always there. And when she felt better, she stopped showing up. After that, when I would go to the barn in the mornings, I'd see her in the pasture or the side yard. "Good morning, Miss Baby!" She would answer me, walking parallel to me on the other side of the fence. She always kept her distance.

I never really understood why she was so cautious of me. I've never gave her cause to fear me. I never cursed her or raised my voice at her. When she was spayed, I always made sure I gave her extra special food and treats. Some cats just never grow accustomed to human contact. That was certainly the case with Miss Baby.

As the cold weather of 2017 closed in, I began to notice a change in Miss Baby. She actually sought out refuge in the barn. I attributed that to the fact we had some new heated cat condo's built and she was just putting them to use. One day, when I was feeding kittens, I stood up to come nose to nose with Miss Baby, who was huddled in one of the cubbies. She furrowed her brow and hissed at me. "Miss Baby! Shame on you! You know your pa loves you!" She flattened her ears to her head and glowered. That was just Miss Baby. But her appearance was changing as well. She seemed thin and over the course of the next weeks, she grew weak and frail. I arrived at the barn early one morning to find her huddled in the soft hay of the feed room. She wasn't running away. "Miss Baby, are you OK?" She didn't even look at me. I rushed back to the house to get a cat carrier. I would try to catch her. If the vets couldn't do anything, at least I could end her suffering. She had just enough juice in her tank to get away, seeking refuge in the heated dog house in the feeding area. "OK, Miss Baby. Daddy's sorry. You rest. I love you, Miss Baby. I'm so, so sorry."

The next morning there was no sign of her. Or that night. I assumed she was gone. The next morning when I put wet food down for barn kittens, here comes Miss Baby! She was slow and clearly weak and obviously very ill. She crouched by the food and ate. "Good Morning, Miss Baby!" No reaction. She was on pure survival now. That night she was in the hay room in the same spot as before. I put on a pair of thick gloves. "Miss Baby, can pa pet you?" I crouched down and with a single gloved finger, stroked her head. She looked at me with dull eyes and gave a half hearted hiss. You could smell the infection. The decay. That was the one and only time in all her years with us, that I ever touched her. She struggled up and moved to the dog house. Before I left, I told her I loved her, one last time. "Poppy always loved you, Miss Baby…even though you never loved me. You rest Miss Baby. You rest. Goodnight, old girl."

The next morning I found her where I left her. In the dog house. She'd passed away overnight. After chores, I collected her remains, bed and all, and carried her to the house. I wrapped her in a soft blanket and later that day she was buried behind the barn. The only home she ever knew. I was going to have her cremated, but in this case, it seemed more proper that she stay right where she lived her life. You don't always get to bury a feral cat. They crawl off and die somewhere else. But in her sickness, Miss Baby finally became a homebody. I would loved to have helped her, but the problem with saving a sick feral is that by the time you can catch them, it's usually too late.

Though we didn't have much of a pet/owner relationship, I still loved her. Her presence was comforting to me. And I lived in the hope that one day, we would be friends. I now know that when I leave this world, Miss Baby will be there waiting for me. And I'm sure she'll greet me with a hiss.

. . .

THE PAST MENAGERIE

We collected various odds and ends from the animal kingdom over the years. Here are just a few.

BENNY THE COCKATIEL

Named after iconic British comedian, Benny Hill, Benny was a comical, funny bird. He wasn't particularly friendly but he was social, if that makes any sense. We could leave his cage open and he'd climb to the top of it like a feathery King Kong. He'd spread his wings and make hilarious sounds. He'd hiss at the dogs and then he'd fly all over the house. The dogs didn't quite know what to make of it but they were entertained, nonetheless. Benny loved having his cage taken into the yard on sunny days for his bath. Gail would turn the hose on a fine mist and Benny would spread his wings like an eagle and rock back and forth. Benny never learned to speak actual words, but if you called him by name, he'd answer with a series of silly blips and chirps. Benny lived a good, long life but finally fell to a heart attack.

BOBBY THE BUNNY

As I recall, I think we got Bobby at Target! She was a sweet little black and white Dutch rabbit, barely a handful. She didn't stay small long. She was our first pet in our first apartment. She was cage trained and very comfortable loose in the house. She became fast friends with our first dog, little Pippit. When we moved to our first rental house, there was a small fenced in yard just off the screened in back porch. Bobby's cage was in the laundry room and she loved to go out the back door and into in the yard. She and Pippit would chase each other around and then relax in the shade together. Bobby came down with pneumonia and we didn't catch it in time. We tried treating it but, sadly, she passed away in her sleep one night. It was so sad.

JEAN AND ROGER, THE BLUE SPINEY LIZARDS

I've always liked reptiles and have been especially fond of lizards. I had a mated pair of Blue Spiney Lizards that were anything but friendly, no matter how hard I tried. One passed away while I was in Vancouver doing a movie and the other passed shortly after I got home.

EMILIO LIZARDO, THE IGUANA

Emilio was a good boy. Iguanas are smart. I managed to teach him how to shake hands. He got quite big, at least three feet plus. He started acting sick and off his food so I took him to the vet. He attacked me in the car and took off my right thumbnail. He was suffering from kidney calcification and it was all she wrote. I had to have him put down. He would be my last reptile.

ACE AND BANDIT, THE FERRETS

They were a very comical addition to our family. They loved the dogs but needed to be monitored when mingling. Dolly was the best playmate for them. When she would get overwhelmed, she would simply sit down on them, which they loved. Ferrets are wild and high spirited. They were very well litter trained and good about going back to their room…sometimes. The rats loved to wrestle and when you got the best of them, they'd hiss and hop around with their backs arched. They'd hide and when they thought you weren't watching they'd leap out and attack. Sadly, both developed some sort of tumors and they both passed away not far apart.

THE KEETS

The Parakeets had their own world going on. When Emilio passed away, we turned his cage into a parakeet paradise. It was better than TV. They'd carry on conversations with each other, argue and make kissy face. Sometimes Gail and I would sit for an hour and just marvel at this small avian community. One little blue keet wound up having a tumor on his chest which was clearly visible. We separated him and put medicine on it. One day while I was doctoring it, it fell out leaving a hole in its chest! It looked like a little egg! The keet swooned and got weak legged, but recovered. Amazingly, he went on to live a good long life. One by one, they passed away. I miss having a parakeet but it's just not feasible with so many cats.

NIBBLES THE GUINEA PIG

Haley was very little and wanted a pet. She seemed drawn to a guinea pig, so we got her Nibbles. Nibbles was a precious little orange and white nugget. Unfortunately, Haley didn't understand that she wasn't a toy. She wound up throwing her to ground, over and over, resulting in her death. A tragic, tragic end for such a sweet little soul.

...

PRESENT

These are the wondrous, crazy, obnoxious souls still with us. Where relevant, I'll include details of how they came to us and any particular quirks and idiosyncracies. Most of the time it will merely be to acknowledge them and honor their presence. I worry that these stories will overwhelm or bore you, the reader. But I choose to include them to show the vastness of this endeavor and the depth of our commitment.

CANINE

GINGER

aka
[Ginger Bear; Dingle; Dingler; Dingle Binx; Gin-Jar-Binx; Golden Dog; Gin Gin]

We'd been in the Mineral Springs house for about a year or so. Gail was learning the back roads in Union County. One day she saw a medium sized yellow dog wandering the roads. She didn't think too much of it. A lot of the people out here let their dogs run free. That's also why you see so many dogs hit by cars. On the way back from lunch with her mom about two weeks later, she spotted that little yellow dog again, sitting all alone in a ditch. Gail had some chicken and biscuits left over so she stopped the car. The little yellow dog was a hard sell, but apparently very hungry. Gail coaxed her over with the food and she gobbled it up. Gail reached down and put her arms around her and put her in the car. Ginger wouldn't have to wonder where her next meal was coming from ever again.

We're not quite sure what Ginger's lineage is. She's about twenty five pounds, golden yellow in color with a wrinkly face and purple spots on her tongue. We guess she's probably got a little Terrier of some sort; a splash of Chow; and maybe a dash of Shar Pei. Whatever she is, she sure is cute. What a funny little thing she is. Her golden face is mostly white now, but you can still see that spark in her eyes.

Once Ginger knew this was her home, we never had to worry about her wandering. Even before we fenced the property, she didn't go very far. She loved her security and didn't want to jeopardize it by wandering off and getting lost. Don't get me wrong. She likes a little adventure. As long as she can still see the house. Her life before us must have been frighteningly uncertain.

Ginger is happy most of the time. Unless another animal gets too close. Ginger is not really a dog's dog. In fact, she doesn't care for most other animals. She's a people dog. She goes with the flow most of the time but she's always been kind of a grouch. We always have to scold her for being irascible. It's gotten worse as she's gotten older. Any other critter gets too close to her and she starts to growl. Not snarl. She doesn't show teeth, she just makes it known she's not interested in being your pal. When it comes to cats, the situation is even more untenable. Cats don't really understand or respect your personal space. They fly past Ginger and she snaps at them. They bound over her and she leaps up and barks. She's never hurt them but who knows what the future holds.

If Ginger has a super power, it's the perfection of "The Low-Butt Run". It's the kind of run that most dogs do where they tuck their tales, drop their butts close to the ground and run around with great abandon. In her younger days, it took very little to get her in Low-Butt mode. I'd stare at her and whisper "Ginger". She'd cut her eyes toward me. I'd make a sudden move towards her and off she went. Run out around the cars, past me a couple of times, then into the garage. I'd wait a second. "Ginger!" She'd explode out of the garage and repeat. These days her poor old knees give her trouble, but every once in a while, she'll just erupt in a Low-Butt fly around. She's the oldest member of the pack now. Seniority gets extra love and special blueberry cookie treats. She's still crabby, but that's just Ginger.

. . .

SKITTLES

aka
[Skittles Marie; Skit; Gittles; Biddles; Piddles]

Josh, Haley's boyfriend at the time, was on his way to our house when he saw a small dog dart into traffic. A car entering the road hit it and sent it rolling into a ditch. Josh stopped the car and ran to her. He found her lying in the ditch shaking. He gently picked her up and brought her to us. She was traumatized, shaking and quivering and panting. Gail examined her and didn't really get a painful reaction to any of her poking and prodding. The next day, Haley and Josh took her back to that area, going house to house looking for an owner. Someone directed them to a house that they'd seen the dog hanging around, but the woman didn't claim her. So we did. I named her Skittles after Haley's favorite candy when she was younger. It was a perfect fit.

Skittles is some sort of Jack Russell mix. Brown, tan and white, with big wet eyes and raptor like dewclaws. She's a solid little girl, even at this age. She can still fly like the wind, but she's not as "acrobatic" as she used to be. In her early tenure with us, she constantly had to be on a lead or a leash. Left unfettered, she'd scale the fence into the pasture and run among the horses, barking like an idiot. Although the horses were unimpressed, it was still dangerous, so we had to keep a tight rein on her. Before the entire property was fenced, Skittles had a very bad habit of dashing into the woods or down the driveway. It's probably how she got displaced in the first place. She'd run into the woods behind the house and poor Haley would have to follow her all the way around the property perimeter, usually ending up all the way down at our neighbors. Calling her didn't help. She was a little shit. One time she ran down the driveway and I had to pursue her, shoeless. Trodding through gravel, underbrush, thorns, with Skittles always staying a few feet ahead of me, her selective hearing tuning out my shouted vulgarities. And once she was captured she'd put on the "fragile, frightened fawn" act. Her eyes got wet. She trembled. But once she knew she wasn't in real trouble, she'd immediately recover. Brat.

Skittle's Kryptonite is, and always has been, thunder, gunfire and fireworks. We always know a storm is coming before any meteorologist has a clue. Skittles, much like Buster before her, has a horrified reaction to loud, cacophonous noises. Her entire little body shakes. She pants like she ran a marathon. Her ears go up and back. There is no consoling her. She usually retires to a corner of the kitchen to hide. I always feel terrible that I can't comfort her. Independence Day and New Years I always prayed for rain so she'd be spared the nightmare of the local's compulsion for shooting off store brand fireworks. Somehow, the night makes it worse for her. Poor Gittles.

Unlike most of our dogs, Skittles has a job. Her life's mission is to make sure the horses don't get any farther than the fence. I'm dead serious. Skittles sits in the yard and scans the perimeter for any unwanted Equine advancement. If they get too close, or even too rambunctious, Skittles races back and forth along the fence row, barking her warnings. Her arch enemy was Kita. Oh, how Kita delighted in tormenting Skittles! She'd see Skittles standing guard and then casually saunter up to the fence, innocently grazing, knowing…KNOWING… that Skittles would lose her mind! Kita would also put her nose right up against the fence, daring Skittles to try and nip her. On occasion, Kita regretted that decision.

Skittles loves her some treats. She doesn't like to wait until you decide it's time for a snack. She paces with her giant ears up in the air, softly growling. She goes over to where the treats are and looks up at the counter, just in case you've forgotten where they are. If you don't move fast enough, you get a bark. Don't even think about ignoring her. She does NOT give up. Whatever you do, don't give her something she doesn't like. She'll spit it out and stare back. "Next!"

Skittles, though well over ten years old, is really not much different than the day she arrived. She maintains her youthful appearance with very little grey around her face. She's a good girl. Ageless and shameless.

...

BJ

aka
[Bird Boy; Mr. Beans; Beej; Handsome Puppy Boy]

It was another one of those major storms that hits the Piedmont in the spring. Lots of rain, thunder and lightning, damaging winds, trees down. The next morning, we were greeted by big white and black stray dog. He looked like a Dalmatian mix of some kind. This was before we had everything fenced and gated so he was right up by the house. He was wearing a harness with a broken lead attached and he was very scared. He wanted to trust us but it was clear he was traumatized by his ordeal. I guessed he was probably an outside dog that was so terrified of the storm that he broke free and ran. Gail and I couldn't touch him, but little Haley Pillars had better luck. She lured him in with some treats and before long we could all pet him. This time, Haley named our latest adoption and he was dubbed BJ.

To me, BJ looked like a dog from the cover of "Field and Stream". His face is mostly white but with a big black patch over one eye. Black eyelashes on one side, white on the other. Thick ears and a thick tail. He has a sweet disposition but in the early days, he proved to be a danger to the cats. He spent time in the side yard on a long lead and a runner anchored in the ground. But if a cat got within reach, he'd grab them. This wasn't a vicious attack. He'd grab them in his mouth and run around like it was a toy. But he was so strong, that sometimes he'd shake his head and severe damage would be done. More than one seriously injured cat escaped his jaws and ran over the fence, into the woods, never to be seen again. It was such a helpless feeling. We managed to save a few, like Turtle, but it was rare. He finally had to be moved to the front yard on a much shorter lead and constantly monitored. These days, he could care less about the cats and is more interested in "yard swimming".

"Yard Swimming" is something that he's done for a while. He'll lay, belly down, in the grass and drag himself around the yard, covering a great deal of distance. He just seems to love it. Always a big, stupid smile on his face. Even though he's neutered, it probably feels good on his weiner. He does it indoors too, but there it's called "Floor Surfing". It's not his only quirk. He does a thing Gail calls "Zen Dog". It's the craziest thing I've ever seen. He goes up to a bush or a tree and sort of shuts down. His eyes glaze over and he starts to move in ultra slow motion. Long, slow, deliberate steps, brushing up against the shrubbery or tree or fence or whatever. We've never known why he does it or what it's about. In a way, it's almost creepy! As far as tricks go, his only schtick is to sit up on his haunches. He's been yelled at so much for jumping up on people, that now he does his little gentleman routine and Gail praises him by calling him "Handsome Puppy Boy!" He's always so proud of himself.

BJ loves toys almost as much as Clover did. But Clover cherished her toys. BJ destroys them! When we were getting prescription meds from Road Runner Pharmacy in Phoenix, they'd always send it in a box. And as an added bonus, they'd always include a toy! How cool is that? The meds were for Dolly or Oliver or Clover, but the toy was for BJ. It got to the point where he'd see that box come in the house and those big, thick ears would go up and his eyes widened. He'd sit there in front of you waiting for that toy. If it was a rope toy or a rubber ball, he'd take it and play with it for a while and forget it. If it was stuffed, it'd last about three minutes. He'd tear it to pieces looking for the squeaker. The floor would be covered in fluffy stuffing and a mangled body of a formerly cuddly playmate. On the rare occasion they actually forgot to include the toy, the look of disappointment on his big, dumb face was pitiful.

With all of our losses the last few years, BJ is the only boy left. I remind him daily that he's the man of the house now. A responsibility he seems proud to carry. As long as toys are involved.

. . .

ANGEL

aka
[Angel Berry Beast; Bane-gel; Angel Pig; Coy Dog]

I was off to run an errand. I'd usually go straight at the stoplight in Mineral Springs, but at the last second, something; or someone; told me to turn left. As I did, about one hundred yards ahead, just past the entrance to the post office, I saw a dog flailing around in the right hand lane. I pulled up as fast as I could, jumped out and ran to the injured dog. She tried to stand, but couldn't. I talked softly to her and extended my hand for her to sniff. She was terrified. Traffic was backing up and I couldn't wait any longer. I scooped her up and put her in the passenger side floorboard. I raced to the clinic in Waxhaw. She was in shock. She pooped and peed all over the floor. I talked to her and told her she was a good girl. It wasn't helping.

The vets said she had a broken hip and a punctured lung. She needed specialized care. So I took her to the emergency clinic at a local veterinary specialist. Not my first choice, but I had no other option. They kept her for a couple days until the lung situation was resolved. Then I brought her home. I named her Angel, because I believed it was an angel that made me turn the corner instead of going straight ahead that day. She's tan with definite German Shepherd blood and maybe some Coyote.

We put a recovery cage in the basement for her. Her movement needed to be restricted so she could heal. It had a big, comfortable bed and clean water and plenty of food. When it was time to go out and potty, we'd open the door to her cage and she wouldn't move. I'd walk over and open the door to the back yard. She'd sheepishly slink out into the yard and do her business. Then she'd come back, her tail between her legs and dash back into her cage. She wanted to be happy but she wasn't sure about her situation. It would take some time to get her comfortable in her new home. When I took her to Atrium, they checked her for a chip. She was indeed chipped. Her name? Angel. Exactly what I'd named her. I was disappointed that after all we'd been through that she'd be returned to her owner. But her owner could never be found. Angel finally had her forever home.

Angel's world changed when we adopted Maggie. They became known as "The Teenagers" or because they were both tan, "The Tan-agers". Maggie is the dominant one, unfortunately for Angel. But Maggie loves her sister, spending a lot of time cleaning her face and loving on her. They fight like most step siblings but are quick to make up. They don't like to be separated. When Maggie spent three days in the hospital, Angel spent a lot of time looking for her. Their reunion was very sweet. Angel tried to love up Maggie and Maggie tried to attack Angel. Everything was back to normal.

These days, Angel spends her days lounging outside during the day. At night, she sleeps with her old dad and Maggie. But only after many tummy rubs and special treats. She's got an inquisitive nature, remarkably smart and a very fast learner. She loves attention and knows how to give hugs. She jumps up on her hind legs and when you hug her, she lowers her head and leans into you. Sweet, sweet girl.

. . .

MAGGIE

aka
[Maggie Bag O'Beans; Maggle; Baggle; Bags; Weirdo]

Maggie was, literally, the dog no one wanted. A good friend called me and told me someone was trying to place a troubled dog. I was told she was a Pugle. The owners had tried to place her several times with no luck. Apparently this dog had some emotional problems. The next stop was the pound. I asked her to have the owners bring her out and they did. The dog that got out of that car was no Pugle. She looked more like a Boxer-Pug mix. Her face is the pefect combination of Pug and Boxer characteristics. She was tan, with a tail curled tightly over her back. She was a nervous wreck. She was too frantic to be social. I managed to pet her and even pick her up but she was far too frightened to really get a read on her. Gail and I agreed that we would at least try to make it work. She was dubbed Maggie.

Maggie was a handful. She would deal with Gail but was terrified of me. I had to corner her in the house, catch her, put a leash on her harness and take her outside and put her on a lead. To bring her in, I had to go to where the lead was attached and reel her in like a sea bass. She fought the whole time. I always took the time to talk gently to her and pet her when I got close, but she was a hard sell. She was damaged goods. Some man, somewhere, sometime, abused her. She would not trust me.

Sleeping was a nightmare. Poor Gail. She would try to sleep in the room with Maggie but she was a maniac. She couldn't relax and wouldn't calm down. Some nights, she was on the go until 3am! Gail was a wreck. She tried putting her in a cage at night. That just made it worse as Maggie would scream and cry all night. Maggie wound up alone at nights because she was such a lunatic. There was no other practical remedy. During the day we let her be in one of the smaller dog runs out in the shade of one of our huge trees. The trick was getting her back in the house. You had to go in the run and corner her, which amped up her fear even more. Then you had to lead her into the house. Dealing with Maggie was exhausting. But I was determined, no matter what, that this would be her last stop. I was going to be bigger than the problem.

It took six long, tiresome, sleepless, maddening months before Maggie started to trust me. Six months of fighting her on the leash and lead. Six months of having to catch her. Six months of patience. One night, I was sitting on the bed in the back bedroom, giving Maggie and Angel treats, she put her paw on my leg. She looked at me nervously with her big, wet eyes. "Good girl, Mags." I rubbed her head. I wanted to hug her, but I didn't want to push it. With Maggie, it was all about baby steps. The next morning, I took her and Angel downstairs and out the back door. Maggie was still skittish but let me pat her head. From there and over the next three months, she became more and more trusting.

Eventually, Maggie became relatively "normal". She still has some quirks. Most significant is her "selective hearing". Maggie hears you, but she doesn't listen. I attribute that to the Pug side of her family. I had these same problems with Sadie. Maggie can be five feet from you and no matter how loud you scream at her or how many obscenities you hurl in her direction, she still gives you the shade. It is infuriating. Many times I have to storm out to her and, in typical Pug fashion, when you get close enough to strike, she strides away with her ears flapping in the breeze. She also bears a remarkable Boxer trait. The post stool celebratory sprint. Our old Rosie would launch into a happy, full body wiggling dash after dropping a stink pickle in the yard. Maggie does the exact same thing. She sniffs and sniffs, looking for the perfect spot. Once she drops that butt torpedo, she explodes in a joyous, growling, high speed sprint. Pure comedy.

Today, Maggie is loving and silly. She loves to cuddle with her dad at night. She wrestles and plays before bedtime. It's taken almost five years to get here. All she needed was time, patience and love. And she finally got it.

...

CHLOE

aka
[Little Dog; Elf; Prancing Fawn; Hot Dog Tail; Fat Back]

January 2014. It was bitter cold out. Coldest winter we'd had in a while. Our neighbor knocked on the door. He was holding a small, very cold, senior dog. "Are you guys missing a dog?" Gail said that we weren't. Apparently, this poor, thin, little dog had been staying on his porch in the bitter cold for a couple of days…and nights. I've never understood how some people can just ignore an animal's suffering like that. Rather than let it go back to that stupid situation, Gail took her in. She was not a pup and hadn't been for some time. She was some sort of Jack Russell mix with enormous ears and a sweet disposition. She was thin and hungry and ate really well for us. Gail named her Chloe. I call her Little Dog.

Chloe the Elf looked like a petite fawn. Mostly white with patches of brown, small emotive eyes, giant bat ears and a docked tail. It wasn't docked short, but about mid-length. Hence, the nickname "Hot Dog Tail". She's very delicate. When she is in anticipation of something, she sits with one paw raised ever so politely. I hesitate to use the word, but she is absolutely precious. We looked all over for "missing dog" signs and nothing ever appeared. Who in the world wouldn't look for this little lost angel? And what kind of monster would simply abandon her in these freezing temperatures? It didn't matter anymore. Chloe would never have to worry about those things ever again.

Once she settled in, her personality really blossomed. She gets freaky excited over the weirdest things. A lot of dogs like to ride in the car. A simple invitation is enough to send some into a frantic frenzy. Chloe doesn't wait to be asked. She goes to the car and wiggles and squirms and tries to entice YOU to want to go for a ride, and, if so, she'd be happy to tag along. There are days where Gail is getting something out of the van and Chloe will leap in and position herself in the farthest possible corner away from her so she can't get her out. Gail finally has to give up and just leave the doors open until Chloe realizes she's not going anywhere. Personally, I love taking her for rides. I put a big, fluffy blanket on the passenger seat and watch her burrow down poke her little head out to get pet and loved on.

Her personality wasn't the only thing that grew. So did her figure. When she came to us, she was very thin. I think it had been a while since she had three squares a day. She learned that the trough is stocked with great stuff. These days, she has a bit of back fat going on and when you pick her up, she feels like a real sausage. Sometimes, I'll pick her up and hold her and just laugh. She doesn't know that I'm laughing at what a pudge she's become, she just knows dad is happy. She turns to me and licks my face with little chameleon tongue.

Another thing that makes her lose control is nap time. Because I get up so damn early every day, I try to catch a nap in the afternoon whenever possible. Chloe knows when I come upstairs in the afternoon, that it's "that time". She leaps about and wiggles like a worm, waiting; hoping; for an invitation. "Come on, Elf!" Boom! She's at the hallway door. Then she scampers to the front door, so she can go do her potties. Then she tippy taps to the bedroom, runs in, gets a drink and then leaps into what used to be my recliner. Now it's hers. She waits for her special treat and then hunkers down for a nap. I don't really understand why this ritual is so special for her, but it makes her ridiculously happy and that's what counts.

Chloe is part of a team with Skittles that we call "The Twins" because they look so much alike. Chloe loves her step sister and the feeling is mutual. Chloe follows Skittles around the yard and wherever Skittles pees, Chloe pees there too. When Skittles takes off towards the fence to bark at the horses, Chloe is hot on her heels, doing the same thing, although you can see on her face, she's not quite sure why. Same goes for a random barn cat that gets too brave and comes into the yard. Skittles is chasing a cat. Chloe is chasing Skittles. It's predictable and hilarious. She's the ultimate tag-a-long.

Chloe is going strong. We're not sure how old she actually is, but even if she lived for another twenty years, it wouldn't be long enough. I love my Elf. Eternally grateful I'm able to make her golden years golden.

. . .

LADY 2
aka
[Apple Head; Little Butt; Bobble Head]

Haley called home and said she'd found two dogs running down the road. She got them into her car and brought them home. They were two King Charles Spaniels. An unneutered boy and an unspayed girl. They seemed healthy enough and quickly made themselves at home, falling in with the rest of the pack like they'd been there all their lives. The little female took quite a shine to Gail. She'd sleep on the table next to her chair and follow her everywhere. Well, a vet trip was in order because the little girl had some serious eye problems. The vet found her to be chipped. As I stood there, they contacted the owner. They were ecstatic. The dogs had escaped their yard when someone left a gate open. They never thought they'd see them again. Gail was a little disappointed, as she'd already bonded with her. We made arrangements to meet the family in front of Farley's Pizza in Mineral Springs. I really got choked up when the family, especially the kids, were reunited. They thanked us profusely for taking such good care of them. I gave them my card and told them if they ever needed a pet sitter, we'd be happy to take care of them. They drove away and I knew that we'd never see them again. But they were home. And that's all that mattered.

Fast forward almost a year. I get an email from the dog's owner. They were moving and couldn't take the dogs. They'd found a home for the boy but not the girl. "Do you want her?" I promised to get back to him. I asked Gail if she was up for it and she said 'yes'. I knew she would, but wanted to make sure. Shortly afterwards, that little black, white and brown sausage was back in Gail's arms. They had named her Lady and even though we'd already had a Lady, we decided that it was probably best to just keep it. It was like she'd never left.

I've never seen a dog assimilate to new surroundings like Lady. She was immediately right back at Gail's side. Sleeping on the table again, right next to her. At night, sleeping in the chair next to Gail's bed. Happily bobbling along with the rest of the dogs. The only problem was her eyes. They were a mess. Her previous owners had been treating her eyes with Visine. What the hell? I'm always dumbfounded by people who claim to love their animals but won't take the most modest steps for their health and welfare. Unfortunately, Lady's eyes are permanently damaged. Her vision will never be normal again. But that doesn't faze her in the least. She sees just well enough to know where she is and what's going on. I'm certain, at some point, she'll be blind, but that's OK. We've had blind dogs before. We'll be just fine.

After we lost our beautiful old Rosie the Boxer, the cats didn't have a dog to call their own. Someone they could climb on and rub against. When Lady came back to us, that all changed. She is a cat magnet. The cats lie across her and cuddle up to her and some of them even try to nurse on her. What does Lady do? Just lays there and lets it happen! At night, there's always a cat sleeping on either side of her. It's all good. Unless, of course, its dinner time. Sometimes Lady takes a while to eat her supper. The only time you'll hear her growl or snap is when a cat gets too close to her bowl. I think sometimes that she does it on purpose so she can screw with their heads.

You can't touch a treat bag or crinkle cellophane without the pitter patter of little fat legs headed your way. Lady is a treat pig. She's crazy for treats. I'm not sure that her previous owners were into the treat thing. For Lady, this has become more than an exciting diversion, it's an obsession. She'd eat the whole bag if you let her. Like some housefrau sitting on the couch with a bucket of bon bon's, pounding them down till she hits bottom. The happy look on her soft little face melts my heart.

Through whatever quirk of fate, I'm just so happy that Lady wound up with us. I can't be certain what her life was like before, but I know for certain, that now, it's better.

FELINE

INDOOR/OUTDOOR CATS

There are a select few that we really trust to go out and come back. With the exception of Molly, these are the lifers that have been with us for good while. They had experience outside before becoming comfortable inside. They know when they want to be out and when they want to be in and we let them come and go as they please.

CLEO

aka
[Cleotis; Closhee; Corleeotis; Mommies Kittie]

Without question, Cleo is everyone's favorite cat. It seems like she's always been here. She's a big, fluffy Maine Coone mix with the sweetest disposition and a passion for play. But her beginnings were tenuous.

Gail was on her way to the barn when she thought she heard a baby bird. Closer inspection revealed a nearly newborn kitten with its umbilical cord dried to the fence. Apparently she was strong enough to crawl through the fence but not strong enough to pull free. The kitten was weak and tired and Gail had to tear the cord off of the fence and take her to the house. It was touch and go for a while, but she made it. Gail named her Cleo after Cleopatra.

Cleo developed some sort of immune disease that made her poor little paws swell up. It was a problem for quite a while. They're better these days, but her claws are very brittle and they splinter which makes them even more lethal when she's in a wrestling mood, which is often. Every morning I'm greeted by her delicate meow and she trots ahead of me to go out for her morning stroll and to keep her dad company during morning chores. The only cat I've ever known that comes when she's called.

. . .

GRACIE

aka
[Grace; Chicken; Chickie; Chicken Neck; Chickle]

Gail's friend, Maryanne, worked at a greenhouse. Periodically, they were forced to "get rid of" all the cats that found refuge there. Maryanne had been feeding one of the mom's and her litter of kittens. Just before the exterminators came, she was able to capture the mother cat and kittens. She found homes for all of them…but one. A little yellow tiger cat. So we took her. Gail named her Gracie, but because she was always so afraid of everything, I called her, and still call her, Chicken.

Gracie is a sweet girl. If she makes eye contact with me and I call her name, she does the "silent meow". She moves her mouth, but she doesn't make any sounds. It might be because she went through a spell with a lump on her throat. Many different rounds of medication, and several months of wait and see, and it eventually went away, but I think it affected her vocal chords. She still makes sounds from time to time, but it hasn't done a thing to her purr. Gracie is a cuddler. She loves to sleep on you and if Gail is sitting outside, look for Gracie perched on Gail's chest, front legs tucked, eyes closed and very happy.

. . .

CINDER

aka
[Chubby Gray; Graybar; Graybarzini; Gray Gray; Cindar the Barbarian]

Gail had been thinking about having a gray cat and, sure enough, she got it. I wish she'd spend some time thinking about winning the lottery. There was an old house on Rocky River Road that had burned to the ground. While she was driving by one day, Gail saw a little gray head poking above the grass in front of the burned out shell. She pulled over and picked her up and home she went. A little gray cat; so gray she's almost steel blue; that she named Cinder.

Cinder, is, in a word, malleable. Easy to pick up and handle. Put her on her back, do whatever you want, and Cinder is cool with it. She has a precious little fat face and a chest rattling purr. But what has always fascinated me is her tail. It never stops moving! She switches it all around no matter what mood she's in. Come to think of it, I honestly don't believe I've ever seen her in a foul temper. She's pretty chill, even with other cats.

Cinder is a kneader. If she's sitting on you, those paws are making biscuits. Sure, it hurts a little. But it makes her so happy. What are you gonna do? Regardless of what kind of crappy day I'm having, seeing Cinder, for whatever reason, always makes me smile.

. . .

MOLLY

aka
[Grape Head; Grape; Princess Grape of Monacat]

Molly is an odd looking grey diluted Calico. She has a small head, hence the nickname Grape Head. Her front legs are short. Her back legs are long. She has a long body and tail. And she loves, loves, loves her dad. She meets me every morning, walking along the counters as I make coffee and get the cat dishes ready. She talks to me if I don't notice her. How she attached herself to me, I have no idea. I love that weird cat. She can't wait to go outside in the morning and has started a silly friendship with Curly Sue. The thing about Grape is I truly believe she thinks she's a dog. If BJ or Ginger decide to walk all the way down the driveway, Grape loves to tag along. When Maggie is out front to go potty, Grape runs and gives her a Ninja kick with all four legs, which sends Maggie running. They chase each other all over the yard. She is an oddball.

...

THE GARAGE CATS

The Garage Cats are the ones who stay primarily in the vicinity of the garage. They don't venture far from it because that's where food, water and shelter are. They are all, with rare exception, quite tame. Most of them are long termers, having been with us for a while. Some are newly arrived due to overcrowding in the barn area.

BIRDIE

aka
[Bird; Dirty Birtee; Miss Bird]

When we were under construction for the now defunct New Pineville Dinner Theatre, we had a big dumpster out back. One day, one of the workers said he heard a kitten in the dumpster. After some rummaging around, I found her. A tiny black, white, grey and brown kitten. We brought her inside and put her in a box with some food and water. At the end of the day, everyone stood around looking at each other. I just shrugged my shoulders and brought her home. Gail named her Birdie.

Birdie is pretty intense, but that's mellowed with age. She has an elevated perch in the garage where she waits for her twice a day feeding. She doesn't get along with many other cats. But if a person sits down outside, Birdie sets on them. It's kind of a rule.

. . .

SPANKY

aka
[Mr. Spank; Banky; Spankers; Mr. Banks]

Spanky is a slender, shiny grey boy. When you reach down to pet him, he helps you by standing on his hind legs. He loves head pets and sleeping on Gail's chest, which he has done since he was a baby. Spanky has health issues that we need to monitor. A virus that will eventually kill him. But for the moment, he's doing fine. I don't know what he lives on. I think I've seen him eat in person six times in the last year.

...

SALTY

aka
[Miss Salt; Salty Dog; Saltine]

Salty is a senior member of our feline crew and the only surviving sibling of the late Oregano and Pepper. She's a grey diluted Calico who is still, after all these years, a bit stand-offish. If you pet her, it's only by accident. But she's not shy about hanging around and doesn't run away when you're near. At dinner time, she politely sits by the feeding table and waits for her food. Sweet old gal.

...

MOMMA GIRL

aka
[Circus Girl; Momma Chubbs; Red Panda]

Momma Girl was a fixture at the barn for years. One of the very first feral cats that made an overture to me for attention. She's like a miniature Maine Coon. Her facial markings make her look like she's perpetually pissed off at something. She's got a shorter tail than most, stumpy legs and a roly poly figure. She's a doll. Our first interactions were at the barn. She would run up the fence post and wait on the crossbeam for attention. I called her Circus Girl. After a couple weeks, all I had to do was say that name and she'd fly up the fence to wait for some lovin'.

She gradually moved up to the cat condos in the pasture and not long after she started jumping the fence to visit the garage. I was worried that she would have an unfortunate run in with the dogs but she wasn't concerned in the least. Now she's a regular fixture. She even lets me pick her up. Her favorite trick is "The Tootsie Roll". That's where she throws herself down in front of you and exposes her curly underbelly and waits for attention. She is absolutely adorable.

. . .

SPYDER

aka
[Miss Pyder; Spyder Bear; Pitter Patter Pyder]

Spyder is a beautiful white cat. Very sleek. She started out as a barn cat. She got the name Spyder by her uncanny ability to vertically climb up into the barn rafters. Most of her young life was spent aloft. Her sibling, Powder, was one who just disappeared one day. Spyder is shy but always very social. She always talked to me when I was at the barn. I'd hear this disembodied meow and would eventually look up to see Spyder in the rafters shadowing my every movement.

With all the new kittens at the barn, Spyder decided to migrate up the hill to the pasture condos. She'd always leap to the roof of the condo so she could eat in peace. When that became an impossibility, she went over the fence and now she hangs out in the garage area. She shows up in the garage window waiting for me to fill her bowl on the sill. I just wish I could break her of the habit of eating all the birds that come to our feeders.

. . .

CEE-CEE

aka
[C-Bond; Big Cee; Miss Cee]

Cee Cee is big boned grey Tiger cat that we found in the barn. Actually, Cee Cee originally stood for "Cleo's Clone" because she looked so much like her. Cee Cee keeps to a pretty tight perimeter. She hangs out on the back patio and garden. Sometimes the pool deck. But she runs hot to the garage when I holler that it's time to eat!

BENJAMIN

aka
[Benjamin Cat; Big Ben; Mr. Ben]

Benjamin is a new addition. He's a big, thick necked, black tomcat with beady eyes and a baby meow. I named him after the cat mascot on "Impractical Jokers". He showed up because of all the females in season. He was terrified of me and always waited until I left the barn to sneak in and eat. One day, he followed me up the pasture at feeding time. He jumped up on top of the condo and sort of sidled up to me. "Well, hey, Benjamin! What are you doing?" He arched his back and showed me his butt, his way of saying hello. I reached over and gently stroked his back. He erupted into a purr. Jackpot! The next thing I know, he's in the garage the next morning, talking and talking. He immediately demanded attention and accepted many pets and neck rubs. It took a few weeks to learn the garage etiquette and he's still learning, but he works really hard at being a good boy. He's staked his claim in the garage and even bravely lies in the driveway among the dogs. He rolls over and offers his belly for scratches and plays and romps like a kitten. A stark change from the furtive, cautious cat I met only months before.

Being a prolific breeder, Benjamin was a priority for neutering. While I'm on the subject, and not to be indelicate, Benjamin had THE biggest set of balls I've ever seen on a cat. It's like he's on his way to a bowling tournament. And even though I "emptied his coin purse", he still loves and trusts his old dad.

. . .

BEAR

aka
[Bear Bear; Baby Bear]

Bear is an enigma. A mystery wrapped in a riddle inside a fur coat. Now you see him, now you don't. That's not dramatic, it's stunningly accurate. Bear was a little blonde muffin from one of the barn litters. He was cuddly and cute with his long, thick beige hair and easy going demeanor. He grew into a big, lumbering puffball. Bear is elusive. He lives atop the cage adjoining to Shemp's old pen, keeping an eye on the property like some sort of feline Batman. The recent addition of an old recliner to the covered area is just another lounging area for Bear. When he deems it necessary to come down from his perch, he runs hot or cold on human interaction. Somedays, he'll jump on your lap or hop up on the table next to your chair and act all kittenish to get attention. Other times, you'll find him in the garage eating and he'll turn and look at you like you caught him in the men's changing room trying on lingerie. I can't be sure, but he might be a ninja.

. . .

CURLY SUE

aka
[Curly Girl; C-Sue]

A relatively new addition, Curly Sue made a rapid migration from the barn to the pasture condos to the garage. She is a dark Calico with white and silver highlights. She is the only cat I've ever seen with a tail that curls over her back like a Pom or a Pug. She got tame very quickly. She went from being super shy to begging for pets on the feeding table. She's very comfortable around the dogs. Silky soft and adorable.

GUMBY

aka
[Miss Gum; Gum Gum; Gumbot; Gumberson]

Gumby is a recent addition to the garage, as well. Gumby is the sister to Pokey. A sleek, all grey, very precious girl. She is the mother to The Pips; Screech, Pee Wee, Star and Monkey. Gumby was quick to make friends early on. When she was little, I made sure that she and Pokey got wet kitten food every morning. She would always jump up where I was getting the food ready and get her neck rubbed and back scratched. When she grew up, she never changed. When she was in recovery from spaying, she loved all the good food and attention. I made sure I kept that up when her convalescence was over. Seems like only yesterday that I'd be on my way to the barn in the morning and all I had to do was yell "Gum Gum!" She'd squeeze through the fence, with her kittens in tow, and run to get her lovin'. She'd follow me from feeding area to feeding area to double dip on chow. Now, she greets me in the garage for breakfast and likewise for dinner. She has the most precious little meow and thinks the world of her old dad.

...

BRAVEHEART

aka
[B.H.]

This is absolutely the worst name for this cat. A bigger coward never lived. I named him Braveheart because he was one of the first young barn cats to make the overture to be pet and loved up. But when I had him neutered, he hid under his bed the entire time he was in recovery. I thought "What a loser!" I'd come in and say "Come on, little brother. Time for dinner." I'd hear this sad little "meow" come from under this fleece bed like some sort of thing from a Mario Bros. game. But once he was released, he became my new best friend. He's a sweet, sweet, pale yellow faded tiger with a precious little meow.

...

ROY

aka
[Roy Boy; Royster Doyster]

A big, awkward, pale yellow tiger cat. Recently neutered. Wants to trust, but very uncertain. I've actually pet him a couple times but usually when he's not looking. He likes to follow me to the pasture condos at feeding time but he always comes back. Always. He's a bit of a knob, but he tries hard.

...

LENNY

aka
[Aka Len; Leonard; Groovy Len]

Lenny is striking brown tiger with white legs and chest. We honestly don't know where he came from because he just sort of appeared in the garage one day. For the longest time we called him "Lilly" because we thought he was a girl! The kind folks at the Spay/Neuter clinic told us otherwise. Who knew? I apologized to him all the way home from the clinic. Started out quite shy but gets more comfortable as every day passes.

FRECKLES

aka
[Freck; Miss Frecky; Count Freckula]

Freckles is such a sweet girl. A grey muted calico, with a slender frame and interesting face but an extremely cautious nature that kept us apart. She was just recently spayed and during her recovery, the feral cat I could never touch, would come out of her cage at feeding time and rub around my legs and asked to be scratched and pet. She enjoyed the attention and loved getting her special food. I looked forward to every day during her two week recovery because I could scarcely believe that she was being so social. For a short time, she was in the room with a then baby Cotton. She was obsessed with him. She'd clean his face and lick and lick him. It's a habit that she carried on with Pinky's kittens. But once she was released, it didn't take long for her to go back to her feral ways, avoiding me and avoiding any sort of contact. In many ways, it broke my heart. She went missing shortly after that. She's done it before, but this time I felt like something had happened. Well, over three months later, I was on my way to the barn one morning and there she was. I couldn't believe it. "Freckles! What the hell? I've been so worried about you, you little shit!" Up went her tail and she followed me to the barn. I smiled the rest of the day.

...

THE HOUSE CATS

Get your feet braced. This is what I have running underfoot on a daily basis.

WIDGET

aka
[Widgey; Widge Piddle; Dum Dum]

Our farm hand, Jeremy, found a pitiful little yellow newborn in the barn aisle one day. Abandoned and alone. Gail named him Dumpling, but I've always called him Widget. Clearly, Fat Andy's son. Big yellow tiger. The single neediest cat I've ever met. In. My. Life. If you sit down anywhere, Widget is right there. He looks at you and cocks his head to the side like a dog. If you don't pet him, he'll make you feel so guilty. He's also possibly the single most uncoordinated cat we've ever had. He routinely knocks things over and falls off tables and chairs. He's not "special", he's just stupid.

. . .

GOOSE

aka
[Gooster]

Goose, Tip and Cookie were litter mates of Widget's. We didn't find them until a week later, huddled next to the lifeless body of poor little Ninja, who had disappeared after being very sick. They were rescued and brought to the house to be raised with Widget. Goose is a husky, thick yellow tiger cat. He is definitely the world champion wrestling cat. He spends his days either sleeping or wailing on Flynn.

TIP

aka
[Tippy; Tip Tip; Dip]

Yellow tiger, like his brothers Widget and Goose, except for a big white tip on his tail. Playful and dopey.

. . .

COOKIE

aka
[Cook; Cool Cat; Cookie Puss]

Cookie is the only one in that litter that wasn't a tiger. Cookie is a silky dark gray and white cat that is so laid back, you sometimes don't even know he's there. Most times you'll find him flat on his back in box or in a similar position on a chair, table or shelf. Chill beyond belief.

. . .

FLICK

aka
[Flicker; Fleek]

Sleek, dark grey boy cat. Got the name Flick because that long damn tail does not stop moving. Rambunctious and rowdy.

. . .

SHADOW

aka
[Shade; Shadow Cat]

Shadow is the spitting image of Flick in appearance and manner. The only way to tell them apart is the tail. Shadow's tail is shorter and thicker.

. . .

MITZI

aka
[Mitz; Mitzers]

Mitzi is Molly's litter mate. They could not look less alike. Mitzi is sturdily built with ornate orange and dark orange markings. Very exotic looking. She has eyes like Jennifer Love Hewitt's. If I make eye contact with her and say her name, she always answers me.

. . .

GOLDIE

aka
[Goldar; Gold Cat]

Goldie is part of another barn litter that includes Spice, Flick and Shadow. Goldie, as you can probably guess, is golden yellow and orange. It's gotten to the point where there are so many yellow cats, you have to work to remember who's who. Goldie looks like a skinny Mitzi. If she ever beefs up, I'll never be able to tell them apart.

SPICE

aka
[Spicy Weiner; Chatty Catty]

I originally called her Stripe because she has a big stripe on her face. She's a petite little muted Calico. Grey, white and orange. She loves to talk. Actually, it's more like chirping. She perches on the back of the kitchen chairs and talks your ear off. Precious little kitten.

. . .

SAMMY

aka
[Sam; Samson; Sammers]

It was a chilly night. I was on the front porch and I swore I heard the unmistakable sound of a kitten. A very young kitten, mewling somewhere in the darkness. I called to Gail to hustle out front and help me find it. There was a big tree that had fallen in the pasture and in the weeds around it was a small grey tiger kitten. Gail scooped it up and held it close to get it warm. Then we heard another kitten calling. We turned towards the house and waddling towards us was another little grey tiger and an all black kitten. The black kitten would become Sammy. The others were name Frank and Dean. They became "The Cat Pack". Sammy is a big chicken. Everyone picks on him. Surprising, considering he's a behemoth, with enormous fangs. Intimidating. However, all for naught. Has a terrible habit of lying wherever you want to walk or sit. Uncanny.

. . .

DEAN

aka

[Deano; Dean Dean]

The only way to tell Dean from Frank is that Dean's back is much, much darker. Handsome, swaggering grey tiger boy. Very cordial and loving.

...

FRANK

aka

[Chairman; Captain Frank]

The Chairman is a good boy. Like Sinatra, he's super cool, but it doesn't take much to see his funny side. Doesn't wield an iron paw. Not a tough guy, but you don't want to push him or he'll light you up like a Christmas tree.

...

GEMMA

aka

[Gem; Gemmers]

Gail was on her way to the vet in Lancaster, SC, and stopped at Hardee's. She saw a couple of kittens behind the store and the cashier at the drive through said they'd been trying to feed them. There were exterminators coming to get rid of all the feral cats living in the drainage pipes back there. With the help of one of the Hardee's employee's, Gail managed to catch only one of the kittens. It broke her heart knowing what lay in store for the other. But you can only save the ones you can save. She was given a box to put her in and she just drove immediately to the vet. On the way there, though it was only a short distance, the terrified kitten escaped and dashed all around the inside of the van. Thankfully, one of the vet assistants was able to help Gail corral her. She got all her shots and came home with Gail, who named her Gemma. Gemma is very shy. She only will allow Gail to touch her. I seldom ever see her and when I do the look on her face makes it seem like she got caught shoplifting high heels. But she gets lots of love from Gail, so I know she's happy.

...

FLYNN

aka
[Brat; Baby Boy; Shit Cat]

I was in the barn one morning and I heard a newborn kitten crying. I looked in the raised cat condos and found Miss Tiger had her kittens. She was in one condo with four of them and there was another one in the adjacent condo. I thought I may have interrupted her in moving them but by the time my chores were done, I realized that she had chosen her four and this poor little guy was out of luck. But it was really his lucky day. I reached in and got him and tucked him in the sleeve of my hoodie. A little yellow pickle, eyes still closed and raising a ruckus. I took him to the house and handed him off to Gail. I wanted to call him Dink, but Gail put the brakes on that. Next was Drax The Destroyer. Nope. Finally, she dubbed him Flynn. He was an infuriating kitten. He fought his bottle like it was an alien invader. He always loved sleeping and cuddling on Gail. Today, he's definitely her boy. He's very gregarious and interacts with everyone, but his favorite thing is doing the rough and tumble. He loves, loves, loves to battle. Once exhausted, he collapses wherever he is and sleeps. For nine or ten hours. What a life. Like I said, lucky.

DORA

aka
[Dora the Explora; Dangerous Dora; DORA! DORA! DORA!]

A recent addition to the flock is courtesy of Miss Slinky, a demure, slightly built cat. How she had six kittens is mind boggling. Apparently, six was too many and Dora got discarded. When I found her, I thought she was dead. It had been cold the night before and I had no idea how long she'd been alone. Slinky was right next door nursing the other five. I reached in to grab the body and her eyes opened and she started talking. She looked like a cross between a dirty Q-Tip and an unmade bed. I hustled her to the house and into Gail's care. "Gail, I'm going to need your help." She didn't even have to ask what it was about. She knew. So, here we go again. Giving the hopeless some hope. Dora is growing up to be a dadgum pistol. Absolutely fearless. A little bundle of grey dynamite. She can't be more than a couple months old and she is right in the other cat's faces. Thankfully, they all love her. They groom her and sleep in the cage with her and play with her. She is a happy kitten. When I'm having a bad day, and that's often, it makes me smile to watch her.

...

THE NEW KIDS

When the plague ran through the barn, some of the kittens dealt with it ok, others didn't. The ones that floundered were brought to the house to be nursed back to health. This is the new crop of knuckleheads.

EGGROLL
aka
[Uncle Egg; Eggsy; Egbert; Oaknut; Eggnog]

The most recent "acquisition", Eggroll is a fat, little monster. A beige dumpling that looks like Phyllis Diller and a Tribble had a baby. Egg is whirlwind. He was a barn baby. He wasn't abandoned, but he was not doing well so I brought him to the house. He recovered nicely and is a wonderfully awkward addition to the family. A friendly, happy little guy that can amuse himself with anything.

...

LITTLE ORANGE
aka
[L.O.; L'orange; Little O]

Little Orange always looks like he just farted himself awake. Slightly disheveled and tufty. Orange tabby with little eyes and a big personality.

GENE

aka
[Eugene; Gino; Gene Gene the Purring Machine]

Gene came to the house at the same time as Eggroll and was not nearly as robust. Gene was a long time in recovery. In fact, Gail had to take him to the vet three days in a row for fluids and wound up on some strong kitten antibiotics. We had to syringe feed him for a week which he took to quite nicely. It took a while, but Gene bounced back. He's a little orange tabby tiger with big, bright eyes and a penchant for cuddling. He's developed quite a purr and isn't shy about using it. Welcome to the family, Gino.

. . .

NUGGET

aka
[Nug; Nuggie; Nug Nug]

You can tell that Benjamin is the true father of all the black cats because they all talk as much as he does. Nugget is no exception. He's a happy, engaged, sleek, slightly built girl. Doesn't like to be held but loves to cuddle on mom.

. . .

FLASH

aka
[Flashy; Flash Pants]

Flash is a charmer. He was one of my early favorites from Slinky's litter. Always happy to see me. Never hated to be picked up and cuddled in the barn. When he got sick, I didn't even bring the carrier. I just cradled him in my arms and walked him up the hill. He's such a delight. He's becoming a big, ambling, spastic clown. He loves his pa. Sometimes.

. . .

BABE

aka
[The Babe; Baby; Babelicious]

Babe is Babette's sister. We weren't sure if she was going to make it. What a little lover she is. She sits on your chest and touches her nose to yours and looks you right in the eye. A look that always says "thank you". That look? That's why I do this.

. . .

JINX

aka
[Jinxie; Jink-a-Link]

Jinx is a beautifully marked dark calico. Haley's favorite kitten. Easy to see why. Jinx is a lover. She can handle herself in a wrestling match with her step brothers, but she'd rather be loving you up. It always makes me smile to watch her cuddle up to Big Benjamin. He loves her back. She's a precious little angel.

. . .

THE BASEMENT CATS

There was an old workroom in the basement with a door to the outside. So we built an enclosure that would allow this bunch to be indoor/outdoor kitties. A cat door in the window lets them come and go as they please. Outside is a myriad of platforms and levels that they can enjoy the weather and get some fresh air. Inside, they have a big cat tree, an easy chair, a sofa and several beds. They are a special bunch.

DOMINO
aka
[The Big D; D Money; Uncle D; Dummy-No; Mr. D; Tub Johnson; Dominose]

Once upon a time, Gail had a dream about white cats because she so badly wanted one. Well she got 'em! Domino is one of a group of five kittens including his brothers Sonny and Romeo (another white cat) and sisters Carmen and Bunny (yet another). When he was a crazy little white kitten, he had a couple of dark spots on his head, which have since faded. That's how he got his name. They all grew up in the feed room in the barn among all the hay bales. Gail and I can't remember who their mother was, but this was in the days when there were so few cats in the barn that they got a lot of attention and weren't afraid of people. They made their move to the house by necessity. We were having a lot of problems with hawks and owls. Gail and Haley were attached to them at this point, so up to the house they came. The whole litter is a pack of knuckleheads.

Today, Domino is "da boss". He is a fifteen pound behemoth with the heart of a fool. And man, is he a love bug. He can't get enough of getting jiggled and jostled and hugged and kissed. He was diagnosed with diabetes over a year ago, but blood work showed that he had outgrown it! I'd never heard of such a thing. But during his time "on the needle", you couldn't have asked for a better patient. He got his shot morning and night and not once did he fuss. We keep his condition in check now with a good prescription diet. He walks into his little feeding cage at mealtime of his own accord. He's a good, good boy. And he loves, loves, loves his special "post feed" treats.

...

ROMEO

aka
[Romers; Romanose; Romey; Romus; Pretty Boy]

To the uninitiated, Romeo and Domino look alike. Romeo is a big, lovable lug of a cat. His distinguishing characteristic is his tail. Most cats' tails stand straight up when they are happy. Not Romeo. It only stands halfway up. Then the top half of his tail lopes back, so it looks like a Shepherds Crook. Romeo was born deaf but it really doesn't affect him. He loves to play in the water dish. I finally had to put a big solid ceramic dish on the counter so he wasn't able to knock it off. I don't know what it is about white cats and the water dish. Romeo spends his days sleeping on his back on the top platform outside or the top of the cat tree inside. He wakes up to eat and get treats. What a life!

...

CARMEN

aka
[Carmeese; Carmen Veranda; Carmus; Carmy Apple; Carmenose]

Carmen is a beautiful, chubby, muted Calico. Grey and silver and white with a splash of orange. She's got big eyes and an intense nature. She loves her lovin' but gets nervous if you try to hold her. She purrs and purrs when she gets her head and cheeks rubbed and if you stop, she reaches out a paw to bring your hand back for more. She's only got three teeth left but that doesn't slow her down at the chow line. She loves her treat times. When I'm on the couch, she's the first in line for attention.

. . .

BUNNY

aka
[Baby Bun; Bun Bun; Bunanose]

Bunny is a pretty, lithe white cat, very unlike her doughy brothers. Bun Bun has unusually big eyes and slight deformity on the right side of her mouth that makes her look like she's giving the Elvis sneer. She's amazingly agile and her vertical leap is unmatched. She loves to be held and purrs so loud you think the mini fridge is on the fritz. Despite her delicate and graceful appearance she can put down the cat food bite for bite with her fat brothers.

. . .

SONNY

aka
[Son Son; Mr. Son; Sonanose]

Sonny is a happy boy. A big, yellow tiger boy with a bright disposition and a perpetual good mood, Sonny is always up for "chuffs". That's where you hold their face and scratch under the jowls. He likes his special treats. When I'm feeding Domino, I always give a few nuggets of the prescription food to an eagerly awaiting Sonny. He never misses it. He loves to lounge in and on things that are logistically way too small for him. He spills over the edges like a too full muffin pan. At the moment, Sonny is the only "Uncle" who puts up with his crazy new nephew, Cotton.

...

MITTENS

aka
[Mitty; Smittens; Smitty; Mitt; Mittenose]

Mittens is pretty gray and white girl. She started out as a feral barn cat. She was sister to Boots and Socks The Cat. But little Mittens got sick. Some sort of bronchial infection. I was able to catch her and put her in a cat carrier. We had some time before we went to the vet so I put the carrier on the bed and lay down next to it. I opened the door and slowly reached in to pet her. She was scared, but she was also so sick she really couldn't fight it. After some gentle loving, she started purring. Mitty fully recovered and over the course of her tenure here, she has grown very tame and accepting of loving and attention.

...

COTTON

aka
[Rotten; Turdzilla; Mr. Dinklepuss; Doucher]

Cotton is the latest addition. His story is told in length elsewhere in this book. He's still an annoying youngster and isn't shy about it. In the beginning, he was a little too insane for his Aunt's and Uncle's, so I kept him in a separate cage until he was big enough to join the general population. Cotton is a crazy little beige puffball. He's got two modes. Lunatic and sleeping. He loves his toys and Little Haley Pillars. He's not really interested in me holding him yet, but he loves Haley. He lays in her lap and wrestles and wrestles. As often as I can, I let him be in the office with me while I'm working. He likes to hang out in the recording booth but his purr is so loud the mic picks it up! So I have to shoo him away until I'm done. He's ridiculous. I love him, dammit! Now that he's a little older, he's loose in the room and enjoys wrestling with his Uncle Sonny and sleeping with Aunt Carmen.

...

THE GREEN ROOM CATS

One of the many "districts" is The Green Room, which is one of the converted guest rooms in the back of the house. It's heated and air conditioned for year round kittie comfort. We've had an outdoor area built, accessible through a cat door in the window, so they can get some fresh air and exercise. In the near future we will build a "fire escape" from the corner window down one floor to another open area outside my office window. This will allow them another avenue of exercise and a chance to come visit dad while I'm working.

TURTLE

aka
[Turtly Turtle; Miss Turt; Turtle Bird; Dirty Lips]

Turtle is a beautiful, old diluted Calico. Orange and black and tan. Almost a tortoise shell type of look. But that's not how she got the name Turtle. I named her after the character on "Entourage" because she was so chubby and ridiculous. She's got bright, bright green eyes with dark shading around her mouth, hence "Dirty Lips". She lost all her teeth to an infection but it makes it easier to play with her because she loves to play bite.

Turtle has run through a few of her nine lives. In her youth, when she was still a feral barn cat, BJ caught her in the side yard and shook her pretty good. He only dropped her when I tackled him. Gail managed to catch Turtle and look her over. She survived with a few scratches. Turtle, not Gail. She was almost stepped on by Ranger in the barn as a kitten. Most recently, she was attacked by Angel in the back bedroom. That was her closest call. That required a trip to the ER and an overnight stay. But she's safe and happy now. And loves her pa.

TEDDY
aka
[Mr. Ted; Teddy Bear; T-Boy; Ted Ted]

A friend found a litter of kittens that someone heartless son of a bitch had thrown over a fence at his job. They were hiding from the guard dog, a big Black Lab, when they were rescued. Two yellow tiger cats, a black and white short hair and an orange and white boy were all delivered to us. Gail named them Max, Dodger, Lacey and Teddy. Teddy was the orange and white boy that looked like a melted Dreamsicle. All of them were sweet. Teddy was the sweetest.

Teddy used to be in the Yellow Room, but the other boys were mean to him. Now, he's the lone boy in a room full of girls and they're mean to him too, just not as much. Teddy is a big, lovable tub. He craves attention and if you pick him up, he's going to be there for a while.

...

LACEY
aka
[Lace; Miss Lace; Lacey Jane]

Lacey is chatty little black and white character. She's small, but not petite. Pretty solid. And a scrapper. Bossy and a bit of a snot. She loves to talk. A lot. If you say her name, she talks. If you talk back, she'll answer. She's a nibbler, too.

...

TINK

aka
[Stink; Stinkerbell; Tinkle Dink; Tinky]

Tink is quiet, stealthy, black and white cat. Not particularly social with people but likes a pet once in a while. Her weakness? Treats. No matter what it might be. Cat treat, pizza crust, graham cracker, you name it.

...

OLIVIA

aka
[Miss O; Oleo; Livvy]

Olivia is a sleek, white girl with exotic, almost Egyptian, features. She's a tad high strung and we have to monitor her for a bad habit of licking all her fur off. Usually from the waist down. Sometimes it looks like she forgot her pants. Loves a lot of attention.

...

DOTTIE

aka
[Miss Dot; Dottie-Too-Snotty; DotSnot]

Dottie is a sweet, long haired white cat. When she was a kitten she had a dark dot on her head, but it has long since vanished. She's a might needy and gets a little aggressive when she gets attention. She's a very elegant looking girl on the surface, but beneath that, she's kind of a doofus.

THE YELLOW ROOM CATS

The Yellow Room is next to the Green Room in the back hallway area of the house. It's similarly appointed with amenities like heat and air conditioning, several cat trees and many beds. One half of the front porch is enclosed so they can cavort according to their desires. An attached doorway leads to another multi-level area and a big PVC tube leads to a tower for some privacy and sunlight.

MAX

aka
[Maxxy; Maxxy Cat; Maximus; Butterball]

Max is one half of the crew I call "The Boy Cats", with his brother Dodger. For the longest time, they looked so much alike I couldn't tell them apart! But Max has sort of porked up and is a darker shade of Tabby. Max is a big boy. Not fat, just thick. He looks like a tiger but as cliché as it sounds, is a real pussycat.

...

DODGER

aka
[Dodge Kitty; Dodgeball; Dodge Podge; Butterscotch]

Dodger is a lighter shade of Tabby than his brother and a tad snugger in the waist, but just as sweet. I never got a chance to spend much time with the Yellow Room Cats until the last three or four years. It has been worth the time to get to know them. Dodger is a favorite. When you pet him, he cranes his head all the way back, exposing his soft neck which he loves getting scratched. He's the first to come for treats and lovin' and the last to leave when it's all done.

POGO

aka
[Poge; Pogie Dokie; Pogemon; Pogo Jones]

Pogo, and his brother Toby, are the two surviving members of Miss Baby's first litter. Gail was trying to finish up trapping in the barn and these were the only kittens in the barn, so Gail snatched them up. Their dad was Mr. Blonde, who had brought Miss Baby to the barn as part of his harem. Pogo was the first out of that litter that let me pet him. He's another in a long line of our black and white cats. Pogo is different because he's mostly black like his late brother, Beau.

. . .

TOBY

aka
[Tobe; Toby Jones; Tobias]

Toby is a mystery. Despite our best efforts, Toby has reverted to his feral state. He looks so sweet with his chubby soft brown tiger stripes and patches of white fuzziness, but he is quick to hiss and growl when he sees me. It might be because he hasn't been neutered. We are planning to try to trap him and have him fixed. Regardless of his attitude towards me, I always talk gently to him and make sure he gets his treats in his special spot every day. I don't know what the future holds for him and me but I really do hope we are able to make some sort of connection someday.

. . .

HALEY'S CATS

There was a litter in the barn that we just could not catch. One day, I called Gail on the cell phone. "They're hiding on the fence line by the side yard!" Gail came out and we were able to capture them. Two girls and a boy. We were at critical mass with cats in the house, so Haley decided to adopt them and became mom to Maize, Lola and Gabby. But when she's gone, it's up to me to keep them fed and happy. They torture poor Haley with their antics; waking her up before dawn to eat, climbing on her head when she's trying to sleep; bringing frogs and giant bugs in from their outdoor tower. For me, they're always so good for their old dad.

MAIZE

aka
[Crazy Mazie; Maze; Maize Jane]

Maize is a crazy looking thing. I remember when she was a kitten, how big I thought her eyes were. She's a pretty Calico. Mostly white, with patches of orange and black. She's also a little mental and she looks it. Like the cat version of Peter Lorre. When she was a kitten, she used to wander into my office from Haley's bedroom and stare at me. Gave me the creeps. But she's a puddin'. So casual and social and chatty.

. . .

LOLA

aka
[Lola Bug]

Lola is a delicate little gray and white girl. She's the only one of the three that hasn't been fixed, since she has a bad reaction to anesthesia. So, when she's in season, she is a monster. It's funny, because she's the smallest one of the three. Bottom line, she calls the damn shots in that bunch. With people, she's sweet as pie. Always quick to talk to me and when my office door is open, she's the first to come in and say hello.

...

GABBY

aka
[Gabbus; Gabbers; Gabalosh]

How this big slab of dopey came from this litter is beyond me! He's a huge boy with giant fangs and thick white, black and grey fur! Clearly part Maine Coon. You'd think he'd be fierce! Nopers. He's the biggest coward in the world. Little Lola wails on his fuzzy ass all the time. It's a shame, too. He's so dang gentle and loving.

...

EQUINE

ABBY

aka
[Abbas; Moe; Abba-do; Abby Magoo]

She was what they call a "throwaway horse". Free to anyone with a horse trailer. She was being boarded as a favor to a horse dealer at the barn where Gail was taking riding lessons. She was very underweight and covered in rain rot, which is a skin condition caused by exposure to rain and humidity. The owner told Gail she could take care of her while she was there. She spent a lot of time brushing and grooming Abby, putting the medicine on her poor skin and giving her lots of treats and extra food. She also devoted time to socializing her with both people and other horses. She eventually started to put weight back on and was leading a relatively normal existence.

The time came when they were going to try to sell her. She had supposedly been taught to be a cross country horse, meaning she would do all sorts of jumps. The problem was she had a reputation for way, way over jumping. Her feet were flat from running on the race track. One shoulder was massively muscled and she was missing part of her right eyelid. It was clear she hadn't been properly cared for. Now, if no one wanted her, she'd be sold for mere dollars to "The Meat Man". Another horse, used and discarded. Criminal. Gail decided she couldn't give her up. She was ours now.

The thinking was that this would be a good second horse, since Haley was getting too tall to ride Kita. Gail had the vet come in and check her out. The vet discovered a tattoo on her upper lip. That meant she was a race horse! The dealer had told Gail she was part Thoroughbred and part Quarter Horse but the vet said there was no way. He read the tattoo off to Gail and she sent the information and fifty dollars to the United States Jockey Club to find out who she was. Her original name was "Arby's Winner", which Gail hated. So, she called her Abby.

Abby is, and always has been, high strung due to her racing days. Gail's friend, Kathy, was riding Abby in some shows one summer and when the bell would ring for them to enter the arena, Abby would immediately go into racehorse mode and leap forward like the green flag just dropped! Kathy could usually get her under control but it was something that she was never quite cured of, even to this day. We live very close to an event in Mineral Springs called "The Steeplechase". And when it rolls around every year; and Abby hears those sounds so close by; her tail goes up and she struts and strides around the pasture, snorting and kicking. Old habits are hard to break.

Abby was equally fanatical about her relationships with other horses. Especially our Quarter Horse, Ranger. Where Ranger was, there was Abby. She took all her cues off him. And when Ranger died, Abby was a wreck. Directionless. She eventually got her ground back, but it took a while. It broke my heart that, for the longest time, she'd come to the pasture in the morning and look all over for Ranger. Calling to him. Waiting for a reply that never came.

That same scenario would be revisited a few years later. When Kita passed away, it left Abby all alone. They'd gotten so close over the last four or five years. As I write this, it hasn't even been twenty four hours since Kita left. Abby is maintaining but we worry about her. She knows Kita isn't coming back. I will endeavor to try to be her new Kita. I'll try to go see her in the pasture at least once a day. I'll go sit on the old stone bench and give her treats. I hate that she's alone now.

Abby is a good girl for her old dad. When I go down in the morning, I ask her if she can be pretty for me. She turns her head to the side and waits for her treats. She loves her carrots and peppermint treats. I hold her face and tell her "I'm gonna kiss you!" She gently closes her eyes and lets me kiss her big, soft cheek. Good pony.

─ FERAL CATS ─

THE BARN BROOD

The ebb and flow of the cast of feline characters at the barn goes on. A few have been there for a very long time. Some are here briefly, either moving on or meeting an untimely end. No matter how much you care; no matter how hard you try to fend for them, such is the life of the feral. This current batch has several unnamed members. I try not to get too attached.

SNICKERS

aka
[Snickerdoodle; Snickety; Schnickersh; Snick]

Snickers is the eldest member of the feral squad. She's been here well over ten years and for a feral, that is impressive. I think at one time I did the math and less than ten percent of all the barn cats survive or stay for the long term. Snickers is a black and orange diluted Calico with a gnarled, nub for a left ear. You will go months without seeing her and then one morning, she'll just saunter around the corner, looking to see what's on the chow line. I've written her off many times, only to be surprised by her reemergence. She's not an easy one to pet, but she knows her name and runs to meet me if I call her. I think I so closely identify with Snickers because we're both loners at heart. We wear our scars with dignity and just keep trying to make it to the next day. There's a quiet comfort knowing she's around. And if I never see her again, I'll just assume that she's out there somewhere.

SOCKS THE CAT

aka
[Socks the Cat]

Socks the Cat is unique because, unlike all the other animals on the compound, she has no other nickname. It always has been, always will be, simply Socks the Cat. She's a long timer, too. She's a simple black and white short hair. he always runs up the paddock from the barn in the morning to meet me. Sometimes she lets me pet her, sometimes not, but she's never shy. Good old Socks The Cat.

. . .

CHICLET

aka
[Chicky; Chick Chick]

She's a black and orange short hair. Very shy, but sweet. Not a people cat, but we get along pretty well. Currently trying to trap her for spaying. She's a smart, cautious kitty. She's gotten to the point where she'll come see me when I'm giving sardines as treats. She always waits her turn. That's a good sign.

. . .

BIB

aka
[Bibby; Bibbity]

Bib is an elusive cat. Yellow tiger with a big bib of white fur around her neck. She's another that's hard to read. She's wary of people, still. With her it's a waiting game.

SLINKY

aka
[The Slink; Stinky; Miss Slank]

Slinky was a real baby maker! It was pure luck I was able to trap her! She's another in a long line of diluted Calico's. She is the only barn cat that allowed me to handle her kittens with no fuss. She's a beautiful girl with a pink stripe down the back of her neck. Since she's been trapped, she's much more at ease with her old dad.

...

HARVEY

aka
[Big Harve; Handsome Harvey]

Harvey is one of our big barn toms. He's just beautiful. Dark orange with light orange highlights and big white puff at the end of his tail. He almost looks like some sort of miniature tiger. He was another elusive tom that I finally trapped. I predict many less tiger cats in the future now that he's been "retired". He's a good boy. Shy. But good.

...

THE BARN KITTENS

Dear Lord, I won't bore you with many details. There's just so damn many.

THE PIPS—Four black kittens born to mom Gumby and dad Benjamin. Screech, Star, Pee Wee and Monkey. Tiny, sleek and lithe. And loud. Very loud. Especially at feeding time. They love to talk to dad. Easily pet when they're preoccupied eating. Star and Pee Wee are now remarkably tame and even let me hold them.

COTTONELLE—Cotton's twin sister. She used to be terrified of me, but now that she's been spayed, she's much more accepting of me. Lets me put her food down right in front of her.

PALEFACE—I guess technically, she's a tiger cat. But she's so pale and washed out, it's sometimes hard to tell. Her face is such a pale yellow it's almost white. Untouchable, as of now, but getting close.

ELVIRA—Jet black long hair. Nice girl. Easy going.

SHMUZZLE—Pretty little yellow and white girl with white all around her muzzle.

MOONEY—Black cat with big, big eyes.

PATCH—Grey, diluted Calico with patches of white and an orange patch over her right eye.

NOODLES—Patch's sister. Same sort of coloration except big white rear legs. Funny cat. Silly.

SPIKE—Slender black male. Almost named him "Parkour" for the way he leaps up the walls and all over the barn.

PERSIA—An elegant looking female. Almost like one of those Egyptian cats. Reserved and smart. Too smart, if you ask me.

FANTASIA—Persia's sister. They look so much alike, I have to look twice to make sure I know who I'm talking to. Fantasia's tail is darker.

MARY BETH BETH BETH—Persia and Fantasia's sister. Diluted calico, as well. Sweet little girl.

SHEENA—Small black female. Very shy and retiring.

SPOT—A big, handsome grey boy with a white spot over his right eye. Sometimes they just name themselves.

TAYLOR—Yellow tiger boy. Got a dark streak down the length of his tail.

HOSS—Little yellow tiger with dark markings on his back that looks like he's wearing a saddle.

CHICK—A pretty and shy little tabby gal. Since spaying she's a little more comfortable with daddy but it's a work in progress.

BICK—Chick's brother. Almost identical except Bick's face is rounder and the tip of his tail is white.

BABETTE—Babe's twin brother. Pudgy and grey and a sweet and friendly girl.

AMAZING LARRY—Larry is light yellow tiger cat who tends to the skittish side. One of the few kittens who hasn't warmed up to dad.

BIG ORANGE—Little Orange's twin brother. Actually, Big Orange isn't quite as big as Little Orange, but hey, who knew?

DUTCH—Little dark calico pudding. Good sport. Likes his dad. Especially when it's time for sardines.

Jeff Pillars

THE CAT CONDO CLICKE

Just outside the front gate to the pasture and under a majestic, old Magnolia tree, is a set of condos just for cats. The last couple of years, the cat population demanded something a little more significant in terms of shelter. Our ultra-handy neighbor, Dave Nickle, built three condo units. Two of them are two bedroom and one big four bedroom. It didn't take long for certain cats to lay claim to these digs. There are visitors from time to time, but these are the steadfast members of the clicke.

TWO FACE

aka
[Two Two; Twofer; Miss Two; Auntie Two]

Two Face has been around for a long time. How long? She was named after "Two Face" in "Batman Forever". Two is a beautiful orange and black Calico, with her facial markings split exactly down the middle. Orange on one side, black on the other. Before her move to the condo's Miss Two was a barn cat. I couldn't touch her, but she did communicate with me. When I'd go to the barn in the morning, I'd call "Twooooo!" And off in the woods I'd hear a baritone meow that was distinctly Two Face. I'd keep calling. She'd keep answering until she could see me. She wasn't afraid of me, but she wouldn't let me touch her.

Since her move to the condo's she gotten to where she won't touch her breakfast or dinner until she gets loved up by her dad. I rub her neck and scratch her back and chuff her cheeks. If I'm slow to show affection, I get to hear that famous meow as a reminder. Once that's done, she's ready to eat. She goes from dish to dish just to make sure that no one is getting anything better than she's getting.

Two Face is the senior member of the condo's and wields her power with a velvet claw. She's the strict Aunt to all the youngsters. She takes zero shit from anyone, including the toms. When the kittens get too rambunctious, especially around meal time, she shuts that nonsense down. Sometimes they gang up and torment her but it's to their everlasting regret. Two don't play that.

. . .

BABY BOOTS
aka
[BB2; Bootsy Boy; Booter]

Baby Boots is grey cat with little white feet. Just like his dad, the late, great Boots, Sr. Baby Boots is Boots last progeny and the resemblance is striking. He's not as friendly as his dad, but I'm working on it.

. . .

PINKY
aka
[Miss Pink; Pank]

Pinky is a sturdy grey cat with a little round face and vibrant yellow eyes. She is the attentive mother to the now grown Ajax and Fish. She's shy but not a wallflower.

. . .

AJAX

aka
[Jax; AJ]

Ajax is another jet black kitten with a short tail. Not a bob tail but only about mid-length. He's stealthy like a Ninja. Since her brothers Bob and Smokey disappeared, she's connected at the hip to her brother, Fish.

...

FISH

aka
[Queenfish; Queenie]

Fish looks exactly like Ajax but he has a normal tail. It's the only way I can tell them apart. Fish seems to be perennially happy. She's always bounding around in the tall grass and being silly with the young kittens.

...

THE GREY BABIES

aka
[Corky, Porky and Dorky]

These are Pinky's latest litter of kittens. Three pudgy little muffins that have been raised away from my control. I'm slowly winning them over. The smallest one, Corky, is a special needs cat. That doesn't keep him from enjoying life and wrestling his cares away! Loves his uncle, Fat Andy.

BUTTONS

aka
[Baby Buttons; Buttons Bear]

Buttons is a very unusually marked girl. She's a patchwork of muted Calico and white. The grey tones almost look like a shade of blue. She's just beautiful. When she was recovering from spaying I was hoping to get closer to her, but no cigar. But at least she doesn't run from me anymore.

...

FAT ANDY

aka
[Ando; Fat Boy; Fandy; Andrew]

Fat Andy is a neutered tom. He's a pale yellow, faded tiger cat. He has a round, gentle face. He's one of the only toms we've ever had that plays with the kittens. He's like Uncle Buck. He hides behind the weeds or the sand pile and the springs out! The kittens scatter and run away. Andy goes right back and hides again and the kittens slowly come out of the barn to look for him. Repeat. Sometimes they even chase him. He plays the tough guy, but when I see that side of him it makes me smile. He's gotten much better about not running from me at meal time. In fact, he always tags along with me when he knows I have sardines. I can now pet him when he's not expecting it. He used to run from that. Now he doesn't. Time will tell.

...

THE CLOVER'S HOUSE CREW

Not a huge contingent, but an interesting story. When Clover passed away, I converted her dog house into a recovery room for spayed and neutered ferals. Inexplicably, it's become "the place to be" for a select few special kitties.

TIGER

aka
[Miss Tiger; Pretty T]

Tiger is a very delicate little yellow tiger cat. She's as sweet as she can be. She was the first cat to be housed in the Clover Recovery House. She was so scared and so sweet. She wanted to trust me. Towards the end of her recuperation, she started coming forward to get her food, which she loved. But when it came time to release her, she didn't run back to the barn, as I suspected she would. Oh, hell, no. She was used to that wet food and decided to hang around. In the mornings, she and Kibby would meet me in the driveway and run crazily down to Clover's House for breakfast. But now that Kibby is gone, she still does the same thing, but alone. Every single day she gets a little closer to me and little bit braver. Just recently she started putting her tail up when she sees me. That makes me smile.

. . .

POKEY

aka
[Pokey Jones; Buzz Balls; Poke]

Pokey is Gumby's twin brother. Steely grey and well muscled. He is also a real pain in the ass because he's so intense. I was finally able to trap him and get him neutered. The time in the recovery house was well spent. It calmed him down and he's become quite friendly. He's still intense but at least he lets me love him up.

. . .

PERSONAL THOUGHTS AND REFLECTIONS

I HAD A DREAM...

I remember the date because I wrote it down. February 24, 2014. The night I had "the dream". I never keep a dream journal but this was so vivid, so real, that I felt compelled to write it down. I hadn't been sleeping well. I'm not sure why. Just hadn't been. That night I finally turned off the TV around 2am. Little Chloe was cuddled under my arm. It seems like I'd just closed my eyes. I don't know how much time passed but I was awakened by the smell of fresh cut grass. I slowly opened my eyes. It was dark. But there was a light under my door. I walked out of the bedroom, into the hallway and for some reason went to the front door. When I opened the door, it was bright midday. The smell of dewy sweet cut grass filled the air. I stepped off the porch and I was in a meadow that went on forever. I was drawn to a large tree off in the distance. As I scuffed through the grass I became aware that I was not alone. I don't know who I saw first, but all around me were my pets who have passed on. There was my old Lassie. She passed when I was in my late teens. To my eternal regret, I wasn't there when she left this Earth. But it didn't seem to matter to her. She ran to me, her crippling arthritis gone. I couldn't believe my eyes. Little Fred the poodle, my beloved Pippit, Lady, Peanut, Katie, Buster, Brownie, Lucky, Sadie the Pug, Buddy the Beagle, all of them. And the cats. Bianca, Blackie, Sassy, Clarkie Soft Face, Boo Boo Biscuit, Beau and leading the pack was Timmy the Tiger! They all came to me, gathering around to greet me. I heard the thunder of hooves and here came old Zoe, Big Head Ranger, Gypsy the Pony and Jessie. Old Jessie alive again! Sneaking up behind me and pulling at my back pocket looking for her treats. We all arrived under the big tree, enjoying the cool breeze. Under the tree were beds. Gloriously and ornately carved wood, adorned with big plush pillows. Above the beds their names were engraved. Alongside them were other empty beds. Beds with the names of all my animals still alive and some I didn't recognize. All engraved in gold and marked with a sign that said "reserved". Then bigger beds. Lounges, really. There were names there too. Mine. My wife. My daughter. Sleeping on my bed was a familiar white shape. Dolly! Dolly Marie! She rolled over on her back and I ran to the bed to wrestle her and pull her soft white lips. I was with all my old animals. I wanted to settle into my big bed and stay but before I could, all my animals went on alert. They pricked up their ears and looked into the distance. Then they looked at me. As if they were telling me something. I didn't want to go. But I knew I had to. With tears in my eyes, I walked away from that beautiful tree and away from my beautiful old friends. I walked toward the sun. In a moment, I was back in my bed. Next to me, Little Chloe was having a bad dream. I put my arm around her and comforted her. She woke up, her little eyes still filled with sleep. She gave me a quick kiss on the nose with her little wafer thin tongue, curled back up under my arm and went back to sleep. And I was back among the living, caring for my creatures. Sent back by my animals long past to care for the remaining pack until it's their time to take possession of their big soft bed, under that magnificent tree where they'll wait for their dad. I thank God for that short trip. I hope it's real. I hope it's not the last time I see them. That bed sure looked comfortable.

VET YOUR VET

If you love your pet, its health is a primary concern. So, it's vital that you shop for a vet like you'd shop for your own doctor. Remember, your pet's life depends on it. Be sure to look at their reviews online and most importantly, talk to other customers about their experiences. Check with the Better Business Bureau. Don't go to a vet blindly just because they're convenient or close by. Ask to interview your vet before making an appointment. If they won't sit for an interview, you don't want them.

It's important to remember that a veterinary clinic is a business. They're there to make money. I totally get that. I'm a very happy Capitalist. But some of them take advantage of pet owners by playing on their sympathies. The operative word here is "some". Like any other business, there are shysters aplenty. Don't let your emotions take over and get played. If you're unsure, get a second opinion. Price shopping is another way to do it. Call the clinics you're interested in and check prices for basics. Rabies vaccine, a general blood panel, dental cleaning, spay and neuter. You'll be SHOCKED at the price differences. For example, one clinic we visit gives a dental cleaning for $150. Another, for a whopping $1300!!!! That's not a joke. One clinic even charges $20 for a simple nail trim while most do it as a complimentary service.

Believe me, if you like and trust your vet, you've struck gold. But sometimes, that vein can run dry. I think every pet owner has had bad experiences with veterinary clinics and veterinarians. We've had our share. One thing I've learned is not to be afraid to tell them what you think. Vets are human, too. They can make mistakes. They miss things. Sometimes, as with people, those mistakes can be fatal. I don't want to repeat myself, but you'll see perfect examples of this in the chapters for DULCIE, DAISY AND ROXIE. Three very good instances of how vets dropped the ball.

Don't be hooked on "Western Medicine." By that, I mean, conventional treatment. Open yourself up to Alternative Medicine. This sort of treatment is cultivated from Chinese medicine with lots of herbal based therapies. I'll give you a very good quick example that's elsewhere in this book. When Dolly was incontinent and wetting the bed, Atrium prescribed something called a "tea pill". Basically, it's an herbal tea in small pill form, about the size of a BB. I believe it was called Suo Qan

Wan. After only a few days, Dolly stopped leaking for good. It was miraculous. From then on, I was hooked on Chinese medicine. Herbals and supplements kept old Rocky alive for another four months after he was given two weeks to live. Don't turn your nose up at it.

Acupuncture and physical therapy is very affordable and works wonders for any number of situations. I've used it for anything from kidney and gall bladder issues to nerve stimulation in the back and hips. They can even do a form of acupuncture with a laser. It's totally non-invasive and actually very quick. Less than ten minutes in some cases. The K-Laser can also be used to reduce inflammation and promote healing. Again, just make sure that whoever is offering these services know what the hell they're doing.

When it comes to an ER, you're sort of limited to options. An emergency sometimes leaves the pet owner vulnerable to overcharges and price gouging. Been there, done that, too many times. There was a wonderful chain of veterinary specialist clinics in our area. They were top notch and the care was remarkable and reasonably priced. Then they were bought out by a bigger entity. Immediately, the prices shot up and the care went down. Luckily, a new hospital opened in Charlotte, NC, about 25 miles from the house. It's farther to go, but, my God, what a wonderful place. They have been our salvation these last few years in good times and bad. We are blessed beyond words to have access to them.

Vets can only do so much. You will also need to accept the inevitability of losing your pet one day. You'll run up against a situation where nothing more can be done and the only thing left to do is say good-bye. It's then that you'll really appreciate your vet. They're the only one who can grant your pet the mercy of peace. And that peace will be yours, as well.

BETTER A DAY EARLY, THAN A DAY LATE...

It's a simple fact that, like us, pets get old. Sometimes they get sick. Very sick. In some cases, you can maintain their quality of life for a while. I've had wonderful success prolonging pets' lives who've suffered from terminal ailments, especially kidney disease. But most are not reversible. You can slow it down, but you can't cure it. If you find yourself in this unfortunate position, a day will come that you will have to make "that decision". It's what I refer to as a "Cruel Mercy".

Sometimes it's difficult to know when it's time. Other times, it's not. But if you know your pet has a terminal illness, there is such a thing as waiting too long. I've been guilty of that on more than one occasion. The post mortem guilt haunts me to this day. If I could go back, knowing what I know now, I'd have done things differently many times. But everyone has twenty-twenty hindsight. It all comes down to understanding quality of life.

Just because your pet is alive doesn't mean they're living. People in coma's still breathe, but they have zero quality of life. When your pet can no longer enjoy the life they once lived, even moderately, it's imperative that you accept that it is time. I'm not saying don't exhaust all other options. But at some point, you will see it in their eyes. The sadness. The emptiness. The plaintiff look that begs you to do something. To ease their pain. They've depended on you and trusted you their whole life. They look to you for answers. Don't let them linger in agony because you can't bear to let them go. If there isn't any hope, it's up to you to give them the only solution you can: Goodbye.

Some people fear the act of euthanasia and they shouldn't. It's not a cake walk for you, to be sure, but it is merciful to the animal, and that's all that matters. It's peaceful and gentle. Take time to say your farewells. Reaffirm that you love them and will see them again someday. Stay with them. Talk to them until they're gone. They might not communicate the way we do, but they understand. But some people will avoid the process. They will choose to do nothing, justifying it by saying "Let God take them back naturally". If this is your mindset, you're a coward and, what's worse, cruel. You choose to let your pet suffer rather than upset your delicate sensibilities by releasing them from their agony. For the love of God, be humane.

There will also be times when the pet seems to be fully functional but things are happening inside their bodies that forewarn of a dramatic downturn within days or even hours. I've been there, too. The hardest thing in the world is to say good-bye when they appear to be fine and alert. You need to understand that they aren't fine and if you wait, the cruel fate that awaits them will be on your head. If your pet means anything at all to you, you will do the right thing.

OH, THOSE FICKLE FERALS

When we moved to Mineral Springs, Gail wanted property with a barn so we could have our horses at home instead of stabled off property. And where there's a barn, there are cats. Some domesticated that visit from neighboring homes, but mostly feral. We've had a bunch over the years. In truth, you don't really own a feral cat. They're just there. You see them every day. You name them. You talk to them. You feed them. You try to help them when they're hurt or sick. Some even let you get close to them. But you have to be careful not to fall in love with them. Because one day, they're gone. Wandered off. Killed by another animal. Died of disease or illness. Sometimes old age. And while it hurts, you have to just accept it.

Adult ferals are hard to get next to. They've been around and seen a few things. You don't get to be an adult feral by being a dope. No matter how nice you are to them; no matter how you sweet talk them, they always give you the stink eye like you stole their last Milk Dud at the movies. So, when there are kittens at the barn, I do my best to get them on my side. Be their pal. Step one, is to get them used to my presence. I don't try to touch them at first. I just talk to them. Not baby talk, just talk. The things I have to do today, the weather, who's being naughty, that sort of thing. And when it's time for breakfast or dinner, I holler "KITTENS! KITTENS! LET'S HAVE SOME FOOOOOOOOD!" After a few days, they put two and two together and when they hear the dinner bell, they come running to meet me. I make sure that the little babies have kitten chow. They seem to know what it is because they crowd around all the dishes. Then I put down big cat food. They seem to know, as well. Then I stand there as they come to eat. I just talk quietly to them. If there's a dust up, I tell them to knock it off. I try to call as many by name as I can. I try to prove to them daily that I'm not a threat.

On nice days or early mornings, I'll take a can of tuna or sardines and I'll go sit on the ground in the paddock in front of the barn. They smell that fish and they know I've got treats. They're cautious, but they come closer. There's always one that's either dumb or brave and they come right up for a treat. Then another. And another. Like squirrels or pigeons, some will eat right out of your hands. I sing to them, sometimes. They seem to enjoy it. One or two will crawl into your lap or on your leg. I never try to pet them. Not right away. They'll let you know when they're ready. Like dating a girl that knows karate, it's always smart to let them make the first move.

Before long, there will be one or two that will let you pet them. A scratch on the head or a stroke down the back. That's it. I don't push it. Nothing major at first. I get them used to touch. Pretty soon, they run to greet me, their tails straight up in the air, a sign of love and acceptance. It sounds stupid, but it makes me so happy to go to the barn in the mornings and see the kittens playing and carrying on and then clamoring up the pasture to greet me and walk down to the barn for food. It's the best part of my day.

The reason I invest so much time in ferals is that you have to be ready to trap them. If you have feral cats on your property, it's imperative that you get them spayed or neutered. There are a lot of places that have Feral Feline programs and many times its low, or no, cost. But it's important that those feral cat populations are kept under control. One year, we dropped the ball and we were overrun with cats. Some sort of virus, probably Coronavirus, ran through the colony and wiped most of them out. It was awful finding their little bodies. As I write this, we're in the process of trapping our ferals. It's a real chore. But you have to do it.

Trapping a feral cat is a psychological game on the scale of playing chess against a computer. Since they're so unpredictable, you have to find a way to get the upper hand. I developed a strategy that has served me well. To start, I take the trap cages and rig them so they won't spring shut. I put a towel over it and fill it with tuna or sardines or wet cat food and I put it in the paddock where they're used to finding food. They're always suspicious at first but they soon discover that the cage is where the food is. At this point, you can't give them the treats anywhere but the cage. Since they can come and go from the cage at will, it gets them used to the idea that it's perfectly safe. The kittens accept it right away. They climb all over the covered cage, playing and carrying on. This sets them up for down the road when they're old enough to be fixed. Males need to be around six months old and females around nine months. Between then and now, they need to accept that I'm their buddy. Once I have their confidence, the job becomes much simpler.

The adults are a different story. Some are extremely enthusiastic. I had a little girl named Freckles that went into the trap before I ever put the food in it! She was a real chow hound. Or chow cat. But there's always a few that are a hard sell on the whole trap thing. Two females in particular, Bib and Chiclet, who basically do the cat version of rolling their eyes. Getting them will be a game of patience and concentration. Like being stuck in an elevator and you have to pee. The feral tom cat is different situation altogether. There are only a few toms around with their junk still intact. They lead a hard, hard life.

Those that survive to adulthood are very cagey. I've found that in the case of toms, luck is your only hope. No matter how many feral cats you have fixed, there will always be more. It's like the TV series "The Walking Dead". Every season the cast changes, but the story remains the same.

The sad epilogue to this chapter is that you rarely get to say good-bye to a feral. They have a precarious place on the food chain because they are both predator and prey. I've had some ferals, long and short timers, that I loved dearly for one reason or another. Then one day, they don't show for breakfast. No big deal. It happens. Then a few days pass. Then a few more. And eventually you know it's time to bow your head and say a prayer for the little one you won't see again. I've done it many times, with many more times to come.

THE VOICES OF ANGELS

For those that believe, this will not be a surprise. To those that don't, I ask that you proceed with an open mind. I will begin by telling you that I've had a number of supernatural encounters. I've been face to face with a ghost. I've seen flying discs and other UFO's. I've even seen a very tiny man in our yard one night. But that story is for another time. Of all of these, the most significant and profound have been with Angels, where my animals are concerned. Now, I'm saying that these are Angels with no real proof other than a feeling. I've always believed in Angels. I've had friends that have actually seen them. My old friend and fellow voice actor, the great Croy Pitzer, was dying in Charlotte, NC and I was stuck in Vancouver, BC, doing "Ernest Rides Again". One morning the phone rang. It was unusual that I was in the hotel room. It was my friend, Lizzie Lawless. Croy had passed away. Then she related that she'd seen him a few days before. He sat up in bed and looked around the room. "Look at all the Angels" he said. Croy, even as sick as he was, was not one for bullshit. I took it as the Gospel.

The House of Goodbyes

My first time experience with the voice is still incredibly clear to me. I was sitting in my office working on a script when, over the drone of the TV, I could hear someone screaming. I jumped up and as I ran out of my office, I could hear that it was Gail yelling from the back yard. Heidi and Daisy were playing and Heidi got her lower jaw caught in Daisy's collar. The collar got twisted and subsequently choked Daisy unconscious. Gail found Heidi dragging her limp body around the yard. Gail held Heidi and I got the collar undone. I looked at Gail and shook my head. "She's gone." As those words left my mouth, I heard a voice. I can't tell if it was male or female but the words were clear. "Breathe for her." I had never done CPR on a dog before but I clamped my hands around her muzzle and blew. I rubbed her chest and blew again. Repeat. Her little eyes fluttered. She took a deep breath. She was groggy, but alive. But would she be if I hadn't listened to that disembodied voice? It took me days to come to terms with the experience. In my mind, there was no other answer other than Daisy's guardian angel.

On another occasion, I was on my way into town. I stopped at the light in Mineral Springs and was planning on going straight ahead, as usual. The second before the light changed, I heard a voice say "Turn left." That was all. Again, clear as crystal. Almost absent mindedly, I cut the wheel left as I hit the gas. One hundred feet in front of me was a small, yellow dog, lying in the road. She was trying to get up, but was clearly unable to. She'd been hit by a car and the driver didn't stay to help her. I did. The vet found that she was chipped. But oddly, all attempts to find her owner ended in a dead end. No one claimed her so she was ours. Oh, and her name on the chipping record? Angel. The irony left me breathless. But the name stayed.

Clover wasn't feeling well, so I took her to the vet that Friday. When Dr. Credit, at Atrium, wanted to keep Clover for a couple days, we both assumed that it was just a simple kidney infection. She'd had one before. I said my goodbyes to Clover and loved her up a bit before I left. I backed out of my parking spot and before I could put the car in drive, I heard a voice say

"She won't be coming home." I paused for a minute. I took in what I'd just heard. Past results had all gone the way of the voice. I closed my eyes and said a prayer that the voice was wrong. That following Monday morning we said good-bye to one of our dog babies for the twenty first time.

That was it. I've only heard the voice three times. But those times were so impactful and profound that I still get goosebumps when I think about it. I think, if I'd heard it more often, I'd just attribute it to voices in my head. No matter what the source, it has affected me deeply. I pray for my animals, domestic and feral. I ask the Angels to comfort them when they're scared; heal them when they're sick; protect them when they're in danger. I feel a connection to…something. I choose to think its Angels. But I probably won't know until after I've shuffled off this mortal coil.

A MIRACLE FOR COTTON

The summer and spring of 2017, we experienced a kitten population explosion. As near as I could figure, somewhere in the neighborhood of twenty five to thirty kittens. But that number will change. Some will be taken by foxes or coyotes or even hawks. Some will get a little older, decide they want to see the world and move on. And some will fall victim to illness.

Coronavirus is an insidious sickness that sometimes breaks out in feral populations. One year, it was bad. Gail hated to go to the barn because of the horror of dead kittens. She was burying sometimes two a day. Last year, I lost my little girl, Ninja and my buddy Peach. When kittens get to be a certain size, it's difficult, and frankly, not safe, to capture them by hand. And when they're that sick, traps don't work that well. We found Ninja in the hay room, her lifeless body surrounded by another cats four kittens, which we rescued. And I was actually able to capture Peach because he was used to me. He seemed to be doing good but died in the hospital. We've only had one cat survive. Boo. Gail was picking her up with the pitchfork and saw her head twitch. She was able to nurse her back to health.

The House of Goodbyes

Of all the new kittens, my favorite was Cotton. Cotton was tiny, with long, fluffy beige fur. His head looked like a big cotton ball, so naming him wasn't exactly rocket science. His head was so fuzzy that it made his face look abnormally small. One of the few long haired kittens I think we've ever had down at the barn. When I came into the barn, Cotton would look at me wide eyed and then scurry under the big saddle cabinet. But after a while, Cotton got used to my presence and would wait by the dish for his kitten chow.

One day I noticed that Cotton wasn't playing and goofing around like the other kittens. He was quite still, actually. I walked right up to him. "Hey, brother, what's going on?" He didn't even look at me. I stroked his head with my index finger. It took him by surprise. He looked up through bleery eyes and hissed and started back toward the barn, his gait unsteady and wobbly. My heart stopped. Could he have rabies? In all our years and all the animals that have come and gone, we've never had a problem. But I rescued a rabid kitten on the road in Waxhaw a few years before and I got a crash course in what to look for. This was one of them. His pupils weren't enlarged and he wasn't exhibiting any other signs. I prayed it wasn't coronavirus. Cotton was the first kitten from this current crop that I named and it broke my heart to think he'd also be the first I said goodbye to. That night, his condition had gotten worse. He didn't go for the food dish. He didn't run to the bowl for fresh water. He sat on the barn floor with his front legs tucked under him, his tiny chin on the ground.

The next morning I arrived to feed the babies and Cotton was in the exact same place and position. I touched him to make sure he was still alive. He stood up. His movements were jerky and his head trembled. I sighed with the reality that my Little Fat Cotton was sick and it was just a matter of time before I'd be burying him. It's macabre, but in my mind I'd already picked out a spot by the blackberry bushes that he loved to nap under. We had a couple old rectangular laundry baskets in the feed room and I clamshelled him between them and carried him into the feed room. I tipped one of the laundry baskets on its side and put an old cushion in it. I placed a weak and dazed Cotton on the cushion. I wanted him to at least be comfortable as he passed. To be safe I put food and water nearby. He struggled to his feet, shaking almost like he had a palsy. His eyes were all gunky and there was goop around his nose. He finally settled down. I went back to the house, knowing that after evening chores, I'd be burying my little pal.

That night, I looked in the feed room and Cotton hadn't moved. I got close enough to see he was breathing so I left him alone. When I was done feeding the cats and horses I sat on a hay bale and just looked at him. He was struggling. "Cotton, your old dad loves you. You don't have to stay. And if you go, you won't be forgotten." I was going to get up but I stayed. I lowered my head. "God, it won't make a difference to the world if this kitten lives or dies. It will matter to him. And to me. But I'm asking you to intervene. I'm asking that you spare Little Fat Cotton. He's done nothing to deserve a pardon. He's also done nothing to deserve this. I've had a rough couple of years, God. Things have been difficult. I could ask for money or health or any number of things. But if you can turn this around; if you can bring Cotton back to me, I'll know that miracles still happen. Because that's what it's going to take to save him. Anyway, bless and keep this little knucklehead, God. He's at least earned that. Amen." I said good night to the kittens and the ponies and went back to the house.

Morning came and Cotton was still in the basket but he had changed positions, so that was something. He was still breathing, though labored. I touched him and was very warm and didn't move. I went about my chores as silently as I could as not to disturb him. I took a last look and headed back. I worked in the office until about one o'clock and I couldn't stop thinking about him. I went down to the barn and looked over the half door into the feed room. Cotton wasn't in his basket. I opened the door and just inside lay Cotton. On his side, rapid shallow breaths and motionless. I scooped him up and took him to his basket. I pet him a couple strokes. I was certain the end was near. There was no change that night or in the morning. "God, either take him or bring him back, but don't put him through this."

I went back to the house and texted Gail. I was distraught because Cotton was lingering and it was so painful to watch. She suggested I take a syringe out of the medicine drawer and trickle some water in his mouth. So, I headed back down to the barn. Cotton had changed positions again. I leaned over and put a couple drops of water on his mouth. He smacked his lips. I gave another couple drops and suddenly Cotton sat up. He looked at me with sticky eyes. I moved the syringe back toward him and he was having none of it. On unsteady legs, he stood and staggered out the door into the barn aisle. He shakily dug a little spot in the dirt and peed. Then he covered it and sat down. Almost like the exertion was too much for him. He wobbled back down the aisle and lay down outside the feeding area. I got the laundry baskets and tried to catch him. He got away and went outside. I pursued and he hopped away! He headed to the fence and scrambled up one of the diagonal beams and sat on the crossbeam hissing at me and giving me the stink eye like I farted in his nachos. I was certain it was adrenaline that propelled him. I didn't want him to go over the fence and into the woods so I left.

That night, when I went to the barn, he was back in his basket. I checked and he was breathing. Again, I quietly did chores and left. In the morning, I found him curled into a ball in the hay. I'd never seen him curled up before. This was how I found my little LuLu passed away. I put my hand under the hay and jostled him a bit. Nothing. I was certain he was gone. I decided to finish feeding and then I'd bury him. I took the shovel out, picked a spot under the blackberry bush and dug the hole. When I came back to get him, he was sitting up. He looked at me and yawned. "Cotton! What are you doing, man?" He blinked and got up, walked a bit steadier to the water dish, leaned in and took a big drink. He walked to the edge of the feeding area, sat down and started grooming himself. This is significant because a sick cat won't groom. After grooming for a minute he walked back to his soft spot in the hay and curled back up and went to sleep. "What the hell is going on here?" Then I remembered my request. Was this my miracle?

That night I came down to the barn to try and trap one of the feral cats. A doozy of a storm was coming and I was pressed for time. I went behind the barn, trap in hand and looked around. For some reason I looked up. There, on top of the hay barn, peering down at me, was Cotton! This was not an easy endeavor for a healthy cat, let alone one that was death's door twenty four hours earlier. He had to climb a tree to make it to the roof! "Cotton! You idiot! What are doing up there?" The rain started and I turned to go back into the barn. By the time I got to the end of the aisle, Cotton rounded the corner. He immediately walked over to the food dish and turned and looked at me. I started to cry. I took his kitten chow over to his dish. "You hungry, pal? You haven't eaten in a couple days." He tucked into his dinner like a champ. It was the first night I slept well since he'd gotten sick.

The next morning, he met me in front of the barn. I was carrying a trap and had a can of sardines. When I set the trap down, he was sitting directly in front of me. "Hey, Big Man. Let me hold a sardine!" He ate two, while I fended off the other kittens. Cotton's eyes were clearing of the gunk. His snotty nose, gone. His gait, steady and kittenish. Cotton was back, baby. Cotton was back. As he and the other kittens turned and headed for the barn, I closed my eyes. "God, you did it. Thanks for giving me Little Fat Cotton back." I was at a point in my life where I was unsure and afraid. The future was uncertain. My world was getting smaller and smaller. But by resurrecting a random little barn cat, God showed me that prayers are heard. And miracles do happen. But the story doesn't end here.

The next morning was my birthday. Fifty nine. I thought I'd celebrate by taking snacks to the barn kittens. "Kiddens!!!!" They all came running. All but one. There was no Cotton. I called and called. Nothing. My heart sank. There is an attrition rate among the feral population. Either illness or being picked off by coyote, fox, owl or hawk. Cotton was so little. He would be unable to defend himself against something like that. So, I solemnly went about my chores, talking to the horses and kittens, but my heart wasn't in it. "Why would you pull Cotton through the fires of hell, God, only to let something awful happen to him?"

I made my way up the paddock and into the pasture to collect cat dishes from the cat condos. There, sitting with the other cats, was Cotton. "Cotton, what the hell are you doing?" He hopped over to me, stopped at my feet and looked up. I'd never picked Cotton up when he was conscious, but I reached down and scooped him up. I expected him to freak out and shred me alive, like most ferals would. Not Cotton. He hunkered down into my arms and purred and purred. That was the day Cotton got his second miracle. A home. An early birthday present for me. I went for a year not sitting in my chair because that was the one I bought for Speck and I. But now it's for me and Cotton. I love it. He could care less.

Today, Cotton is a fat, crazy kitten who loves his dad and his aunts and uncles. He gives me nose kisses and sleeps in ridiculous positions on his cat tree by the office window. Someday we'll have to say good-bye. But not today. Not today.

THE SHORT LIFE AND PEACEFUL DEATH OF SHARPIE

On the way to the barn one evening in October, I spotted a black kitten, sitting all alone, in the middle of the paddock. It was perfectly still, not even moving when Gail drove by on the four wheeler. I walked over to it. The little black kitten looked up at me. I bent down and picked it up. The previously silent kitten hissed. Not only hissed, but growled. "Okay, tough guy." I'd never seen this particular kitten before but was struck by its appearance. It was jet black with several silver hairs peppered throughout his coat. Its little ears had a higher concentration of the silver coloring. It was plain as day that its father was a pre-neutered Benjamin, whose markings are very similar. Apart from the hissing and growling, it was adorable. "Here you go, pardner. I don't want any trouble." It scampered towards the barn. The second I let it go, I had reservations. Something seemed a bit off about it but after having lost another kitten earlier in the week, I put it down to being gun-shy.

The next morning, just as the sun was coming up, I was entering the paddock to feed the horses and kittens. I stopped short. There was the little black and silver kitten sitting right where I found it the night before. I walked up and it didn't move, looking right up at me. Right into my eyes. I could sense something was just not right. I bent down and picked it up. Whatever fight was there the night before was gone. It was cold to the bone. I held it to my chest and cupped my hands around it. I found a bucket in the feed room and made a nice bed of hay. I placed it gently into the soft hay. "Give me one minute, buddy. I'm going to take you home."

I wrapped up barn duties quickly and took my new little charge in hand. I got a nice cage set up in a cat carrier on the kitchen table. I added a hot water bottle wrapped in a soft towel. "I'm going to call you Sharpie". It looked right into my eyes. "You hungry, buddy?" I made some kitten milk replacer and some wet kitten food and made a warm gruel. Sharpie tied into his breakfast and ate almost the whole thing. I tried to sex the kitten but it was so young it was impossible for me. It had teeth but his eyes were still blue. I couldn't tell how old it was. Rather than keep calling the kitten "it", I decided, for better or worse, Sharpie was a "he". Once he was done chowing down, he didn't want to go sleep it off. He wanted to be held. He wobbled out of his carrier and sat down right in front of me. My arm was resting on the table and he stood up on my arm. I held him to my chest and, though you couldn't hear it, you could feel the tiny rumble of a purr in his chest.

Sharpie loved to cuddle on his hot water bottle with a little stuffed elephant. For the next few days, whenever Gail or I

The House of Goodbyes

would open his door, he'd amble down to see us, ready for some food and attention. He'd lap at his formula and peck at the wet food like a bird, taking little kitten bites. His strength would ebb and flow, sometimes giving us hope that he was going to survive his ordeal and other times, we were certain he was losing ground. I was optimistic over the first few days as he gobbled up whatever we put in front of him. We made sure to keep him hydrated by dribbling water in his mouth with a syringe. I took him outside a couple times and he didn't want to be too far from me. I was hoping the sunshine and fresh air would do him good but when left to move around freely you could easily see he was weak and struggling.

I took every opportunity to sit with him. He was strong enough to crawl out of his cage. Gail and I would take turns holding him. He was so thin and frail, I know the cuddling was a comfort to him. I'd stroke his boney back and use a finger to pet his head. Every single time I put him back, I'd kiss his little head. "Poppy loves you, buddy. Poppy loves you. He does." He'd dutifully wobble back up on his water bottle and settle in for a nap. So, so precious. On his fifth day with us, I sat with Gail at the kitchen table. Little Sharpie was sitting between us. I looked at her. "Sharpie isn't going to make it, is he?" She shook her head. Gail was seldom wrong. That night while I worked, Gail held Sharpie on her chest like she did every night. He'd cuddle against whatever other cat was there. He seemed so content. I came up from the office and made a saucer of kitten formula with some wet food on the side. He lapped at the formula and ate a few bites of food, but it was obvious his heart wasn't in it.

I didn't sleep well that night. I had Sharpie on my mind. I got up at 5am and went out to the kitchen. I sat at the table and opened the door. Out came Sharpie. He was very weak. He wasn't interested in food. He just wanted to be held. So, I held him. I held him against my chest for ninety minutes. I told him everything was going to be ok. I told him how much I loved him and how happy I was that he was part of our family. I tried not to cry but the more I talked to him the more the tears flowed. "Poppy will never forget you, brother. You will always be in my heart. Mommy's too. I'm so sorry, Sharp. I'm sorry I won't get to see you grow up. I'm sorry that you won't get to know all your brothers and sisters and cousins and aunts and uncles. Most of all, I'm sorry I couldn't save you, Sharpie. Poppy tried. But I couldn't save you. I'm so sorry, brother." I kissed his head and put him on his water bottle. He stretched and settled in. I covered him up with his soft towel. I looked at him for a minute. Then I headed back to finish chores.

When I was finished with the mornings work, I headed to kitchen to check on him. Gail was just getting up and around and was letting the dogs out. I got a cup of coffee and sat down by Sharpies carrier. I opened the door. For the first time since he came to the house, he didn't come to see me. I reached in and picked him up. "Gail....Sharpie died." Little Sharpie was gone. His body was already starting to become rigid so he must have passed shortly after I put him down. Although I was expecting it, I was heartbroken. I had really bonded with that pitiful little kitten. I was always so touched when he would put his front legs on my arm and with his needful stare, tell me he wanted to be held. I held his tiny, fragile body for a few minutes, then I wrapped him in his favorite little soft blanket. For the second time that week, I was a one man funeral procession. Sharpie was preceded by Blinky, who I found in the barn early one morning and though I got her back to the house quickly, she was too far gone and actually passed away in my arms only hours later. I buried Sharpie out back next to Blinky. Several of the barn cats attended the funeral. I'm sure they had no idea what was transpiring, but they could see I was upset and that wasn't typical "dad behavior". I spoke a few words in Sharpie's honor.

"God, that's two this week. If you're trying to show me that I can't save them all, I get it. It was sad to lose Blinky, but Sharpie was different. Thank you, God, for letting Sharpie know what it was like to have a home. What it was like to be loved. What it was like to be part of a family. Thank you for letting us be his vessel to the other side. Thank you for giving us the opportunity to make a real difference in a kittens' transition to the next world. So many, God; so many die out there somewhere, without knowing love or warmth or safety. For five whole days, Sharpie had what so few of them will ever know, no matter how long they live. Five days doesn't seem like much, God, but for Sharpie…it was an eternity. Take care of him, God. I want to see him again."

I tried to sing a few verses of "Amazing Grace" but my voice broke and as I stood over those two small graves, little Star Baby, my newly neutered little male, came up to rest his head against my legs and meowed to me. "It's okay, old man. I'm still here." I bent down and picked him up. I kissed him on his face. "You take care of yourself, Starfish. Poppy doesn't want to do this with you for a long time." I walked back through the barn aisle, surrounded by little lives. I looked at them all and spoke softly to them. "Your old dad loves you." Several little tails went up. I realized then how lucky I was.

Godspeed, Sharpie.

THE DARKEST OF HEARTS

If there is anything controversial in this book, it will be this chapter. To be blunt, I find few people more contemptible, vile and loathsome than those that abuse animals. Not just domestic animals but any animals. Social media has given a platform to scumbags who would display their cruelty for the world to see. It has reached epidemic proportions. A man smiling broadly in front of his dog hanging from a noose. A woman with a bucket full of puppies throwing them one after the other into a fast moving stream. A veterinarian posing with a cat that she'd killed with a bow and arrow. A young punk cutting the head off of a two hundred year old snapping turtle with a jigsaw. There was even a website dedicated to videos of people running over puppies. I could literally fill pages with the monstrous acts of abuse I've seen. It quite literally hurts my heart and worse, fills me with a rage that is nearly uncontainable.

Where do these monsters come from? Is it how they're raised? A misfire of synapses? It's well documented that serial killers and mass murderers have a history of abusing and killing animals as children. Was nothing done to correct this behavior? Bottom line, I believe there is an intellectual disconnect with compassion for living things in certain individuals. And it's usually the tip of the iceberg in regards to other reprehensible behavioral issues. I mean, if they would do these unspeakable acts to a defenseless animal, what won't they do? It appears to be a psychosis that doesn't stop at just one event. It's like they're addicted to it. I can't tell you how many times I've read about a serial animal abuser who was supposedly rehabilitated, only to go on to commit further, sometimes even more heinous, acts. When I hear people defend Michael Vick saying he's "rehabilitated", I want to choke slam them through a table. Someone doesn't do those things and just change overnight. Michael Vick needed to lose everything he ever worked for and everything he ever loved for the horrific things he did to those dogs. With a good, solid ass whipping as the cherry on top.

Question: What sort of human trash takes part in dog fighting? Answer: Scumbags. Dogs fighting to the death for fun and profit. There's no profit for the dogs and I can't imagine its much fun for them either. And if they don't die in the fight, when they've outlived their usefulness, they're killed. Not humanely, by the way. Shot. Electrocuted. Drown. Absolutely monstrous. The fighting isn't the only cruel part. To train these dogs to fight, they use what is referred to as "bait dogs". Dogs that are either picked up at the pound, off the side of the road or sometimes even stolen from a yard; from a family that loved them and considered them family; and are used to teach the fighting dogs to kill. The culture and sub-culture of this practice is an abomination and those involved are below the lowest level of shit on the bottom of the flattest shoe. If I could work my will, every single person, male or female, that is caught in the commission of this crime, should be sentenced to be stripped naked, thrown in a pit and forced to fight others of their kind to the death. The one that survives gets life in prison. Sound harsh? Yup.

There's also the cruelty of neglect. Those people that "need" a dog, but when it's not a cute puppy anymore or becomes more trouble than they anticipated, it goes into a pen, or worse, on a chain, leaving the once beloved family pet wondering what happened. Hoping against hope that today; maybe today; they'll be brought back to the house to be part of the only family they've ever known once again. Why would their family cast them out? What had they done to deserve this? Then to add insult to injury, they're barely given the minimum of care; cheap food and dirty water; inadequate shelter; not even minimal veterinary care. It's as if the owner is too cowardly to just have the animal put down. They just slowly let the animal linger in poor conditions until they finally die. Burial is usually optional.

It requires the darkest of hearts to hurt an animal. To look at a defenseless creature and decide that brutally torturing and murdering it would produce some sort of personal euphoria is beyond my comprehension. I'm not talking about hunting. I get that. But to victimize dogs or cats or any animal is an evil only the most vile human filth engages in. Some states are finally making laws to address this but too many times the perp goes unpunished. Many of them are never, ever brought to justice. When I read or see these things, it makes me fantasize about an animal version of "Death Wish". Put Hammurabi's Code into full effect. An eye for an eye. Put these upright walking stool samples on notice that while their heart may be dark, a darker heart exists. One that has their sights set on them.

I'm probably a little long in the tooth to do something like that. Probably. I can only hope that Karma comes to pay them a visit someday. And you know what a bitch she can be.

NO GOOD DEED...
THE COST OF COMPASSION

I almost called this chapter "Full Heart...Empty Wallet", but the cost of this thirty odd year journey has gone beyond the mere dollar. You can put a price on goods to purchase, but to affix a monetary exchange on things like emotional and mental fatigue can be rather nebulous. I'm not just referring to the stress of losing a pet, it's the anticipation of it, as well. It's gotten to the point that every time we suffer a loss, the first thought in my mind is "Who's next?" Trying to navigate my day to day responsibilities without wondering if today will be the day Gail calls me, in tears, to tell me something has happened to one of the dogs. If this is the morning I find one of the horses down in their stall. Or find an outdoor cat or kitten dead. All of these have happened. Many times. And for that reason, I live day to day expecting the worst. That's a horrible way to live.

There is a physical cost. I do about four hours of chores in the mornings starting at 5:45am. Every morning. No days off. Then another hour, or so, at night. In between and after all this, I try to earn a living. These old bones don't take the wear and tear like they used to. There are always injuries to deal with. I've been bitten by cats. Real bites. Fangs in up to the hilt, bites. I've had my flesh scratched open by playful dogs. Had to have rabies vaccinations. I've gotten E-Coli from handling dirty kitty litter. And the Sunday after my fifty ninth birthday, I cracked two vertebrae in my back dragging my old horse Kita 180 degrees so she could stand up. Now, my back is severely compromised. But I still have to do my chores. That is simply another price I pay for the duties I've accepted.

There has been a cost of freedom. It's hard to travel or vacation as a family when there are so many little lives to account for. There are medications to administer and special care to be given to one or more at any given time. There's the ongoing maintenance. Stalls and litter boxes to clean. Kittens and cats and goats and horses to be fed and watered. At the moment,

I'm the only one physically capable of doing the heavy lifting. Gail's arthritis makes it difficult for her to get around and little Haley Pillars has her own life to live. Sometimes it gets to be just too much. It would be nice to get away for a couple days, but it's not practical. I make the best of it by seeing a movie now and then, and that seems to be enough.

There is the cost of guilt. I'm sure this should probably be listed under "emotional cost", but I think it's significant enough to warrant its own designation. Anytime we lose an animal, the guilt of doubt lingers long after they're gone. "Did I do enough? Did I miss something? Was it something I did?" Then there's the overwhelming guilt I feel towards my family. I'm sure Gail didn't sign on for this three decades ago. She's had to live such a "little life". So confined. Restricted. It is a horrible burden for her, but for me, it's a torture of conscience. Half of her life has been hamstrung because of animals. I know that life's not fair, but this seems to be an abuse of that axiom.

There is the guilt of negligence. With so many little souls to care for, it's extremely difficult to spend quality time with all of them. They crave human attention and my time is so limited. It haunts me constantly that they might wonder why I'm so absent in their lives. Let's not forget the guilt of resentment. Even though my situation is entirely of my own doing, there's many times I resent them all and I feel horrible for it. Understand this. Despite how noble you may think this life of mine has been, I'm far, far, far from perfect. I have cursed their very existence on more days than I care to admit. I have pushed them away. I've yelled at them. I've spanked them. I've hated them. I've blamed them for all of my woes. But I've never hurt them. I've never stopped loving them. I've never stop caring for them and as long as I'm breathing, I never will.

The most impactful cost has been the financial. I'm not ashamed to say, I make a very good living. In all honesty, it's probably too good for my level of skill. But it costs a lot to care for all these souls. I think we spend more to feed the critters than we do ourselves. Medical care fluctuates with the health status of the flock but none of it, even routine care, is cheap. What can I do? I can't not take care of them. They count on me. But it can be overwhelming. Smothering. Just when we get one of our Care Credit cards paid off, another emergency happens. You can set your watch by it. All this spending has pretty much guaranteed I'll never be able to retire. We're so far in debt that many necessities have to take a back seat.

The homestead is in various stages of disrepair and dilapidation. Unless it's a catastrophic situation, we just live with it. Or rather, without it. Our geothermal AC and heat went out years ago and we couldn't afford to replace it. We get by with window AC units in the summer and space heaters in the winter. The sink in my bathroom leaks and the fixtures are so old they don't even make the replacement parts anymore. I just use the shower to wash my hands and brush my teeth. The kitchen cabinets are falling apart, so we tape some of them shut. The ovens are old and outdated and really don't work properly. Our over the stove microwave doesn't work anymore, so we just use it as storage space. The kitchen floor is buckling and peeling apart. The shitty laminate flooring in the rest of the house has been peed on so often that it's just rotten in places. The house is a mess. It's hard for Gail to get around well enough to keep up with the housecleaning and I simply don't have time. We have a mouse problem so significant that the cats can't even manage it. We can't put down poison traps because we can't risk the cats getting a hold of a poisoned mouse. That would mean another hospital bill, at best. A private cremation, at worst.

Transportation is an issue. I drive an old 2006 Hyundai Sonata with 200,000 miles on it. Though I take good care of it, I know its days are numbered. Thanks to a voice over windfall, I splurged and got my wife a used Dodge Ram Minivan a couple years ago. It's the newest car she's had since we got married over thirty years ago. She was long overdue. The cars aren't the only thing that could use repairs. Gail needs cataract surgery and knee replacement. I'm living with three broken teeth.

Even with insurance, fixing all this is out of our price range. Ironically, there's a good chance I'll lose my insurance through Screen Actors Guild soon. To qualify for my insurance I need to work a certain amount of SAG/Aftra work. But I can't really do that because I can't be away from home for an extended period. I'm needed here to care for the herd. It's a Catch 22 of biblical proportions.

But the animals don't know any of this. All they know is that they're loved and happy. That's the sole consolation for all this misery. We don't starve. We aren't cold in the winter or too hot in the summer. Our vehicles run. We have more than most and less than some. I have my hot coffee every morning. A cold cocktail every night. I have cable so I can watch the news and "Impractical Jokers". We don't thrive, but we get by. Maybe someday, I'll hit my pot of gold. Maybe not. Probably not. But as long as I've got breath in my body, this motley, mismatched brood that God has sent to me will be cared for as best I can. No matter the cost.

I BEG OF YOU...

I have learned painful lessons on this journey. Some I'll always be thankful for. Others that will haunt me to my grave. Hard earned knowledge gained through often unpleasant experiences. If I can offer you anything, it is some simple wisdom. I beg of you...

Teach your children early about respect for animals. Teach them to be gentle. They might not understand that some of the things they do can hurt them. Teach them that animals have feelings. Cruelty is never the answer. All these animals really want is to be accepted and loved, the way they accept and love you. There is no better way than showing them by your example.

Don't ignore animal abuse or cruelty. Never take things into your own hands if you can help it. Report abuse and neglect to the authorities. Hold their feet to the fire to do the right thing. If you don't, who will?

If you can't afford to properly care for a pet or you have a lifestyle where the pet will always be alone, please don't get one. A pet should always be a member of the family, not an accessory. Remember that they aren't an object, they are a sentient being.

If the only way you can keep a dog is on a chain outside, please reconsider. Put yourself in the animals place. That is no life for a creature that wants your love and companionship. Pets are family whether you think so or not.

Spay and neuter your pet. There will always be plenty of dogs and cats that need homes. Don't make more.

Abandoning animals should be punishable by life in prison. How on earth could you abandon any animal and sleep at night? There are other avenues if you can't keep your pet. Abandonment is lazy and cruel. Don't be surprised if Karma doesn't come knocking on your door if you do something so despicable.

Don't tell me that you can't have a pet because you couldn't bear to lose them. If you do, I will expect you to stay single and never have children for the same reason. It's OK to admit you're selfish, just don't lie to me.

Help the lost, abandoned and forgotten. Open your heart to those animals less fortunate. There is no more faithful, loving animal than one who is rescued.

Don't get your dog or cat from a breeder. Visit the shelter or rescue one. Puppies and kittens from a breeder will always find homes. But there are so many high kill shelters full of dogs and cats who desperately want a home, any other options are basically negligence.

If you give to animal charities, do your research. There are some real dirtbags out there who will play on your emotions to get your money and then only use a fraction of your dollar for the "good" they purport to do. By all means, help any way you can. But help the right people. Help the good people.

Foster, rescue or volunteer. It will make you and your heart happy.

Learn to "read" your pet. Don't ignore changes in their behavior, even what you may deem minor ones. It could be something serious. Please, don't wait.

If you're not a vet, don't medicate your pet. For one thing, it's stupid. Don't let your stupidity cost your pet their life. I get so worn out reading of people giving their animals human drugs that destroy organs and shorten their lives. Smarten up.

Don't spare your child the experience of a pet's passing. It's important that they understand what's happening. If you need to get counseling for them or yourself, do so.

And finally, if you can help it, don't let your pet pass alone or surrounded by strangers. There will be times when it's unavoidable, but if you must euthanize your pet, your presence will comfort them. Remember, you have been the focus of their entire life. Put your fears aside and respect your pet. This isn't about you, it's about them. Suck it up. Be there. No matter how much it upsets you.

...

POEMS

TWO OLD DOGS

Two old dogs out doing chores.
One on two legs, one on four.
Side by side, they water and feed.
Caring for others daily need.

Two old dogs make their rounds
Well worn paths on familiar grounds.
To greet the day or say goodnight
Side by side, their friendship tight.

Two old dogs with dish and pail.
Singing songs and wagging tail.
Slower now, than in the past
But that just makes the good time last.

Two old dogs, both muzzles grey.
Aging joints sometimes curb play.
Companionship a simple joy.
His old dad; Dad's old boy.

Two old dogs, and then one day
One old dog has gone away.
The other left to carry on
Two legs to barn and field and pond.

One old dog, eyes full of tears
Still feels his old friend walking near
A reminder in the morning dew.
Just one path, instead of two.

When one old dog has no more chores
And walks through heaven's golden doors
He'll see that face he can't forget.
His blood; his kin. Not just a pet.

Two Old Dogs, together again.
Dogs Best Man; Man's Best Friend.
Side by side, still doing chores.
One on two legs; One on four.

. . .

THE QUESTION

Dear God, I have a question
That I really need to ask.
About my earthly journey
And the mission I've been tasked
To take in all these creatures;
Give them homes until the end.
I have to know, I have to ask
Will I see them again?

I've heard all about the Rainbow Bridge
That every pet must cross.
They leave behind a grieving heart
Left empty from their loss.
But their departure might be easier
If I but only knew

That a reunion will be had one day.
Please tell me that it's true.

They're so important to our lives
Like family, not just pets.
The good times are so very good.
The bad, as bad can get.
Only you know when and where
We have to say good-bye.
Lord, find some way to let me know
It's not over when we die.

That night as I lay sleeping,
An old, familiar bark
Woke me from my slumber
And somewhere in the dark
An unseen muzzle found its way
Into my empty hand
Then a chorus of soft purring
I said "yes, I understand"

They're all there waiting for me.
Somewhere on the other side.
We'll be together there one day
I smiled and softly cried.
My question had been answered.
And my pet fraternity
Will always be together.
Here and in eternity.

. . .

FAREWELL

No more needles.
No more pills.
No more aches and pains and ills.
It's time for us to take that ride
And see what's on the other side.

It seems like seconds
The years all passed.
Not knowing that they wouldn't last.
Yet here we are, my dear old friend.
I'll stay right here until the end.

With tearful eyes
I'll do my best
To share my thoughts before your rest.
Everything that's in my heart
That you should know before we part

I didn't know you
As a pup.
You came to my world all grown up.
It wasn't always a perfect fit
But I loved you so, in spite of it.

You scratched your way
Through many doors.
You left me "presents" on the floor.
You chewed the sofa all to bits
You gave your poor mom sneezing fits.

Not a single trick
You ever learned.
Potted plants you overturned
You hogged both sides of the bed.
Slept with your butt right by my head.

Jeff Pillars

You ate the meals
Meant just for me.
You chased the cat into a tree
You ate my favorite pair of shoes
And the paper before I read the news.

But not one time
In all these years
Did you ever give me cause for tears.
Forgive me now, if I start to cry
I just don't want to say good-bye.

No more needles.
No more pills.
No more aches or pains or ills.
I know I'll see you once again.
I love you and farewell, old friend.

. . .

BOXES OF ASHES

Boxes of ashes
Placed here and there
A paw print in clay
A soft lock of hair.

A solemn momento
That's left to remind
The unconditional love
They all left behind.

A quiet memorial
With collar and tag
Worn by a friend
With a purr or a wag

Each speck of dust
Is a memory kept
Of laughter and love
And bitter tears wept

A small, simple urn
A sad souvenir
Next to a picture
Of the one you loved dear.

Boxes of ashes
I'll keep till the end
When my ashes are placed
Next to my best friend.

. . .

THE OLD MAN AND THE KITTEN

A lonely old man on his porch just sittin'
Sees off in the distance a little stray kitten.
Tiny and yellow and oh, so alone
Going door to door, looking for home.

In the morning just as chores he was quittin'
There on the wood pile that little stray kitten.
Hungry and scared and oh, so alone.
Hoping that this would be his new home.

Soon his breakfast the old man was splittin'
With a very happy little stray kitten.
A dish of warm milk and a big fat sardine.
Both of them sitting in front of plates, clean.

Pets in the house he wasn't permittin'
But that didn't stop a little stray kitten.
Before long the old man's favorite chair
Was covered all over in stray kitten hair.

At night, when the sack he hoped to be hittin'
There on his pillow, a little stray kitten.
The old man's nose itched from stray kitten fur
His lullaby the song of a stray kitten purr.

There was never a moment of hissin' or spittin'
From that rapidly growing little stray kitten.
He seemed to be able to read his old mind.
Where the old man was, kitten not far behind.

This wasn't a wish that he'd been transmittin'
But a prayer was answered with that little stray kitten
His days and his nights are lonely no more
With a pesky stray kitten he just can't ignore.

Although no stories will ever be written
A happier ending could not be more fittin'
It was hard to tell which one was more smitten
A lonely old man or his little stray kitten.

. . .

A BALL OF FUR

She was a ball of fur from a litter of four
Born to the dogs that lived next door.
Her Dad was Mo, a feisty Pom
And Shayna, a Spitz, was her funny Mom.
Picked by my daughter and plopped on my chest
This was the one that she liked best.

Her name was Dolly. A real live wire.
She'd fly 'round the yard like her tail was on fire.
She was white as snow with big dark eyes.
And a spirit easily six times her size.
Active and bright with a curious mind.
And a big, fluffy tail that curled up behind.

The House of Goodbyes

She found her place among the pack.
Always exploring the yard out back.
Run ins' with wildlife and neighbor kids.
Some dogs would back down but she never did.
Fearless and funny like none of the rest.
I didn't know then, but my life was blessed.

Things got busy as things often do.
The years disappeared and time really flew.
A new house in the country with acres to roam.
Acres of pasture. A dog's ideal home.
But all the land meant more chores to be done.
There just wasn't much time for dogs to have fun.

When some of the pack began passing away,
Dolly hung in there, not aging a day.
Immortal it seemed. So sturdy and strong.
Then one day I noticed something was wrong.
Dolly was injured and not able to walk.
I scooped her up and went to the Doc.

"Six months, at best" was the terrible news.
"She'll keep getting worse and you'll have to choose.
Will you just let her suffer or will you let her go?"
The answer to both questions was simply a "NO!"
Surely there was something that I could do.
I had six months to unlock a clue.

New age medicine revealed
Techniques that would help her heal.
Acupuncture and Chinese Herbs
Special massage to stimulate nerves.
The road was hard but she stayed on track.
In very short order, Dolly bounced back.

The evidence was very clear.
Her six month sentence disappeared.
Once again she ran and played.
Amazing progress she had made.
But she wasn't the only one made whole.
Dolly Marie had cleansed my soul.

Through her, I saw the will to win.
To never give up and never give in.
In her spirit, I found inspiration
Sent from God, perhaps divination.
Keep your head down and just persevere.
Ignore the skeptics; face your fear.

For over three years, she was at my side.
My muse, my baby, my joy, my pride.
Circumstance had forged a bond.
That would last in this world and worlds beyond.
But time is a thief who steals your heart
When one day you must surely part.

I don't recall when I knew for sure.
But there was something missing in my ball of fur.
She didn't jump up when I came back home.
She didn't seem to want to roam.
Or sniff and search for some strange scent
That not long before she'd ne'er relent.

I could see the "tired" in her eyes
And hear it in her long deep sighs.
When her steady gate would start to wane
Her little body showing pain
She'd look at me as if to say
"It's alright, Daddy. I'm OK".

But I knew in my heart it was not the case.
The joy of life was leaving her face.
So I held her and sang her favorite songs
Knowing I wouldn't have her long.
The Angels came on a Saturday
And on silent wings, took my friend away.

I miss the funny positions that she'd sleep in.
The wrestling matches she let me win.
Her eager gaze when treat time came
Her happy trot, though she was lame.
Her favorite spot where she'd rest her head.
The endless hairs that she would shed.

Now I walk alone our once shared paths.
Remembering how she made me laugh.
It will be quite some time, I fear.
When I can think of her without a tear.
Someday I'll be together once more
With that ball of fur from a litter of four.

. . .

I HATE CATS

It wasn't my idea to bring you in the house
But my wife says you're injured…or something.
So, I'll feed you and make sure you have clean water.
Even though it goes against my nature.
I think you should know that I hate cats.

I see you're feeling better and you've managed a purr
Or two. You don't have to rub your head against my hand
While I'm trying to feed you. You won't sway my opinion.
No matter how soft your fur is and how helpless you appear.
It doesn't change a thing. I hate cats.

Good morning, cat. Time to come out and get some exercise.
I guess you're probably bored in that cage all day. So stretch your legs.
But no matter what, do not come into my office while I'm working.
I don't need any distractions when I'm trying to work.
And if you do come in, use that bed I put in the corner. I hate cats.
Wife calls you Muffin, but I'm calling you Dink. That fits.
I'm going to try and catch up on my reading.
This is my chair, not yours. If you're going to jump up here,
lay on the blanket I put here on my left.
I hold my book on the right. And don't fall asleep.
I don't want to be Stuck here all night.
It's one of the reasons I hate cats.

It's your turn to be the caretaker, Dink.
Doc says I'll be stuck in bed for a while.
Everyone else is too busy but I figure you owe me.
If you lay on my chest I can't see the TV.
And that purring is putting me to sleep. Come back up here
On the pillow. And rest your head on my shoulder like you do.
I can't sleep without it. Thanks, Dink. But I still hate cats.

It's been fifteen years, Dink. Fifteen years.
Why did I ever let you in this house?
And in my heart? I made this same mistake years ago.
His name was Dink, too.
Now what am I going to do? He was my best friend, Dink.
My very best friend.
After all those years, you filled that void. I know you have to go.
I love you, Dink. This good-bye is the reason…I hate cats.

You're lucky I stopped the car. You shouldn't be out in traffic like that.
I guess I'll take you home and see if I can find someone to take you in.
You can't stay with me, pal. Been there, done that.
I don't care if you're scared,
Don't curl up on my shoulder.
Boy, do you have a loud purr for such a runt.
In case you hadn't guessed by now, I hate cats.

THE OLD STONE BENCH

There's an old stone bench
On the side of a hill.
Overlooking a pond
Calm and still.

An old stone bench
Where dog and man
Share time that only
Best friends can.

That old stone bench
Where friends could stay
In the early morn
Or end of day.

Our old stone bench
A place to meet
Man on the bench
Dog at his feet.

That old stone bench
At the edge of the shade
Where a lifelong bond
Was stronger made.

The old stone bench
Upon that hill
Sits empty now
A bitter pill.

A simple stone bench
Now a monument
To memories
Of time well spent.

A memorial of
A friendship true
A symbol of my
Love for you.

...

OLDER DOGS

Older dogs
And getting older
Notice how the nights are colder
Little solace in the dawn
Save a weary stretch and yawn

Older dogs
Are not as agile
Bones and joints seem frail and fragile
No longer runs to fetch a toy
A simple walk replaced that joy.

Older dogs
With vision fading
Still makes out his masters shading
Graying head seeks gentle hand
Seems to slow times shifting sands.

Older dogs
Have trouble hearing
Deer and duck in nearby clearing
But older dogs still can tell
Who comes and goes by sniff and smell

Older dogs
Might not remember
If it's May or it's November
Might forget familiar ways
Confusion comes with hair that grays

Older dogs
Need much more petting
Lest one day you'll be regretting
The absence of that loyal friend
Who gave their heart until the end

Older dogs
And getting older
I notice, too, the night is colder
I know what you're going through
For I'm an older dog, like you.

...

THE MISSING PIECE

Every time I lose a pet
I lose a piece of me.
It's nothing that's discernible;
Not something you can see.
It's a little portion of my heart
A section of my soul
And every time I say good-bye,
It leaves a little hole.

They take that little piece with them
Upon their final ride.
And make sure it's kept safely
There on the other side.
And one day, when the last one goes
And my final piece is gone
I'll at last be ready
For a journey of my own.

A journey where I'll find the love
I lost down here below.
Loves I lost quite recently
And loves from long ago.
Back together once again
As we were in life
Dog and cat, horse and bird
My daughter and my wife.

But for the moment I still have
Some pieces left to give.
I'll endure the pain to give them
As long as I shall live.
It's just the price one has to pay
For love so pure and free.
I'm thankful for that in my life.
Though it costs a piece of me.

. . .

WHERE ARE YOU, MILLIE?

Where are you, Millie?
Are you behind those empty eyes
That used to smile and dance at the sound of her name?
Is there another world in your head that I'm not a part of?
You walk through the yard now,
Like a stranger in a strange land.
Fog bound. Absent, although present.

Where are you, my old black dog?
Our realities are different these days.
I long for the days when the world we shared was the same.
Your toothy smile and happy gate just months ago, given way
To a vacant expression and awkward ambling.
Here, but not here. Dead, though alive.

Where are you, sweet old friend?
Do you know my face today?
Do you recognize the hand that strokes your head?
Can you hear my voice saying "I love you…
Please come back to me"?
Do you know all you've forgotten?
The life you had? The you you were?

Where are you, Millie?
What I would give to see you whole
One last time, jumping, running, diving in the pond.
We are so close to goodbye, though you said good-bye long ago.
All I can give you now is peace.
Till we meet again. And you know me once more.

. . .

MY OLD GIRL

Sometimes, in the wee hours of the morning
I hear a bark. At least I believe I do,
A familiar old voice from the past. My past. Our past.
I sit up to look for you, knowing you're not there.
But hoping. Hopeful.
And then hope is gone and memories return.
Smile. Laugh. Tears.

A year removed from our 4am strolls.
Sometimes I walk outside and in the moonlight
Expect to see a spot of shiny white
Moving along the fence. Sniffing. Another adventure.
My mind lets me see what is no longer there.
I almost call to you. Like a thirsty traveler
Praying the mirage is real. If only for a moment.
But memories will have to suffice, kept sharp by repetition.
Afraid to let go. To forget makes me afraid.

I return to bed. To sleep. But before I do
Cannot resist the temptation to
Caress the empty collar. Touch the empty bowl
You loved and put a hand on that simple wooden box
That holds what's left. Tiny coffin.
Hard. Unyielding. Unlike your soft white fur
Which always seemed to be right there to be touched.
Held. Loved. Remembered.

So I go on. Because that's the way it works.
More beasts large and small to shepherd
Through their earthly journeys. They come.
They go. All too soon. Most of all you.
My old girl. My Scooby Doo. My Gibbers.
My heart. Aches. And is always more empty
When I hear that bark at 4am. Teasing your daddy.
Spoiled. Some things never change.

I miss you every day.
Love, Poppy

. . .

IF I CROSS THE BRIDGE BEFORE YOU

If I cross the bridge before you
I don't want you to fear.
Although you will not see me
I promise I'll be near.

I'll be right there beside you
As you go throughout your day
An angel on your shoulder
That never goes away.

The House of Goodbyes

You'll feel me as the morning sun
Falls warmly on your face.
You'll see me as the gentle breeze
Gives fallen leaves to chase.

You'll hear me in the distant call
Of lonely whippoorwills.
You'll sense me when the evening sky
Is clear and bright and still.

I know it will be scary
When I'm no longer here.
And all you have are memories
Of one you loved so dear.

But one day you will understand
When your earthly time is through.
And it's your turn to cross the bridge
Where I'll be waiting there for you.

I'll have a brand new collar
And the toys and treats you love.
We'll never be apart again
In that paradise above.

So if I cross that bridge before you
And we have to be apart.
Just know I won't be far away
I'll be right there…in your heart.

. . .

THE MISSING MEOW

The long trip home. A quiet ride.
Emotions difficult to hide.
The family thinned by one voice now.
The silence of the missing meow.

No more to hear that catterwall
A loud, demanding feline call.
That says "I'm past due for my chow!"
All that's left is the missing meow.

The empty spot in your favorite chair
The few remaining fine, shed hairs.
I guess one more tear I'll have to allow
In honor of that missing meow.

When time has passed I'm sure I'll smile
When I think about you once in a while
And when I do, one thing I vow.
I'll never forget that missing meow.

. . .

IF I'D KNOWN...

If I'd known it would be the last time I saw you…
That we would so soon be separated
By the gulf of eternity; if only I had flawless foresight
To even glimpse the sadness that awaited… If I'd known…

If I'd known, I would not have passed you by without
Taking a moment to give you the only thing
You've ever asked of me. Love. I wouldn't have assumed
I could just do it later. Because now, I can't. If I'd known….

The House of Goodbyes

If I'd known, I wouldn't have ignored your adoring gaze. I'd have
Turned off the TV and turned to you. My free time should've
Always been ours. A ride in the car or a walk in the woods or any
Of the simple things you cherished. If I'd known...

If I'd known, I wouldn't have raised my voice to you. I would
Never want your final memory of me to be one that made
You sad or fearful or ashamed. I would have given you only
Words of kindness and assurance. If I'd known...

If I'd known how this day would end... Holding an empty collar
Full of regrets. Wondering where the years went and why you
Weren't here for more of them. Searching my mind for memories
Instead of this steady stream of regrets. If only I'd known...

. . .

THE EMPTY CHAIR

Our big, soft chair in the corner
Has been empty for on a year.
I still can't look at it very long
Without having to shed a tear.

It's where you and I would end our day
And quiet time we'd share.
Free from all our worries
Free from that day's cares.

Just a tired old man and a feral cat
Bonded through life's many struggles
And the world was right and good again
When we sat in that chair and snuggled.

The love I'd see in those big green eyes
The lullaby of your purr
The way you rubbed your face on mine
The softness of your fur.

All just a memory for me now.
Of happier days gone by
To have to sit there all alone
Would only make me cry.

One night I scrolled through photos
Of you and I sitting there
When the sudden urge was upon me
To sit once more in our chair.

I settled in like I used to do
When you were by my side
All those electric memories
I used to set aside

To my surprise I cracked a smile
To see you once again
Movies of a happier past
With my very special friend

So, now when I'm missing you
The chair is where I go
A sanctuary from the world
Like it was so long ago

In imagination you are here
In the chair with me again
Though not in flesh, it will suffice
Until we meet again.

. . .

THE POM

Somewhere up in heaven
There sits a little Pom.
He's anxious and impatient
'Cause he's looking for his mom.

"I saw her just a day ago!
She must be here somewhere!"
He looks and looks and looks some more
But can't find her anywhere.

An Angel sees the little Pom
And tries to ease his mind.
"Your Mom won't be here for awhile.
She had to stay behind."

"She's got a lot to do just yet.
A big, full life to live.
But one day, in a time far off,
She'll join you here, to live."

The little Pom was still upset.
He didn't understand.
This isn't how it all should be.
It wasn't what he planned.

The Angel smiled and stroked his head.
"It will all be clear one day.
She'll walk across that bridge right there.
You'll be together every day."

"You'll run and play and take long naps
And never be apart.
She won't have to miss you anymore.
You'll mend her broken heart.

"A broken heart? What did I do?
I didn't mean to go!
I hope she won't forget me.
Please say it won't be so!"

The Angel smiled and picked him up.
"Let's go, my little Pom.
I'll show you just how much you're missed.
Let's go and see your Mom."

The Angel spread his mighty wings
And in a flash of light
They were in a small apartment
In the middle of the night.

They stood next to a great big bed
Beside a sleeping girl.
"That's her!" The little Pom exclaimed.
"My Mom! She's my whole world!"

"Look around", the Angel said.
"And tell me what you see."
Beside the bed, a little box.
Engraved with "T" and "C".

"TC! That's MY name", he said.
"And pictures of us, too!
That's me when I was older
And in that one, I was new!"

"I want to wake her up!" he said.
"At least to say hello!:
"I'm sorry" said the Angel.
"But that just can't be so."

The Angel saw the Pom was sad.
"But there's something you CAN do.
You can step inside her dreams
For a minute...maybe two."

The House of Goodbyes

The little Pom jumped in her dream
And found her right away.
She held him close and shed a tear.
There were no words to say.

They looked into each others eyes.
Nothing needed to be said.
And then the Pom was back again.
The girl, back in her bed.

The Angel said "Just look, my friend."
That smile that's on her face.
You'll always be a memory
Too precious to replace."

"You can come back from time to time
And sneak into her dreams.
She won't know it's really you.
It will be our secret scheme."

"That's good enough. I understand,"
The little Pom replied.
"If I can do that once in awhile
I'll be satisfied".

With his little heart at peace at last,
The anxious little Pom
Stood at his post, so that one day
He'd be there to greet his Mom.

And sure enough, that day did come.
And that patient little Pom
Got to spend eternity
With his much beloved Mom.

For my Pickle

• • •

Jeff Pillars

THE RIDE

Come on, there, pup. Don't be afraid.
We're going for a ride.
Hop up here on my front seat
And sit right by my side.
How'd you come to find yourself
On a roadside all alone?
I'll take you to a special place
It's your forever home.

Come on, girl. You little brat.
Let's take a little ride.
We're going to the groomers
So, don't dare try to hide.
I know you love to roll around
In everything that stinks
Don't be afraid, I'll stay with you.
You'll be clean quick as a wink.

Saddle up, my sweetest friend
Let's take your favorite ride.
We're going to the park today.
It's beautiful outside.
You're not as fast as years before
You're not as quick to run
But as long as we're together
We always have some fun.

Let me help you up, old gal.
Let's take our weekly ride.
We'll see your favorite doctor
See what's going on inside.
I'm sure you'll be just fine, my love.
But only time will tell.
I'm on my knees every night
Praying you'll get well.

Come on, old girl. Don't be afraid.
We're going for a ride.
I'll lay you here on my front seat
And sit right by your side.
You're going to a special place
Where once more you can roam.
I'll see you again one day.
In your eternal home.

...

SOMEONE'S WAITING...

Someone's waiting for me
At the Rainbow Bridges end.
A face I haven't seen in years
A dear, beloved friend.

I promised when we said goodbye
We'd meet again one day.
And now, it seems that day is nigh
I'll soon be on my way.

I'll be shed of earthly coils
And free from fear and pain.
Off to the beyond beyond
With my best friend again.

We'll make up for long times lost.
Walk heaven's fields of gold.
Rest by streams of azure blue
Just like in days of old.

We'll have no schedule to keep.
No place we have to be.
It's a perfect place for pals
To spend eternity.

So do not waste your bitter tears.
Don't fret and cry and grieve.
You'll see me again one day
When it's your turn to leave.

We'll both be there to greet you
Me and my best friend
And your best friend will be there too
At Rainbow Bridge's end.

. . .

OLD HANK

I knew him only as "Old Hank"
Just a beggar on the street.
His clothes were torn and tattered
He barely had shoes on his feet.

Sometimes I gave him money.
And then sometimes not.
He was there when it was freezing
And when it was boiling hot.

One day our paths crossed at the store.
He walked directly down one aisle.
He loaded up on sardines
Smiling all the while.

My interest piqued, I followed him
Along a winding trail
It took a while because Old Hank
Was limping and quite frail.

He reached his destination;
An old abandoned shack.
Beside a spreading oak tree
And a rundown barn outback.

The House of Goodbyes

Old Hank sat down beneath the tree
And unpacked all his cans
Suddenly from everywhere
A hundred cats all ran.

Old Hank sat there gleefully
Feeding every single one.
They all stayed there beside him
Even when the food was done.

I saw Old Hank the very next day
Panhandling on the street.
So I went to the store and back
And laid some sardines at his feet.

A tear ran down his wrinkled cheek
He thanked me from his heart
I asked him what the story was
He was happy to impart.

"For years I've lived here on the street
And I've been all alone.
I stayed one night in that old barn
But it was someone else's home."

"It was full of cats of every size.
They were all alone like me.
I decided then and there that this
Would be my new family."

"The money people give me
Goes to feed them and their care.
Would you like to come and meet them?
They've got lots of love to spare."

As I drove Old Hank to the rundown barn
He told me about his life
Drink had robbed him of his job
His money and his wife.

Jeff Pillars

But now he's found redemption.
Giving all that he can give.
In some forgotten feral felines
He's found the will to live.

When we arrived, Old Hank called out.
And here came all those cats.
Some very young, some very old.
Most skinny, few were fat.

He'd given each one their own name
And introduced each one.
It was clear from his toothless grin
Old Hank was having fun.

From that day on I made sure
I stopped by Old Hank's.
I brought him food and those sardines.
His laugh and smile said thanks.

I got to know the cats by name
And they accepted me.
I got a veterinarian friend
To tend this flock for free.

One day I stopped to see Old Hank
With some groceries and some treats.
He'd actually started to gain some weight
With proper food to eat.

I called out hello to all the cats
But not a single one ever came.
I found them huddled in the barn
Near Old Hank's lifeless frame.

Old Hank had passed away that day
Leaving all his cats behind.
They were standing vigil at his side
And I joined with them in kind.

The House of Goodbyes

    I paid for Old Hank's funeral
    I was the only person there.
    But that's not the end of the story.
    I've my own tale to share.

    I rebuilt that house and fixed the barn
    Just for my feral kin.
    It's cost me near an arm and leg
    And I'd do it all again.

    On starry nights, beneath that tree
    Surrounded by those cats
    I feel Old Hank's spirit near
    And I'm comforted by that.

    Old Hank is gone, but I'm still here
    And here I'll stay, I vow
    See, I was alone just like he was
    And this is my family now.

. . .

THE WORTHY SHEPHERD

    Lord, let me be a worthy shepherd
For this motley, mismatched flock you've sent to my door.
  Grant me the grace to accept what you expect of me
    And let me be deserving of the unconditional love
      That they give so freely, fully and faithfully.
There are many they could give it to, but they have chosen me.

    Let me be worthy, Lord, to be their protector
    Their provider and their parent, though we are not
  Of blood, but of one family by chance and by choice.
    Bless me with kindness of heart and gentle hand;
To be worthy of the trust others have so cruelly betrayed.
  Let me prove that they have found love, safety and home.

Fill my heart, Lord, with gladness and joyful wonder
At the little lives I have touched, am touching and will touch.
These tender souls who have allowed me into their world
Either as active part or merely as spectator from afar.
Help them understand the meaning of my smile
And that they are the composers of the music of my laughter.

Lord, I'm an imperfect person in a far from perfect world.
But let there be perfection in the blending of our worlds.
Allow me to meet their meager needs, even if I go without.
To shield them from storms, though I am drenched.
Let me be the person, not that I see, but that they see.
Lord, let me be a worthy shepherd.

...

AN OLD PAINT PONY

Just an old paint pony, well past her prime.
But still with a gleam in her eye.
She wasn't as spry as she once used to be
But she always seemed to get by.

There was a mischievous heart in that weathered old frame
A prankster seasoned by time.
The years never hobbled her devilish ways
Or hampered her comical crimes.

No clown ever lived with a sillier face.
She could tell a joke with a twitch of her ear.
Her quivering lips were a punchline.
She was like a Muppet with no puppeteer.

But there was soulfulness in those weary old eyes.
She'd speak volumes to me with a glance.
Everything from "I love you" to "Where's my treat?"
I knew what she thought in advance.

But time is a thief that comes unawares
She robs you as she passes by.
And for that old paint pony time finally ran out
And with those old eyes she told me good-bye.

There's an empty stall in the old barn now
Where an old paint pony once stayed.
There's a big wide pasture that's missing a friend
Where an old paint pony once played.

But that old paint pony will always be here.
Thanks to memories we never shall part.
And until I see her again one day.
She'll wander the fields of my heart.

Better trails, Kita Belle.

. . .

ALONE

She stands patiently in an ever more empty pasture.
Nose to the breeze. Searching.
Hoping to spot someone who will never return.
Where there was once many, there is now only her.

I watch her, unable to help. Unable to explain.
To make sense of death for her.
It was easier before. When there was someone left.
A kindred spirit to share the loss.

Now, she's alone. Going through the motions.
Grazing. A casual trip to the trough.
Some time at the hay roll. Exciting sounds and smells
Not as stirring when you're alone.

I spend too much time wondering what she must think.
When is my friend coming back?
Was it something I did? I'm sorry. Please come back.
Can I come to where you are?

Still she looks. Every morning and every night.
A quick glance in an empty stall.
Just in case. Perhaps an old friend will visit.
She tries not to look too disappointed.

There will come a day that she will see them once again.
Reunited with that ridiculous herd of misfits.
The band will be back together.
And this time, no one is leaving.

. . .

THE PERFECT GIFT

I can still remember your first gift
When you were just a little pup.
A fancy leather collar,
Which you instantly chewed up.

I spent a pretty penny
On a plush and fuzzy bed.
But my old dirty slippers
Are where you chose to lay your head.

I bought you many funny toys
To pass the time away.
But my favorite pair of dress shoes
Were your instrument of play.

I chose an upscale groomers
To keep you clean and fragrant.
But after that you rolled in trash
Till you smelled just like a vagrant.

The House of Goodbyes

When it came to giving treats
I tried to pick the best.
But only poop from the litter box
Could pass your palate's test.

I always wanted to make sure
You had the best that I could give.
That you had everything you'd ever want
As long as you would live.

But now I have one final gift
To give you, my best friend.
The gift of peace and sweet release
As you come near the end.

It's the last thing I can do for you
After all you've done for me.
A cruel, yet tender mercy
That will set your spirit free.

So, look into my eyes, old friend
And let me hold your face.
Soon, you'll be whole again
In a much, much better place.

You don't understand it now
But as the angels wings give lift,
You'll see what I have given you
Is, at last, the perfect gift.

. . .

Jeff Pillars

JUST A DOG?

Did I hear you say "It's just a dog"?
You self-righteous, boorish ass.
What you consider just a mongrel,
Surpasses you in class.

To you this might be just a mutt
But one thing is for sure.
When it comes to grace and breeding
His pedigree's more pure.

When loyalty is brought to bare
The dog bests you again.
It's you that proves exactly why
Man isn't man's best friend.

A good man knows to trust a dog
With his home and with his life.
Men like you pat someone's back
While holding on a knife.

Its true there's things a dog can't do
And one of them is lie.
The same cannot be said of you
Truth isn't your ally.

In the end the lowly dog will be
Mourned when he is gone.
But a day without the likes of you
Will serve a better dawn.

Just a dog? It's trash like you
Who seek to deride and debase.
It's why their company I seek
Instead of the human race.

. . .

A FERAL FUNERAL

The haze of dawn
A tiny corpse
Kitten gently shrouded
A funeral procession of one.
This short life remembered
By someone who cared
A brief eulogy.

Named for posterity
Named for all those
Who die unnamed.
Mental snapshot
Of happier times.
Dulls the pain
Blur the greyness of death.

Cruelty of chance.
Why you, little buddy?
The strong survive
The weak don't.
Pondering life
Between verses
Of Amazing Grace.

The service lightly attended
By survivors and kin
Unaware the same fate
Awaits them. Sometime.
Somewhere. Till then
Life goes on.
Who wants breakfast?

• • •

STAY WITH ME

Stay with me.
You know I'm scared of the dark
And the light is fading.
But when you're here
I'm not afraid.
Of the dark. The storm.
Or the way I'm feeling now.
Stay with me.

Stay with me.
Touch my face and remind me
Of all the adventures we had.
Large and small.
Memories fade for me
But you remember.
So remind me.
And stay with me.

Stay with me.
Let my cloudy eyes see your face
And my muffled ears hear you laugh.
Tell me you forgive me
For all the things I did wrong.
Sing that song you made up
With my name in it.
But stay with me.

Stay with me.
But before we have to part
Let me feel you kiss me
And scratch that spot behind my ear
That made me smile and my leg twitch.
Hold me like you did when we watched
Old movies and ate ice cream.
Still stay with me.

Stay with me.
Until I'm gone and then
Stay a while longer, just in case
I can't find my way.
I will always be with you, even when I'm not.
Watching and waiting till the day
I see you again and you can forever
Stay with me.

...

EPILOGUE

This book has been a labor of love. I wrote it to honor those both here and gone. In truth, there is probably so much that isn't chronicled in these pages. Things I've long forgotten that I'm sure I'll remember once this tome is printed. I've laughed out loud remembering things that have slipped my memory. I've cried bitter tears over resurrected memories of loss. I've seethed with furious anger at the thoughtless cruelty of my fellow man. I have also counted my blessings many times and know them all by heart. I'm thankful I've been given the means to care for this gaggle of misfits. Appreciative that I was receptive to the serendipity of the fates that brought us all together. Hopeful that I've learned the lessons that each one's life taught me. In spite of the personal pain my family has shared, I've been blessed that they ended their run here with us, rather than the circumstances we took them from.

If I have one fear, it would be that some of them will outlive me. At this point, it is most likely a certainty. All too often I see these stories plastered all over social media. Pleas from a grieving family for someone, anyone, to take in an animal left behind. It makes me shudder. I wouldn't ask anyone to make the sacrifices that we have. I pray that God, who has tasked me with this, will help me see most of them across the finish line before I go. It would be fitting, but I don't pretend to know what the future holds. But I wouldn't trade the past for anything.

...

ABOUT THE AUTHOR

Jeff Pillars makes his literary debut with "The House of Good-byes", a chronicle of love and loss in a lifetime of rescued animals. Quite a departure for someone who's spent the last several years amusing the masses with his vast array of characters and song parodies via the nationally syndicated radio show "The John Boy & Billy Big Show". Jeff spent many years as a stage and film actor but these days can be heard all over the world as a much in demand voice actor, doing everything from videogames to national commercials to annoying voices on apps you've probably had and deleted. Feel free to check it out at www.jeffpillars.com. When he's not going broke buying pet food at Walmart and trying to save every animal in the world, he's enjoys watching "Impractical Jokers" and "I'm Sorry" on Tru TV. He lives on a farm in rural Mineral Springs, North Carolina, with his long suffering wife, Gail, and perpetually irritated daughter, Haley and way too many dogs, cats, horses and goats. And that damn possum that won't get out of his garage.

. . .

Made in the USA
Columbia, SC
07 June 2018